Saturday Night Thoughts

by
Orson F. Whitney

Saturday Night Thoughts
by Orson F. Whitney

Copyright © 2023

All Rights reserved.

No part of this publication may be reproduced, stored in a retrieval system, or transmitted in any form or by any means, electronic, mechanical, photocopying or Otherwise, without the written permission of the publisher.
The author/editor asserts the moral right to be identified as the author/editor of this work.

ISBN: 978-93-59329-66-6

Published by
DOUBLE 9 BOOKS
2/13-B, Ansari Road
Daryaganj, New Delhi – 110002
info@double9books.com
www.double9books.com
Tel. 011-40042856

This book is under public domain

ABOUT THE AUTHOR

Ferguson, Orson Whitney, born in Salt Lake City, Utah Territory, was a member of the Quorum of the Twelve Apostles of the Church of Jesus Christ of Latter-day Saints (LDS Church) from 1906 until his death on May 16, 1931. Horace K. Whitney and Helen Mar Kimball raised Whitney. Whitney's father, Horace, fixed type for the Deseret News' first publication and served as a printer for the newspaper for 21 years. Whitney was a professor, politician, journalist, poet, and historian. Whitney began his writing career as a young man in 1878 with the Deseret News' commercial office, ultimately becoming a reporter and the city editor. Whitney was a missionary for the LDS Church in Pennsylvania and Ohio. During his LDS Church mission in Europe from 1881 to 1883, he served as editor of the church newspaper Millennial Star. Whitney taught English and theology at Brigham Young College in Logan, Utah, in 1896 and 1897. Whitney acquired the job of Assistant Church Historian in 1899 and held it until he was called as an apostle. Whitney was also interested in Salt Lake City and Utah politics.

CONTENTS

NAMES AND ABBREVIATIONS 9

PART ONE
OUR PLACE IN HISTORY

ARTICLE ONE
THE SATURDAY EVENING OF TIME 10

ARTICLE TWO
THE WATCH ON THE TOWER 14

ARTICLE THREE
CONCERNING NAMES AND VOCATIONS 18

ARTICLE FOUR
THE CHOICE SEER 22

ARTICLE FIVE
THE LAND OF ZION 27

PART TWO
SEERSHIP AND PROPHECY

ARTICLE SIX
WHAT JOSEPH BEHELD 31

ARTICLE SEVEN
WHAT JOSEPH FORETOLD 38

ARTICLE EIGHT
LOOKING WESTWARD 43

ARTICLE NINE
THE PLACE OF SAFETY 48

PART THREE
A MARVEL AND A WONDER

ARTICLE TEN
THE WISDOM THAT PERISHES 55

ARTICLE ELEVEN
THE GOD STORY 60

ARTICLE TWELVE
THE GREAT VICISSITUDES 66

ARTICLE THIRTEEN
THE GOSPEL DISPENSATIONS 73

PART FOUR
A GLANCE DOWN THE AGES

ARTICLE FOURTEEN
THE ADAMIC AGE 78

ARTICLE FIFTEEN
ENOCH AND HIS CITY 83

ARTICLE SIXTEEN
NOAH AND THE DELUGE 88

ARTICLE SEVENTEEN
ABRAHAM AND THE HOUSE OF ISRAEL 93

ARTICLE EIGHTEEN
MOSES AND AARON 99

ARTICLE NINETEEN
TO THE ENDS OF THE EARTH 104

PART FIVE
IN TIME'S MERIDIAN

ARTICLE TWENTY
THE LAMB OF GOD 110

ARTICLE TWENTY-ONE
    THE SPECIAL WITNESSES 117

PART SIX
THE ERA OF RESTITUTION

ARTICLE TWENTY-TWO
    THE CALL OF THE SHEPHERD 123

ARTICLE TWENTY-THREE
    THE ZION OF LATTER DAYS 132

ARTICLE TWENTY-FOUR
    REDEMPTION BY POWER 138

ARTICLE TWENTY-FIVE
    CLEARING THE WAY 143

ARTICLE TWENTY-SIX
    GOD'S HAND UPON THE NATIONS 149

ARTICLE TWENTY-SEVEN
    THE CONSUMMATION 155

PART SEVEN
POWERS AND PRINCIPLES

ARTICLE TWENTY
    EIGHT-THE PRIESTHOOD 161

ARTICLE TWENTY-NINE
    CHURCH GOVERNMENT 167

ARTICLE THIRTY
    THE LAW OF OBEDIENCE 173

ARTICLE THIRTY-ONE
    THE DIVINE DOORWAY 177

ARTICLE THIRTY-TWO
    THE SECOND BIRTH 182

ARTICLE THIRTY-THREE
    MEANING AND MODE OF BAPTISM 188

ARTICLE THIRTY-FOUR
    THE GOSPEL'S ACCESSORIES 195

ARTICLE THIRTY-FIVE
    WHAT ARE MIRACLES? 202

ARTICLE THIRTY-SIX
    THE MAINSPRING OF POWER 208

PART EIGHTH
BEYOND THE HORIZON

ARTICLE THIRTY-SEVEN
    THE SPIRIT WORLD 212

ARTICLE THIRTY-EIGHT
    SPIRIT PROMPTINGS 217

ARTICLE THIRTY-NINE
    DO THE DEAD RETURN? 224

ARTICLE FORTY
    THE GOAL ETERNAL 231

NAMES AND ABBREVIATIONS

The usual Bible abbreviations are retained.

Hist. Ch. stands for History of the Church.

D. & C. for Doctrine and Covenants.

Nephi, Jacob, Omni, Mormon, Mosiah, Alma and Ether, will be recognized as names belonging to the Book of Mormon.

The Book of Moses, shortened to Moses, and the Book of Abraham, abbreviated to Abr., will be found within the lids of the Pearl of Great Price.

Other abbreviations, such as vol. for volume, p. or pp. for page or pages, v. or vv. for verse or verses and ib. for ibid (the same) are in such common use as scarcely to require mention.

PART ONE
OUR PLACE IN HISTORY

ARTICLE ONE
THE SATURDAY EVENING OF TIME

The Sixth Day.—Saturday, in Christian lands, is a day set apart for house-cleaning, a time for "putting things to rights," in preparation for the Sabbath, the sacred day of rest. Preliminary to the condition of purity, order and quietness especially desirable on that day, the house, in domestic parlance, is "upset"—"turned topsy-turvy." Furniture is moved and dusted, floors are scrubbed, windows cleaned, and stoves polished; the body is bathed, all rubbish burned, and everything done that ought to be done, so that when night is past and glorious morning dawns, the rising sun can smile approvingly on a renovated, sweet and wholesome scene, and the Lord's Day be kept, as He intended it should be, in cleanliness, which is "next to godliness." Is there not something symbolical in all this—something suggestive of things higher?

All Things Symbolical.—"All things are in a scale," says Plato; "and begin where we will, ascend and ascend. All things are symbolical; and what we call results are beginnings." [1] If this be true, then is there a symbolism in small things as well as in great, in endings as well as beginnings, including the ending and beginning of the week. Saturday and Sunday are both symbolical, each suggesting and pointing to something above and beyond.

The World's Sabbath.—Who among men first recognized in the seventh day a symbol of Christ's Millennial reign, I know not. The reign itself was the theme of a revelation as early as the days of Enoch. [2] But it is obvious that the symbolism of the seventh day does not stand alone. The idea of a greater Sunday carries with it the idea of a greater Saturday, of which all lesser Saturdays are typical; a time of agitation, of strenuous toil and strife, during which all will be made ready for the blest sabbatic era, the period of universal peace. The World's Saturday Night must necessarily precede the World's Sunday Morning. [3]

The Apocalyptic Book.—The symbolism of the Sabbath, and the symbolism of other days as well, is plainly indicated in the writings of Joseph Smith. In one place he says—or the Lord says through him: "All things have their likeness, and are made to bear record of Me." [4] We need not be surprised, therefore, to find among the Prophet's teachings this—I quote now from his Key to the Apocalypse:

"What are we to understand by the book which John saw, which was sealed on the back with seven seals? [5]

"We are to understand that it contains the revealed will, mysteries, and works of God; the hidden things of his economy concerning this earth during the seven thousand years of its continuance, or its temporal existence.

"What are we to understand by the sounding of the trumpets, mentioned in the 8th chapter of Revelations?

"We are to understand that as God made the world in six days, and on the seventh day he finished his work and sanctified it, and also formed man out of the dust of the earth; even so, in the beginning of the seventh thousand years will the Lord God sanctify the earth, and complete the salvation of man, and judge all things—unto the end of all things; and the sounding of the trumpets of the seven angels are the preparing and finishing of his work in the beginning of the seventh thousand years—the preparing of the way before the time of his coming." [6]

Seven Great Days.—The "days" here referred to were not ordinary days of twenty-four hours each, based upon earth's diurnal revolutions. He who "made the world" before placing man upon it, had not then appointed unto Adam his reckoning. [7] They were not man's days, but God's days, each having a duration of a thousand years.

"The book which John saw" represented the real history of the world— what the eye of God has seen, what the recording angel has written; and the seven thousand years, corresponding to the seven seals of the Apocalyptic volume, are as seven great days during which Mother Earth will fulfill her mortal mission, laboring six days and resting upon the seventh, her period of sanctification. These seven days do not include the period of our planet's creation and preparation as a dwelling place for man. They are limited to Earth's "temporal existence," that is, to Time, considered as distinct from Eternity.

According to Kolob.—The Prophet's translation of the Book of Abraham explains that these greater days are "after the time" or according to the reckoning of Kolob, a mighty governing planet nearest the Celestial Throne, a planet revolving once in a thousand years. [8] This period, then, is a day upon Kolob. One might well suppose such a day to have figured in the warning given to Adam: "In the day that thou eatest thereof thou shalt surely die;" [9] for Adam, after eating of the forbidden fruit, lived on to the age of nine hundred and thirty years. [10] St. Peter may have had the same thing in mind when he wrote: "One day is with the Lord as a thousand years, and a thousand years as one day." [11]

At the Week's End.—According to received chronology—admittedly imperfect, yet approximately correct—four thousand years, or four of the seven great days given to this planet as the period of its "temporal existence," had passed before Christ was crucified; while nearly two thousand years have gone by since. Consequently, Earth's long week is now drawing to a close, and we stand at the present moment in the Saturday Evening of Time, at or near the end of the sixth day of human history. Is it not a time for thought, a season for solemn meditation? Morning will break upon the Millennium, the thousand years of peace, the Sabbath of the World!

House-Cleaning in Progress.—Marvel not, therefore, that all things are in commotion. War, famine, pestilence, earthquake, tempest and tidal wave—these are among the predicted signs of the Savior's second coming. [12] Tyranny and wickedness must be overthrown, and the way prepared for Him who, though gracious and merciful to all, and forgiving to sinners who repent, "cannot look upon sin with the least degree of allowance." [13] Earth must be freed from oppression and cleansed from all iniquity. It is God's House; and He is coming to live in it, and to make of it a glorified mansion. House-cleaning is in progress, and Saturday's work must be done and out of the way, before the Lord of the Sabbath appears.

Footnotes

1 . "Plato," Emerson's "Representative Men," Altemus edition, 1895, p. 71.

2 . Moses 7:48, 61, 64.

3 . "Rabbinical commentators have expressed the opinion that after six millenniums of years, there will come a seventh, with rest and peace. Paul (2 Thess. 1:7) points to the coming of Christ as the time when the Saints would find 'rest;' and

he also argues (Heb. 4:1-11) that there remaineth a 'rest' to the people of God. The word he uses means a 'sabbathism' or sabbath observance, and he refers to the coming of the Lord."—J. M. Sjodahl.

4 . Moses 6:63.

5 . Rev. 5 and 6.

6 . D. and C. 77:6, 12.

7 . Abr. 5:13.

8 . Abr. 3:4.

9 . Gen. 2:17.

10 . Ib. 5:5. This, of course, refers to the temporal life. Adam died spiritually as soon as he had transgressed the divine command. Shut out from the Heavenly Presence, he was dead as to the things of the Spirit. (D. and C. 29:40, 41.)

11 . 2 Peter 3:8.

12 . Matt. 24; D. and C. 87, 88.

13 . D. and C. 1:31, 32.

ARTICLE TWO
THE WATCH ON THE TOWER

"Haunted Houses."—Several years since, a learned gentleman was lecturing in some of our Utah towns, taking for his theme "Haunted Houses." That was his way of describing the situation of those who put faith in prophets, visions and revelations, as among the means whereby God communicates with man. He invited all such to come out of their "haunted houses," and build for their souls "more stately mansions," founded upon the rock of reason and scientific truth. The lecturer had special reference, of course, to the followers of the Prophet Joseph Smith.

A Fundamental Belief.—A belief in prophets and in spiritual gifts, whereby come visions, revelations, and miraculous "signs," following and confirming full and true belief, [1] is fundamental with the Latter-day Saints. We regard the founding of our Church as a fulfillment of prophecy, [2] and recognize in the decadence of long established systems of religion, a result of failure to be guided and governed by the teachings and warnings of men divinely inspired. "Where there is no vision, the people perish." [3] Where there is no revelation, spiritual darkness reigns.

Not a Chance World.—We are not living in a world of chance. Things do not occur haphazardly, without the care or cognizance of the omniscient and omnipotent Ruler. Not a sparrow falls to the ground without his notice. Design, not accident, governs the universe. Neither man nor Satan, though exercising to the full his free agency, can possibly thwart the Divine Will. With all their schemings and strivings, they are powerless to destroy or disarrange God's Plan, or to hinder the fulfillment of prophecy. All things, both the evil and the good, are overruled in a way to subserve one and the same great end—*What Eternal Wisdom decreed before the foundation of the world.*

The Function of Prophecy.—The need for prophecy must be evident to any pious and reflective mind. Prophets are as watchmen on the tower, noting the time of night, telling of the approaching dawn. "Surely the Lord God will do nothing, but he revealeth his secret unto his servants the prophets." [4] This means, as I interpret it, that the all-wise Dispenser of human affairs will neither cause nor permit any event to take place, concerning which the world need to have fore-knowledge, until he has communicated with his chosen servants, his oracles among men, and has given them due notice of its approach.

To warn mankind of impending judgments; to prepare His people, and through them the world at large, for changes that must come in the carrying out of the divine program—changes necessary to human progress—is the function of those who see into the future and make known the word and will of the Universal Father.

Time for Preparation.—Even without the Prophet Amos and his inspired utterance, we have every reason to feel assured, from what we know of the divine attributes, that God, in his dealings with man, harbors no intent to take what is known as "a snap judgment." His object being to save, not to destroy, it is very far from his design that the world shall be caught unawares, that men or nations shall be involved in trouble of which they have had no warning, and for which, consequently, they could make no preparation. The promised sending of Elijah the Prophet "before the coming of the great and dreadful day of the Lord," was in order that certain things might be done which, if left undone, would cause that "coming" to "smite the earth with a curse." [5]

Not that the Lord wishes to curse. His object, even in chastisement, is to bless. [6] But a want of preparedness can change a blessing into a curse. Messiah's glorious appearing will be a wonderful blessing to the earth and its inhabitants, provided they are made ready for it. But a lack of readiness on their part would convert the boon into a calamity. Hence the need of preparation and of previous notice. Whether weal or woe is wending its way earthward, it is only fair that men should be told of it in advance.

The Supernatural Discredited.—But there is a proneness in human nature to discredit the Heaven-sent messenger. Almost invariably the supernatural is discounted, if not derided, by ultra-practical minds. All miracles are myths to the agnostic intellect. "The natural man is an enemy to God."

Dead Prophets Preferred.—Even those who revere the prophets of the past are tempted to ignore the prophets of the present. It seems natural to turn from What Is and bow down to What Has Been. Not only prophets, but poets, philosophers, and other wise and worthy teachers have been treated in this manner.

> "Seven cities claimed the birth of Homer, dead,
> Through which the living Homer begged for bread."

The Savior reproved the pious unbelievers of his generation for "garnishing the sepulchres of the righteous," the dead seers and revelators, and at the same time rejecting the living worthies, as their fathers had done before them. [7] A professed reverence for Moses and the old-time prophets was a prominent characteristic of those who spurned the greatest of all prophets, the very Son of God, concerning whom Moses and other seers had testified. And this same spirit, the spirit that crucified the Christ, has caused the martyrdom of His servants in all ages.

Counterfeit and Genuine.—For the widely prevalent distrust felt toward men who come burdened with a message from on High, false prophets and the mischief they have wrought are largely responsible. But distrust, no less than credulity, can be overdone. Caution against imposition is commendable, but doubt that rejects truth is to be deprecated and condemned. All prophets are not false. There can be no counterfeit without a genuine; and to proclaim against the one is virtually to concede the existence of the other.

A Test of Prophecy.—A simple and sure test of prophecy is furnished in the following passage of Holy Writ: "When a prophet speaketh in the name of the Lord, if the thing follow not nor come to pass, that is the thing which the Lord hath not spoken, but the prophet hath spoken it presumptuously." [8] By this standard of judgment can be tested all that prophetic inspiration has ever uttered. Given enough time, "the thing" will clearly demonstrate whether or not it was "spoken presumptuously."

A Serious Situation.—Ponder upon this, ye who hear the testimonies of the Elders of Israel, preaching the restored Gospel of the Kingdom as a final witness to the nations. And when you see coming to pass, in these days of war, pestilence and calamity, the predictions of ancient and modern seers, give a thought, a serious thought to the situation. Ask yourselves if you can afford to be classed, either with those who look upon believers in spiritual gifts as deluded dupes living in "haunted houses," or with those who extol the prophets of former ages, and persecute or ignore the prophets of the present time.

Footnotes

1. Mark 16:17.
2. Isa. 29:14.
3. Prov. 29:18.
4. Amos 3:7.
5. Mal. 4:5, 6.
6. Prov. 3:11, 12.
7. Matt. 23:29.
8. Deut. 18:22.

ARTICLE THREE
CONCERNING NAMES AND VOCATIONS

Is Not This The Farmer's Son?—Some such paraphrase was probably in the mind, possibly upon the lips, of more than one opponent of the religion termed "Mormonism," when its supposed author, Joseph Smith, started out upon his remarkable career. And it was deemed by them, no doubt, a sufficient answer to his extraordinary claims.

True and False Standards.—"A tree is known by its fruit." This proverb, accepted by the wise and just almost as a truism, seems to have no place in the philosophy of some people, especially when a servant of the Lord is the object of their critical contemplation. "What do men say of him?" is frequently the only criterion by which such a character is judged. And is it not manifestly unfair? When a prophet comes from God with a message for mankind, what matters the name given to that message, or to that messenger, by those unfriendly to the cause he represents?

"The Carpenter's Son."—Those who rejected the Man of Nazareth when he proclaimed himself the Son of God, doubtless thought they had disposed of him effectually by referring to him sneeringly as "The carpenter's son;" this slight, with others put upon him by his neighbors, causing Jesus to remark: "A prophet is not without honor save in his own country and in his own house." [1]

Effect of Nearness.—His nearness was against him. There was no "distance" to "lend enchantment to the view." His name and humble vocation made his marvelous claims seem impossible. It could not be that God would make a prophet out of a carpenter's son—a prophet mightier than Moses or any of the ancient seers—and give to him such a common name as Jesus, another form of Joshua. [2] It was unbelievable, absurd, to most. Therefore were they justified, as they supposed, in withholding from him recognition and honor. "And He did not many mighty works there, because of their unbelief."

History Repeats.—As with the carpenter's, so with the farmer's son—each was objected to upon similar grounds. Nor was it a new thing in human experience. That which called forth criticism had occurred many times in other ages when God had raised up prophets and seers. Probably most of them were selected from among the plain people, and were comparatively unknown to men when the Lord called them.

Moses an Exception.—Moses was a signal exception. He had been reared as a prince in the palace of the king of Egypt; but that was because Pharaoh's daughter, having found the homeless infant at the water's edge, thenceforth had charge of him and his education. Prince he was, regardless of that princely training; but he was not the only prince in Israel. They were "a nation of kings and priests," though most of them walked in ways that were lowly.

A Herdsman Prophet.—Prophets are not chosen for their worldly culture or their social position. A plain-going farmer, no less than a college professor, may be gifted with prophetic power and be called to exercise it for the good of his fellows. Amos, according to his own statement, "was no prophet," nor "a prophet's son." That is to say, he had not been trained in any school of the prophets, such as existed in Old Testament times. [3] He was not, like Jeremiah, the son of a priest. [4] He was a herdsman and a fruit-gatherer when the word of the Lord came to him: "Go, prophesy unto my people Israel." [5]

Prophets Foreordained.—A prophet's name, his place of birth, and the character of his everyday calling, are matters of little moment compared with other things pertaining to him. What of his state and standing before he came on earth? This is a far more important consideration. God's prophets are chosen before they are born, [6] and are sent into the world as He needs them. Their aims are high and holy. They desire the welfare and happiness of the race. Yet almost invariably their motives are misunderstood, and they and their followers are opposed and persecuted.

The Vital Question.—Does this man come from God? That is the only question worthy of immediate attention, when a prophet, or one professing to be such appears. And his word alone need not be taken as conclusive. There are ways and means of testing a prophet's claim—and that, too, without awaiting the fulfillment or non-fulfillment of some prediction by or concerning him. Honest, prayerful men and women, with even moderate discernment, need not be deceived by any pious or impious pretender. God would not leave his children at the mercy of imposters. The sheep have a right to be protected from the wolves.

"Try the Spirits."—"Many false prophets are gone out into the world." [7] But there is a Spirit that discerns between true and false, between spurious and genuine, and anyone who seeks it aright may have "the inspiration of the Almighty," which giveth to the spirit of man "understanding." [8] Moreover, the Letter as well as the Spirit is a guide. What has been revealed in times past helps to interpret what is now revealed. Truth is always consistent with itself. Heaven-inspired men do not contradict one another. Their teachings harmonize and are dependable. The spirit of contention is essentially evil. [9] "To the law and to the testimony: if they speak not according to this word, it is because there is no light in them." [10]

"Old Joe Smith."—Were these tests applied to Joseph Smith in the early part of the nineteenth century? Yes, by some; and they received the promised testimony of the Truth, the absolute evidence of the divinity of this Prophet's mission. But by far the greater number of those to whom he fain would have ministered, rejected him summarily and without investigation. To them he was only "Joe Smith"—"Old Joe Smith"—old indeed in wisdom, though young in earthly years, yielding up his life as a martyr at the early age of thirty-eight. His claim to being an oracle of God was deemed preposterous, blasphemous; and his religion, the pure Gospel of Christ, was denounced as the world's worst delusion and snare.

Badges of Honor.—But bad names, wrongly bestowed, hurt the giver, rather than the receiver. Blame and ridicule, when applied to the righteous, are badges of honor, worn by true prophets and true principles in all ages. It does not do away with a man of God to pelt him with nicknames and opprobrious epithets. Persecution may end his earthly career, but it cannot confute his claim nor invalidate his testimony. The name of the martyred modern Seer, despite the clouds of calumny enveloping it, shines out from amidst the darkness that comprehended him not. His glorious Lord and Master, crucified as an imposter, put to death for maintaining that he was more than the world believed him to be, gave the only Name given under heaven whereby men can be saved.

Footnotes

1. Matt. 13:55-57.

2. "Jesus" is the Greek form of the Hebrew "Joshua," frequently met with in Ezra and Nehemiah. It was

pronounced "Joshua" by the early Jews. Other forms of the name are "Hosea" or "Hoshea," "Oshea" and "Jehoshua."

3 . 1 Sam. 10:10; 19:20. 2 Kings 2:3; 4:38; 6:1.

4 . Jer. 1:1.

5 . Amos 7:14, 15.

6 . Abr. 3:23; Jer. 1:5.

7 . 1 John 4:1

8 . Job 32:8.

9 . 3 Nephi 11:29, 30.

10 . Isa. 8:20.

ARTICLE FOUR
THE CHOICE SEER

A Prenatal Naming.—Let us now take a closer view of this marvelous man, Joseph Smith, the most extraordinary character that has appeared upon our planet in the past two thousand years. His coming into the world fulfilled a prophecy uttered many centuries before his birth—a prophecy concerning "a choice seer," to be raised up "out of the loins" of Joseph who was sold into Egypt. The seer's name was likewise to be Joseph, and this also was to be the name of his father. [1] That prophecy was fulfilled in Joseph Smith, Jr., the founder of the Church of Jesus Christ of Latter-day Saints. "Joseph the Seer"—so is he designated by divine revelation. [2]

Like great Cyrus, who liberated the Jews from their captivity in Babylon, [3] the Lord's anointed in modern times, raised up to begin the work of Israel's final and complete redemption, was named and his mission outlined long before he had tabernacled in the flesh. Why he came gifted with the power of seership, was made manifest at the very beginning of his career.

Birth and Parentage.—Joseph the Seer was born at Sharon, Vermont, two days before Christmas, in the year 1805. When only a lad, living with his parents, Joseph and Lucy Smith, honest farm folk in the backwoods of Western New York, his career as a prophet began.

In Quest of Wisdom.—Partly from the effects of a religious revival held in his neighborhood, he became much concerned upon the subject of his soul's salvation, but was bewildered and unable to make choice of a church or creed, owing to the diverse and conflicting claims of the various Christian sects. While in this mood, he chanced upon the following passage of scripture: "If any of you lack wisdom, let him ask of God, that giveth to all men liberally, and upbraideth not; and it shall be given him." [4] Deeply impressed with the sacred words, he forthwith resolved to ask from God the wisdom of which he stood in need.

The First Vision.—Retiring to a grove near his father's home, he knelt in prayer to the Most High; but had scarcely begun his humble and earnest petition, when he was seized upon by a power that filled his soul with horror and paralyzed his tongue so that he could no longer speak. So terrible was the visitation, that he almost gave way to despair. Yet he continued to pray—in thought, with "the soul's sincere desire"—and just at the moment when he feared he must abandon himself to destruction, he saw, directly over his head, a light more brilliant than the noonday sun. In the midst of a pillar of glory he beheld two beings in human form, one of whom, pointing to the other, said: "This is my beloved Son, hear Him." [5]

All Churches Astray.—With the appearance of the Light, the boy found himself delivered from the fettering power of the Evil One. As soon as he could again command utterance, he inquired of his heavenly visitants which of all the religious denominations was right—which one was the true Church of Christ? To his astonishment, he was told that none of them was right; that they had all gone out of the way. Their creeds were an abomination, and their professors corrupt. "They draw near to me with their lips, but their hearts are far from me; they teach for doctrine the commandments of men, having a form of godliness, but they deny the power thereof." So spake the Son of God concerning the churches. [6] He declared that he did not recognize any of them; but was about to restore the Everlasting Gospel, with the powers of the Eternal Priesthood, and establish his Church once more in the midst of mankind.

Such was Joseph Smith's first vision and revelation. It came in the spring of 1820, when he was but a few months over fourteen years of age.

The Divine Personality.—The greater part of this wonderful manifestation was the part that did not speak—the silent revealing of the personality of God; a truth plainly taught in the Scriptures, but ignored or denied by modern Christianity. The object worshiped by the sects was defined in their theology as a being "without body, parts or passions." [7] That was the popular concept of Deity throughout Christendom when Joseph Smith and "Mormonism" came forth. In line with this tenet and teaching, an English poet of the eighteenth century had represented God as a "Mind" or "Soul" that

> Warms in the sun, refreshes in the breeze,
> Glows in the stars, and blossoms in the trees,
> Lives through all life, extends through all extent,
> Spreads undivided, operates unspent. [8]

These beautiful couplets admirably describe the Spirit of the Lord—that all-pervading energy or essence which proceeds from the Divine Presence, fills the immensity of space, is everywhere present, and is immanent in all creation. But they give no adequate idea of the Great Creator, "the father of the spirits" of men, [9] who sent into the world his Beloved Son, "the brightness of his glory and the express image of his person", [10] that men might see in him the Father and worship God aright. The Son of God, walking as a man upon the earth, plainly indicated what kind of a being God is; and when his disciple, Philip, said to him, "Lord, show us the Father," Jesus replied: "He that hath seen me hath seen the Father." [11] Could anything be plainer?

But these teachings were lost upon the modern Christian world. They had turned from the truth "unto fables", [12] forsaking the God of their fathers, and substituting for him as an object of worship, an ideal of their own creation. And it devolved upon Joseph Smith to shatter the false doctrine of a bodiless, passionless deity, and bring back the lost knowledge of the true and living God.

The True and Living God.—What is meant by that? Who is "the true and living God?" He is the God of the Bible, the God of Abraham, Isaac and Jacob, the God of Adam, of Enoch, of Noah, of the patriarchs and prophets and apostles of old—the God described by Moses in the first chapter of Genesis, where it is written: "God created man in his own image, in the image of God created he him, male and female, created he them." This is equivalent to saying that God is in the form of man, and that we have a Mother as well as a Father in Heaven, in whose image or likeness we are, male and female.

Of the divine Three who hold supreme power and preside over the universe—three distinct personalities, yet one God or Godhead, one in will, wisdom, power and authority—of these, the Father and the Son, according to Joseph Smith, are personages of tabernacle. They have bodies "as tangible as man's;" while the Holy Ghost "is a personage of spirit." [13]

The Idol of the Sects.—Proceeding forth from them, is that all-pervading essence or influence which is immanent in all things—the light of the sun, moon and stars, the light also of the human understanding, quickening and illumining, in greater or less degree, "every man that cometh into the world." In it we live, move and have our being; for it is the principle of life throughout creation. This is what the poet was describing, when he portrayed Deity as a "Soul" that "warms in the sun, refreshes in the breeze," etc. And this is what the Christian sects were worshiping at the beginning of the nineteenth century. Not God, but a spirit sent forth from God; not Divinity, but an emanation from Divinity. In a word, they were practicing idolatry—or something dangerously akin to it.

What Constitutes Idolatry?—"Idolatry is every worship that stops short of the Supreme." [14] It is "the paying of divine homage to false gods or images; also, adoration of created or imaginary beings or natural objects or forces." [15] This is precisely what the ancient world was doing when the book of Genesis was written. The Canaanites worshiped the sun and moon—Baal and Ashtoreth—ascribing to them the powers of creation. The Egyptians adored the crocodile, the bull, the goat and the beetle (scarabeus). Among the Hindus the seasons were deified—spring, summer, autumn, winter; as were also the passions—love, hate, fear, anger and revenge. All these were revered as deities. Then came Moses, who had seen the living and true God, and had conversed with him face to face, receiving from him the Decalogue or Ten Commandments unto Israel. The first commandment reads: "Thou shalt have no other gods before me."

Modern Christendom's Position.—The world in Joseph Smith's day—the Christian world at least—did not worship the heavenly bodies; did not deify beasts and reptiles, did not regard the seasons and passions as divine. Yet it had turned from the true God, ignoring or misinterpreting what Moses and the prophets had written concerning him. According to its dictum, the age of miracles was past; prophets were out of date, and angel messengers obsolete; the heavens were sealed, the canon of scripture was full, and God would never again communicate with mortals. Then came the vision of the Father and the Son—two glorious beings in the form of man—and from the hour that the boy Joseph beheld them, there was at least one person upon this planet who knew what kind of a being God is. It was a virtual reassertion of the first commandment in the Decalogue: "Thou shalt have no other gods before me."

To worship anything that God has made and given, in lieu of the Maker and Giver, is to worship an idol. They who turn from the Creator to the creature, who forsake God and adore a gift or an emanation from God, are idolaters, almost as much as if they worshiped the sun and moon, or bowed down to goats and crocodiles.

Like to Elijah.—To restore the acceptable worship of Jehovah, and begin a work that would sweep away idolatry and all things connected therewith, was the mission of Joseph the Seer. Against him, as against Elijah of old, the priests of Baal raged in impotent fury. Despite their tongues of slander and their weapons of violence, he accomplished all that had been given him to do. This time, however, the All-Wise permitted his servant to be sacrificed— to the end, no doubt, that his innocent blood, affixing to his testimony the red seal of martyrdom, might give added power to the great propaganda then and still in progress for Israel's redemption—the gathering of the scattered sheep preparatory to the Shepherd's coming.

Footnotes

1 . 2 Nephi 3:6-15.

2 . D. and C. 21:1. See also headings to most of the sections in this book.

3 . Isa. 44:28; 45:1-5.

4 . James 1:5.

5 . Hist. Ch., Vol. 1, Chap. 1, p. 5.

6 . Compare Isa. 29:13.

7 . Church of England Articles of Religion, Presbyterian Confession of Faith, etc.

8 . Pope's "Essay on Man," Epistle 1, lines 271-274.

9 . Heb. 12:9.

10 . Ib. 1:3; Gen. 1:26, 27; Philipp. 2:6; Col. 1:15, etc.

11 . John 14:9.

12 . 2 Tim. 4:4.

13 . D. and C. 130:22. Compare 1 Nephi 11:11.

14 . F. H. Hedge, "Ways of the Spirit," Essay 8, p. 215.

15 . F. W. Standard Dictionary.

ARTICLE FIVE
THE LAND OF ZION

The Angel Moroni.—Three years after that wonderful vision in the Grove, the youthful Seer received a visitation from an angel, a messenger from the presence of the Lord. This Angel gave his name as Moroni, and declared that while in mortal life he had ministered as a prophet to an ancient people called Nephites, a branch of the house of Israel—not the Lost Tribes, as is frequently asserted by the uninformed, but a portion of the tribe of Joseph, mixed with a remnant of the tribe of Judah. The former had crossed over from Jerusalem about the year 600 B. C.; the others a few years later. These blended colonies had inhabited the Americas down to about the beginning of the fourth century of the Christian era, when the civilized though degenerate Nephites were destroyed by a savage faction known as Lamanites, ancestors of the American Indians.

The Book of Mormon.—The Angel further stated that a record of the Nephites would be found in a hill not far from Joseph's home—a hill anciently called Cumorah; and upon that spot, four years afterward, Moroni delivered the record into his hands. It was a book of metallic plates "having the appearance of gold," and covered with strange characters, "small and beautifully engraved"—characters known to the Nephites as "the reformed Egyptian." [1]

By means of "interpreters," discovered with the plates, and consisting of "two stones in silver bows," the youth translated the unsealed portion of the record and, with the assistance of a few friends, published to the world the Book of Mormon. It was so named for its compiler, the Nephite prophet Mormon, whose son and survivor, Moroni, had buried the plates where Joseph Smith found them. The date of discovery was September 22nd, 1823. [2]

The Hill Cumorah is situated between Palmyra and Manchester, in the State of New York. For their belief in the Book of Mormon, the Latter-day Saints were termed "Mormons," and their religion "Mormonism." It proclaims itself the restored fulness of the Gospel of Jesus Christ.

History and Prophecy.—The Book of Mormon is a sacred history of prehistoric America, and a prophecy of the wondrous future of this chosen land. It tells not only of the Nephites and Lamanites, but also of a more ancient people, the Jaredites, who came from the Tower of Babel at the time of the confusion of tongues. Becoming extinct, the Jaredites were succeeded by the Israelitish colony, led from Jerusalem by a prophet named Lehi, whose sons Nephi and Laman became, respectively, the heads of the two nations that sprang from him and were called after their names. The Jewish remnant that mixt with the descendants of Lehi was headed by Mulek, one of the sons of King Zedekiah, whom the Babylonian conqueror, Nebuchadnezzar, overthrew.

The New Jerusalem.—The Jaredites, as well as the Nephites, had a knowledge of the Christ and of the principles of his Gospel, revealed to them prior to his coming. To both these nations it was made known that America is the Land of Zion, the place for the New Jerusalem, a holy city to be built "unto the remnant of the seed of Joseph." [3] Likewise was it shown to them that the Old Jerusalem would be rebuilt "unto the house of Israel" in the last days. All this before the Savior's second advent—the glorious mornbreak of the Millennium.

A Nursing Mother.—Among the many interesting features of the Book of Mormon, is an ancient prophecy of the discovery of America by Columbus; the migration of the Pilgrim Fathers and others to these western shores; the war for American Independence, and the founding of the republic of the United States, a nation destined long before its birth to play the part of a nursing mother to the restored Church of Christ. [4]

And let me interject, that whatever may be said of the persecutions suffered by the Latter-day Saints under the Stars and Stripes in various States of the Union—persecutions inflicted, not because of the Flag, nor of the Constitution, nor of the genius of the American Government, but in spite of them—persecutions inflicted by lawless force, by mob violence, ever to be execrated and condemned by every true patriot—whatever may be said of such deplorable happenings, still must our noble Nation be credited with what it has done in the direction of fulfilling its God-given mission. It is extremely doubtful that in any other land, or in any other nation upon this land, would the Lord's people have been treated with the same degree of consideration. In no other country on earth, without special divine interposition in its behalf, would this great and marvelous work have been permitted to come forth.

A Land of Liberty.—America, according to Nephite prophecy, is to be a land of liberty to the Gentiles—modern peoples, not of Israel, now possessing it—provided they serve the God of the Land, who is Jesus Christ. So long as they shall follow righteousness, and maintain the pure principles upon which this Government was founded, just so long will they prosper and enjoy the favor of Heaven. America, if true to her mission, is promised divine protection, and will be invulnerable to every foe. God "will fortify this land against all other nations," and they who "fight against Zion shall perish." [5]

The Alternative.—If, however, the Gentiles, lifted up in pride, shall harden their hearts and reject the fulness of Christ's Gospel, Liberty's perfect law, another destiny, and a sad one, awaits them. No king but Christ shall reign upon Zion's Land. No people occupying this choice ground can practice evil with impunity. The nation founded here must be a righteous nation, or like the Jaredites and the Nephites, who perished because of their wickedness, it will be swept from the face of the land when the cup of its iniquity is full. So the God of Heaven hath decreed. [6]

Joseph's Blessing.—Another name for America, authorized by the Book of Mormon, is the Land of Joseph, referred to by the Patriarch Jacob in blessing his twelve sons, [7] and by the Prophet Moses in his farewell benediction upon the twelve tribes of Israel. [8] Jacob's allusion to Joseph as "a fruitful bough by a well, whose branches run over the wall," was fulfilled in the migration of Lehi and his companions from Asia to America over the Pacific Ocean. It is hardly necessary to add, in further exegetical comment, that one of the main features of these western continents are those mighty mountain ranges, the Andes and the Rockies, well termed by the Hebrew Patriarch "the everlasting hills," nature's depositories for "the precious things of the earth"—gold, silver, and other minerals—and for "the precious things of heaven"—the sacred records that have already been discovered, and others that are yet to come forth.

Joseph and Judah.—The Book of Mormon has a divine mission in connection with the Hebrew Scriptures, "unto the confounding of false doctrines and laying down of contentions." [9] It is "The Stick of Joseph," referred to by the Prophet Ezekiel, that was to be one with "The Stick of Judah" (The Bible) "in the hand of Ephraim." They were also to be one in the hand of Jehovah, symbolizing the reunion of the two great branches of the Israelitish race, after many centuries of separation. "And I will make them one nation in the land upon the mountains of Israel," saith the Lord, "and David my servant shall be king over them." [10]

Zion and Jerusalem.—David's ancient empire, which parted in twain, forming the Kingdom of Judah and the Kingdom of Israel, may it not have been a foreshadowing of God's greater empire of the last days, which will consist of two grand divisions—two in one? Here upon the Land of Zion, "a land choice above all other lands," [11] the children of Joseph, the descendants of Ephraim, are even now assembling to make preparation for Messiah's advent. The Jews will greet him at Jerusalem. Christ's Kingdom will have two capitals, one in the Old World, one in the New; one in America, the other in Palestine. "For out of Zion shall go forth the law, and the word of the Lord from Jerusalem." [12]

Footnotes

1 . Mormon 9:32.

2 . Hist. Church, Vol. 1, p. 15.

3 . 3 Nephi 21:23, 24; Ether 13:3-8.

4 . 1 Nephi 13:10-19; 22:7, 8.

5 . 2 Nephi 10:11-13.

6 . Ether 2:8-12.

7 . Gen. 49:22-26.

8 . Deut. 33:13-15.

9 . 2 Nephi 3:12.

10 . Ezek. 37:16-24. The king here mentioned is not David, son of Jesse, but "another by the name of David" who is to be "raised up out of his lineage."—Hist. Ch., Vol. 6, p. 253.

11 . Ether 2:10.

12 . Isa. 2:3.

PART TWO
SEERSHIP AND PROPHECY

ARTICLE SIX
WHAT JOSEPH BEHELD

Seer and Prophet.—"Seer" and "Prophet" are interchangeable terms, supposed by many to signify one and the same thing. Strictly speaking, however, this is not correct. A seer is greater than a prophet. [1] One may be a prophet without being a seer; but a seer is essentially a prophet—if by "prophet" is meant not only a spokesman, but likewise a foreteller. Joseph Smith was both prophet and seer. [2]

Like Unto Moses.—A seer is one who sees. But it is not the ordinary sight that is meant. The seeric gift is a supernatural endowment. Joseph was "like unto Moses;" and Moses, who saw God face to face, explains how he saw him in these words: "Now mine own eyes have beheld God; yet not my natural, but my spiritual eyes; for my natural eyes could not have beheld; for I should have withered and died in his presence; but his glory was upon me; and I beheld his face, for I was transfigured before him." Such is the testimony of the ancient Seer, as brought to light by the Seer of Latter-days. [3]

Spirit Eyes.—Let it not be supposed, however, that to see spiritually is not to see literally. Vision is not fancy, not imagination. The object is actually beheld, though not with the natural eye. We all have spirit eyes, of which our natural or outward eyes are the counterpart. All man's organs and faculties are firstly spiritual, the body being but the clothing of the spirit. In our first estate, the spirit life, we "walked by sight." Therefore we had eyes. But they were not our natural eyes, for these are not given until the spirit tabernacles in mortality. All men have a spirit sight, but all are not permitted to use it under existing conditions. Even those thus privileged can only use it when quickened by the Spirit of the Lord. [4] Without that, no man can know the things of God, "because they are spiritually discerned." [5] Much less can he look upon the Highest unspiritually, with carnal mind or with natural vision. "No man"—no natural man—"hath seen God at any time." [6] But men at divers times have seen him as Moses saw him—not with the natural but with the spiritual eye, quickened by the power that seeth and knoweth all things.

By the Holy Ghost.—The seeric faculty, possessed in greater degree by some than by others, is the original spirit sight reinforced or moved upon by the power of the Holy Ghost. By this means certain persons, peculiarly gifted and sent into the world for that purpose, are able, even while in the flesh, to see out of obscurity, "out of hidden darkness," and behold the things of God pertaining both to time and to eternity. Joseph Smith possessed this ability—this gift, but it was the Spirit of the Lord that enabled him to use it. By that Spirit he beheld the Father and the Son; and by that Spirit, operating through the same marvelous gift, he translated the cryptic contents of the Book of Mormon.

How the Book of Mormon was Translated.—The reputed method of translation was as follows: The Seer, scanning through the "interpreters" (Urim and Thummim) the golden pages, saw appear, in connection with the strange characters engraved thereon, their equivalent in English words. These he repeated to his scribe—Oliver Cowdery most of the time—and the latter wrote them. It was a peculiarity of the process that, until the writing was correct in every particular, the words last given would not disappear; but on the necessary correction being made, they would immediately pass away and be succeeded by others. [7]

The Priesthood Restored.—The greater part of the Book of Mormon was translated at Harmony, Pennsylvania, the home of Joseph's father-in-law, Isaac Hale. While the Prophet and his scribe were thus employed (May 15, 1829) John the Baptist, as an angel from heaven, conferred upon them the Aaronic Priesthood. [8] Soon afterward they were ordained to the higher or Melchizedek Priesthood, by three other heavenly messengers, the Apostles Peter, James and John. [9] By virtue of this authority, and pursuant to divine direction, the two young men, associated with a few others organized the Church of Jesus Christ of Latter-day Saints.

Petty Persecution.—During their sojourn in the little Pennsylvania village, Joseph and Oliver suffered considerable annoyance at the hands of mischievous persons who, having no faith in their work and regarding it as a hoax, seemed bent upon rendering their situation as disagreeable as possible. Learning of their unpleasant situation, and desiring to help along the sacred task to which they were devoting themselves, Peter Whitmer, Sr., a farmer living at Fayette, Seneca County, New York, sent his son David with a team and wagon to bring them to the Whitmer home.

David Whitmer's Account.—"When I arrived at Harmony," says David Whitmer, "Joseph and Oliver were coming towards me and met me at some distance from the house. Oliver told me that Joseph had informed him when I started from home, where I had stopped the first night, how I read the sign at the tavern, where I stopped the second night, etc., and that I would be there that day before dinner; and this was why they had come out to meet me. All of which was exactly as Joseph had told Oliver; at which I was greatly astonished." [10] It was at the Whitmer farmhouse, in Fayette, that the Church was organized, April 6th, 1830.

Newel K. Whitney and the "Stranger."—Another instance of Joseph's use of the seeric gift connects with the occasion of his arrival at Kirtland, Ohio, where the Church, at an early day, established its headquarters. A few months prior to that time, Oliver Cowdery and three other Elders, on their way to preach the Gospel to the Lamanites, or Indians, had tarried for a season at Kirtland, where they converted a number of the white dwellers in that region. Among these were Sidney Rigdon, Newel K. Whitney, and others who became prominent in the "Mormon" community. The Saints in Ohio, learning that the Church would probably move westward, began to pray for the coming of the Prophet.

The prayer was soon answered. About the first of February, 1831, a sleigh, driven into Kirtland from the East, drew up in front of the mercantile store of Gilbert and Whitney. A stalwart young man alighted and walked into the store. Approaching the junior partner and extending his hand cordially, as if to an old and familiar acquaintance, he saluted him thus: "Newel K. Whitney, thou art the man!"

The merchant was astonished. He had never seen this person before. "Stranger," said he, "You have the advantage of me; I could not call you by name as you have me."

"I am Joseph the Prophet," said the stranger, smiling. "You have prayed me here, now what do you want of me?"

Joseph Smith, while in the State of New York, had seen Newel K. Whitney, in the State of Ohio, praying for his coming to Kirtland; and therefore knew him when they met. [11] The purpose of this vision, in all probability, was to pave the way for a meeting between the Prophet and the man who was to have the honor of entertaining him during the first weeks after his arrival in Ohio.

Vision of the Three Glories.—One of the most glorious manifestations ever vouchsafed to mortals, came to Joseph Smith and Sidney Rigdon, in the month of February, 1832. They were at Hiram, Portage County, Ohio, where the Prophet, assisted by Elder Rigdon, who had been a Campbellite preacher, was occupied with revising the English translation of the Hebrew Bible—a circumstance that may have given rise to the oft-refuted story of Rigdon's authorship of the Book of Mormon. [12] The manifestation referred to was a vision of human destiny, including the three general conditions of glorified man—celestial, terrestrial, and telestial. Concerning this marvelous vision, Joseph and Sidney thus testify:

"We, Joseph Smith, Jr., and Sidney Rigdon, being in the Spirit on the sixteenth of February, in the year of our Lord, one thousand eight hundred and thirty-two, by the power of the Spirit our eyes were opened and our understandings were enlightened, so as to see and understand the things of God . . . .

"Of whom we bear record, and the record which we bear is the fulness of the Gospel of Jesus Christ, who is the Son, whom we saw and with whom we conversed in the heavenly vision." [13]

Thus is furnished an additional proof that it is by the power of God, and not of man, that mortals behold the visions of eternity.

The Greenville Incident.—In May of the same year, Joseph Smith, President of the Church, and Newel K. Whitney, Bishop of Kirtland, were returning from a visit to Jackson County, Missouri, where, since the summer of 1831, a "Mormon" colony had been laying the foundations of the City of Zion, upon grounds consecrated by the Prophet for that purpose. The returning visitors were detained several weeks at Greenville, Indiana; the Bishop having a broken leg, caused by leaping from a runaway stage coach. Surrounded by unfriendly people, some of whom he suspected of an attempt to poison him, the Prophet proposed that they forthwith leave that dangerous neighborhood. His record goes on to say:

"Brother Whitney had not had his foot moved from the bed for nearly four weeks, when I went into his room, after a walk in the grove, and told him if he would agree to start for home in the morning, we would take a wagon to the river about four miles, and there would be a ferry-boat in waiting, which would take us quickly across, where we would find a hack which would take us directly to the landing, where we should find a boat in waiting, and we would be going up the river before ten o'clock, and have a prosperous journey home. He took courage and told me he would go; we started the next morning and found everything as I had told him." [14]

A White Lamanite.—Still another instance. In 1834, while the "Zion's Camp" expedition [15] was on its way to Missouri, some of the party exhumed from an ancient mound the skeleton of a man having a stone-pointed arrow between two of his ribs. The Prophet, in a vision of the past, discovered the identity of this skeleton, and informed his brethren that the man's name was Zelph, that he was "a white Lamanite," [16] and had been killed in battle by the arrow found between his ribs. [17]

Kirtland Temple Visions.—By this same power Joseph Smith and Oliver Cowdery, in the Temple at Kirtland, Ohio (April 3rd, 1836), beheld Jehovah, the God of Israel; also Moses, Elias and Elijah, who committed to them spiritual keys necessary for carrying on various phases of the Lord's work. [18]

Adam's Altar.—In 1838, after the main body of the Church had moved to Missouri, the Saints built several towns and projected others in Caldwell and other counties of that State. One of those towns was at Spring Hill, Davis County, where the men who made the survey for a new settlement came upon the ruins of an ancient altar, situated on a wooded hill overlooking the surrounding country. Straightway they reported to the Prophet their interesting find. He, upon beholding it, said to those who were with him: "There is the place where Adam offered up sacrifice after he was cast out of the Garden." [19]

The Old-New World.—America, according to Joseph Smith, is the Old World—not the New [20]. The primeval Garden was in the part now called Jackson County. Our First Parents, after their expulsion from Eden, dwelt in the place where this altar stood. The Lord named it Adam-ondi-Ahman, "because it is the place where Adam shall come to visit his people, or the Ancient of Days shall sit, as spoken of by Daniel the Prophet." [21]

All this by the power of seership—all this and more; for many other instances might be given. But these will suffice to show the nature of this rare and precious gift, and the manner of its exercise by the mighty Seer and Prophet holding the keys of this Gospel dispensation.

Footnotes

1. Mosiah 8:15.

2. Such men as Ralph Waldo Emerson, the American philosopher, and Count Leo Tolstoi, the Russian writer, are sometimes referred to as "seers;" it being thought by those who so designate them, that the power to think profoundly and express wise and intelligent opinions, especially on

the future, constitutes seership. It is in this sense that the term "vision" is so much used. But a great thinker is not necessarily a seer; though a seer is apt to be a great thinker. Joseph Smith was both; not so Ralph Waldo Emerson; not so Count Tolstoi. They were great philosophers, but there is nothing in the life-work of either to indicate that he possessed the power of a seer.

3 . Moses 1:11. Moses further declares that he could look upon Satan "in the natural man," but, says he: "I could not look upon God, except his glory should come upon me and I was strengthened before him."

4 . D. and C. 67:11.

5 . 1 Cor. 2:9-14.

6 . John 1:18.

7 . David Whitmer's "Address to all True Believers in Christ." p. 12; and Martin Harris' Statement to Edward Stevenson, Millennial Star, Vol. 44, pp. 86, 87.

8 . D. and C. 13.

9 . Hist. Ch. Vol. 1 pp. 39-42, Note.

10 . David Whitmer's Statement to Orson Pratt and Joseph F. Smith, Mill. Star, Vol. 40, p. 772.

11 . Hist. Ch., Vol 1, pp. 145, 146. Note.

12 . Sidney Ridgon had never so much as seen the Book of Mormon, until several months after it was published, when a copy of it was handed to him in Northern Ohio, by Parley P. Pratt, one of the Elders of the Lamanite Mission. Parley and Sidney corroborate each other in their separate accounts of this incident. Moreover Sidney's acquaintance with Joseph Smith did not begin until almost a year after the Book of Mormon came forth. Yet he was charged with creating it, with converting a religious history into a secular romance entirely dissimilar in character and style from the Nephite record—a romance written by one Solomon Spaulding. A full account of this discredited theory of the origin of the Book of Mormon may be found in George Reynolds' "Myth of the Manuscript Found," and in "Whitney's History of Utah," Vol. 1, pp. 46-56.

13 . D. and C. 76:11, 12, 14. See also Article Forty, this Series.

14 . Hist. Ch. Vol. 1, pp. 271, 272.

15 . See Article Twenty-four.

16 . 3 Nephi 2:14-16.

17 . Hist. Ch. Vol. 2, pp. 79, 80.

18 . D. and C. 110.

19 . "Life of Heber C. Kimball," p. 222; Taylor's "Mediation and Atonement," pp. 69, 70; Whitney's "History of Utah"— Biography A. O. Smoot, Vol. 4, p. 99.

20 . The Prophet's inspired declaration to that effect finds confirmation in the writings of Thomas Jefferson, Alexander Agassiz, and John Fiske.

21 . D. and C. 116.

ARTICLE SEVEN
WHAT JOSEPH FORETOLD

The Proof of Prophecy.—To prove one a prophet, it is necessary to show, not only that he prophesied, but that things predicted by him came to pass. Measured by this standard, Joseph Smith's claim to the title is clear and unimpeachable. I shall not attempt to enumerate all his prophecies, but will mention some of the more notable, as demonstrating his possession of the wonderful power to unlock and reveal the future.

Earliest Predictions.—The Angel Moroni's promise to the boy, that he, an obscure and unlettered country lad, should live to do a work that would cause his name to be known among all nations, [1] has been often cited—too often to require extended comment here. The same may be said of Isaiah's familiar declaration, that in the presence of God's wondrous work, the wisdom of the wise should perish and the understanding of the prudent be hid. [2] These promises are fulfilling daily. Passing them by with this brief mention, I take up one of the best known of Joseph Smith's predictions, namely, the "Revelation and Prophecy on War."

An Ominous Christmas Gift.—This tremendous forecast, relating not only to the fierce internecine struggle between the Northern and Southern States of the American Union, but to other and mightier upheavals as well, some past and some yet future, was launched at Kirtland, Ohio, on the 25th of December, 1832. It may be said, therefore, that it came as a solemn Christmas gift to the inhabitants of the world, warning them to prepare for terrible events.

War and Other Calamities.—The Prophet declared that war would "be poured out upon all nations," beginning at a certain place. That place was South Carolina. The Southern States, divided against the Northern States, would call upon Great Britain, and Great Britain would call upon other nations, for defensive assistance against hostile powers. Slaves, rising against their masters, would be "marshalled and disciplined for war;" and the red remnants "left of the land" would "become exceeding angry" and "vex the Gentiles with a sore vexation." By bloodshed and famine, plague, earthquake and tempest, the inhabitants of the earth would mourn and "be made to feel the wrath and indignation and chastening hand of an Almighty God." The Prophet exhorted his followers to "stand in holy places and be not moved, until the day of the Lord come." [3]

For nineteen years this prophecy remained in manuscript, though copies of it were carried by "Mormon" missionaries and read to their congregations in various parts of the world. In 1851 it was published at Liverpool, the first edition of "The Pearl of Great Price" containing it. Therefore, it was a matter of public note and printed record long before the dire fulfillment began.

Beginning of the Fulfillment.—The revelation had been in existence twenty-eight years, three months, and seventeen days, when, on the twelfth of April, 1861, the Confederate batteries in Charleston Harbor, South Carolina, opened fire on Fort Sumter, thus precipitating the war between the North and the South. As is well known, it arose over the slave question, a circumstance fulfilling another of Joseph Smith's predictions—one dated April 2nd, 1843. [4]

Southern States call on Great Britain.—How eleven of the Southern States, bent upon withdrawing from the Union and establishing an independent government south of the Mason and Dixon Line, called upon Great Britain, and were accorded a measure of encouragement by the ruling classes of that country, need scarcely be told here. The arrest and release of the Confederate commissioners, Mason and Slidell, who had been sent across the Atlantic to present the case of the seceding States at the Court of St. James; and the subsequent payment by the British Government of the Alabama claims ($15,500,000), for damages sustained by United States commerce at the hand of Confederate privateers, built and fitted out in British ports, tell in part the story.

The Negro and Indian Questions.—It is also a matter of history, that many of the negro slaves, set free by President Lincoln's edict of emancipation, and trained as troops, fought in the Northern armies against their former masters. Whether or not this was a complete fulfillment of the forecast concerning the once enslaved people, remains to be seen. The race question was not entirely settled by the Civil War; it still hovers as a dark cloud on our national horizon. As for Indian troubles, many of which have arisen since Joseph Smith prophesied concerning them, while apparently they have ceased to "vex," more may yet be heard from that quarter before the problem is finally solved.

An Effort to Avert Calamity.—Joseph Smith's last public act of a political character was an effort to save his country from the awful calamity that he saw impending. To some it may appear strange, even inconsistent, that a prophet, after making a prediction, would try to prevent it from coming to pass. But it is only a seeming inconsistency. It should be remembered that divine promises and prophecies are conditional. There is always an alternative, expressed or implied, hinging upon a change of attitude or conduct on the part of the person or persons toward whom the prophecy is directed. Deem it not incongruous, therefore, that this Prophet, after predicting the Civil War, should endeavor to open a way of escape from the evils he had foreseen and foretold.

In January, 1844, only five months before his martyrdom, Joseph Smith became a candidate for President of the United States. One of the planks of his political platform was a proposition to free the slaves of the South—not by confiscation, thereby despoiling their owners, but by purchase, making their freedom a gift from the General Government; the funds necessary for the purpose to be realized from the sale of public lands. This just and humane proposition, repeated eleven years later by Ralph Waldo Emerson, [5] and favored also by Abraham Lincoln, was ignored; and it cost the Nation a million of lives and billions of treasure to despise the counsel of a prophet of God, and adopt instead what the hate-blinded politicians of that period deemed "a more excellent way." [6]

How Stephen A. Douglas Fulfilled Prophecy.—Closely connected with events immediately preceding the Civil War, is another prophecy of Joseph Smith's, uttered May 18, 1843, and recorded at the time in the journal of his private secretary. On the date given, the Prophet dined with Stephen A. Douglas, at the home of Sheriff Backenstos, in Carthage, Illinois, the same town where the brothers Joseph and Hyrum afterwards met their tragic death. Judge Douglas was holding court there. The principal topic of conversation after dinner was the persecution of the Latter-day Saints in Missouri, not only the Jackson County affair of 1833, but the more sanguinary tragedy of 1838-1839, culminating in the mid-winter expulsion of the entire Church—then numbering twelve to fifteen thousand members—and its establishment in the adjoining State of Illinois. An account of these events, at the Judge's request, the "Mormon" leader gave. His narrative included a recital of the ineffectual attempts made by him and his people to obtain from the Federal government a redress of grievances.

Douglas was deeply interested, and strongly condemned the conduct of Missouri. He was very friendly with the Prophet, who, continuing the conversation, predicted trouble for the Nation unless those wrongs were righted. Then, addressing Douglas, he said: "Judge, you will aspire to the Presidency of the United States; and if you ever turn your hand against me or the Latter-day Saints, you will feel the weight of the hand of the Almighty upon you. And you will live to see and know that I have testified the truth to you, for the conversation of this day will stick to you through life." [7]

God's Hand Against Him.—Judge Douglas reaped the full fruition of those fateful words. The prophecy concerning him was first published in the Deseret News, at Salt Lake City, September 24, 1856, and on February 26, 1859, it appeared in the Millennial Star, at Liverpool. Between those dates, Stephen A. Douglas, then a United States Senator—made such by the aid of "Mormon" votes in Illinois—turned his hand against his old-time friends and supporters. Joseph Smith was dead, but his followers, driven from the confines of civilization, were out in the wilderness, laying the foundations of the State of Utah. In a political speech, at Springfield, Illinois, June 12, 1857, Senator Douglas, basing a reference to the "Mormons" upon certain wild rumors afloat concerning them, virtually accused them of all manner of crimes and abominations. The speech was looked upon as a bid for popular favor.

Then came the Senator's race for the Presidency. His prospects at the outset were favorable. His party held the preponderance of the national vote, and he was the idol of his party. In June, 1860, he was enthusiastically nominated by the Democratic Convention at Baltimore. Men shouted for him, worked for him, and on election day voted for him; but all in vain, God's hand was against him! His party, torn by dissension, divided its strength among three candidates, and was overwhelmingly defeated. "The Little Giant" was "snowed under," and his great rival, Abraham Lincoln, elevated to the Presidential chair. A few months later Senator Douglas died at his home in Chicago. He was only in the prime of life—aged forty-eight—but he had lived long enough to realize that God's prophets do not speak in vain.

Footnotes

1 . Hist. Ch. Vol. 1, pp. 11, 12.

2 . Isa. 29:14.

3 . D. and C. 87.

4 . Ib. 130:12, 13.

5 . Josiah Quincy, who visited Joseph Smith at Nauvoo shortly before the martyrdom, says of him and his views on slavery:

"Smith recognized the curse and iniquity of slavery, though he opposed the methods of the Abolitionists. His plan was for the nation to pay for the slaves from the sale of the public lands. 'Congress,' he said, 'should be compelled to take this course, by petitions from all parts of the country;

but the petitioners must disclaim all alliance with those who would disturb the rights of property recognized by the Constitution and foment insurrection.' It may be worth while to remark that Smith's plan was publicly advocated, eleven years later, by one who has mixed so much practical shrewdness with his lofty philosophy. In 1855, when men's minds had been moved to their depths on the question of slavery, Mr. Ralph Waldo Emerson declared that it should be met in accordance 'with the interest of the South and with the settled conscience of the North. It is not really a great task, a great fight for this country to accomplish, to buy that property of the planter, as the British nation bought the West Indian slaves.' He further says that the 'United States will be brought to give every inch of their public lands for a purpose like this.' We, who can look back upon the terrible cost of the fratricidal war which put an end to slavery, now say that such a solution of the difficulty would have been worthy a Christian statesman. But if the retired scholar was in advance of his time when he advocated this disposition of the public property in 1855 what shall I say of the political and religious leader who had committed himself, in print, as well as in conversation, to the same course in 1844? If the atmosphere of men's opinions was stirred by such a proposition when war-clouds were discernible in the sky, was it not a statesmanlike word eleven years earlier, when the heavens looked tranquil and beneficent."—"Figures of the Past," pp. 397, 398.

6. President Lincoln, toward the close of the Civil War, "wrote a message to Congress, proposing to pay the slaveholders $400,000,000 for their slaves, if the South would only cease fighting. All the Cabinet objecting, with a sigh he put the message in his drawer." See article, "Lincoln in Victory," by James Morgan, Deseret News, May 10, 1920.

7. William Clayton's Journal, May 18, 1843.

ARTICLE EIGHT
LOOKING WESTWARD

Why the "Mormons" Migrated.—Foreseeing that the Nation would turn a deaf ear to his patriotic appeal for a peaceful and just settlement of the slave question, the Prophet began to contemplate the removal of the Church from close proximity to the scenes of strife and carnage that were about to be enacted. It was highly necessary that a people chosen for such a purpose—to prepare the world for the ushering in of the Reign of Righteousness—should remain upon earth to accomplish their mission. In order to so remain, they must be out of the way of the troubles that were imminent, and, so far as possible, keep out of the way until the divine judgments predicted had gone forth and done their work. This was one reason why the Latter-day Saints migrated to the Rocky Mountains.

Driven to their Destiny.—Their cruel expulsion from Missouri had indirectly contributed to their safety; for when the war-cloud which had long been gathering finally burst, it poured out much of its fury upon those very lands from which the Saints had been driven. [1] And now, their enforced pilgrimage into the all but untrodden wilderness of the Great West likewise preserved them from many trials that would have fallen to their lot had they tarried within the area seriously affected by the stern events that followed.

Fleeing the Wrath to Come.—It was a next-best course that the fugitive people pursued. Originally they were cast for a very different role, but not being ready to enact that role, another part was assigned them, one destined to prepare them for the greater performance that is yet to follow. In order that the community might survive, and accomplish, when the time came, the mighty task of "redeeming Zion," it was imperative that they should "flee the wrath to come."

The Exodus Foretold.—The removal of the Saints to the region of the Rocky Mountains, was the theme of a prophecy uttered by Joseph the Seer nearly two years before his death, and nearly four years prior to the beginning of the famous "Mormon Exodus." Nauvoo, Illinois, where he then resided, is on the east bank of the Mississippi River, and on the west bank, just opposite, is the little town of Montrose. From the Prophet's personal history, I now quote an entry of Saturday, August 6th 1842:

"Passed over the river to Montrose, Iowa, in company with General Adams, Colonel Brewer and others, and witnessed the installation of the officers of the Rising Sun Lodge, Ancient York Masons, at Montrose, by General James Adams, Deputy Grand Master of Illinois. While the Deputy Grand Master was engaged in giving the requisite instructions to the Master-elect, I had a conversation with a number of brethren in the shade of the building, on the subject of our persecutions in Missouri and the constant annoyance which has followed us since we were driven from that State. I prophesied that the Saints would continue to suffer much affliction, and would be driven to the Rocky Mountains. Many would apostatize, others would be put to death by our persecutors or lose their lives in consequence of exposure or disease, 'and some of you will live to go and assist in making settlements, build cities, and see the Saints become a mighty people in the midst of the Rocky Mountains.'" [2]

Anson Call's Narrative.—One of the men who heard that prediction was Anson Call, afterwards a prominent colonizer in various parts of the Rocky Mountain region. His account, descriptive of the Montrose incident, follows:

"A block school-house had been prepared, with shade in front, under which was a barrel of ice water. Judge Adams was the highest Masonic authority in the State of Illinois, and had been sent there to organize this lodge. He, Hyrum Smith, and J. C. Bennett, being high Masons, went into the house to perform some ceremonies which the others were not entitled to witness. These, including Joseph Smith, remained under the bowery. Joseph, as he was tasting the cold water, warned the brethren not to be too free with it. With the tumbler still in his hand, he prophesied that the Saints would yet go to the Rocky Mountains; and, said he, 'this water tastes much like that of the crystal streams that are running from the snow-capped mountains.' .... I had before seen him in a vision (i.e. while having a vision), and now saw, while he was talking, his countenance change to white—not the deadly white of a bloodless face, but a living, brilliant white. He seemed absorbed in gazing upon something at a great distance, and said: 'I am gazing upon the valleys of those mountains.'" [3]

The Seeric Power.—Joseph Smith, at that time, was standing on the west bank of the Mississippi River, fifteen hundred miles from the Rocky Mountains; yet he saw these grand old hills, crowned with unmelting snows, and seamed with rugged gorges down which the crystal torrents were flowing as they flow today. He actually beheld, with spirit vision, these objects—beheld them so vividly, that had he been permitted to carry out his partly formed purpose of leading his people to their new home in the wilderness, he would have recognized this land, and would have been able to say, as Brigham Young said, upon beholding Salt Lake Valley: "This is the Place." [4]

Another Prophet and Seer.—But Joseph did not live to accompany his people upon their historic journey. Another mighty leader was raised up to pilot modern Israel to their promised land. Of Brigham Young it is related, that while crossing the plains west of the Missouri River, in the spring and summer of 1847, he had a vision of the region that he and his fellow pilgrims were about to inhabit. He saw a tent settling down from heaven over the Valley of the Great Salt Lake, and heard a voice proclaim: "This is the place where my people Israel shall pitch their tents." Such is the testimony of Erastus Snow, [5] one of the principal men who came with President Young to the Rocky Mountains. Consequently when the great Pioneer said, "This is the place," he was repeating words that had been spoken to him—repeating them while viewing with natural eyes a scene that his spirit eyes had already beheld.

Human Wisdom vs. Divine Guidance.—What availed, after that, the pessimistic forebodings of the mountaineer, James Bridger, who camped with the Pioneers just after they passed the Rocky Mountains, and whose laconic speech, "I would give a thousand dollars if I knew an ear of corn could ripen in Salt Lake Valley," has been often and variously quoted? What availed the roseate account given of the California Coast by the ultra-optimistic Samuel Brannan, who, after sailing with a "Mormon" colony from New York and landing at the Bay of San Francisco, crossed the Sierra Nevada, met the Pioneers on Green River, and endeavored to persuade them that the flowery slopes of the Pacific were a better place of abode for the exiled people than the parched alkali wastes of "The Great American Desert?" Brigham Young knew better than Colonel Bridger or Elder Brannan what was for the best. Looking past the present into the future, he had for all such warnings and persuasions, one reply: "*This is the place.*"

Prophecy Fulfilled and Vision Verified.—Brigham Young was not the man to ignore divine guidance. His own vision was before him, beckoning him on; and Joseph Smith's prediction behind him, urging him forward and pointing out the way. The Latter-day Saints were to "become a mighty people"—not in California, not along the Pacific Coast, but "in the midst of the Rocky Mountains."

Footnotes

1 . The history of guerilla warfare and its merciless suppression along the Missouri-Kansas border, amply bears out this assertion.

2 . Hist. Ch. Vol. 5, p. 85.

This prophecy began to be fulfilled early in February, 1846, when the first companies of the migrating Saints left Nauvoo for the West, crossing the frozen Mississippi on the ice. About the middle of June they reached the Missouri River, then the frontier of the Nation, where their further progress was delayed for a whole season by the enlistment of the "Mormon" Battalion—five hundred men—who responded to a call from the Government and volunteered to assist the United States in its war with Mexico.

3 . "This was followed," continues the Call narrative, "by a vivid description of the scenery of these mountains as I have since become acquainted with it. . . . . It is impossible to represent in words this scene which is still vivid in my mind—the grandeur of Joseph's appearance, his beautiful descriptions of this land, and his wonderful prophetic utterances as they emanated from the glorious inspirations that overshadowed him. There was a force and power in his exclamations of which the following is but a faint echo: 'Oh the beauty of those snow-capped mountains! The cool refreshing streams that are running down through those mountain gorges.' Then, gazing in another direction, as if there was a change of locality: 'Oh the scenes that this people will pass through! The dead that will lie between here and there.' Then, turning in another direction, as if the scene had again changed: 'Oh the apostasy that will take place before my brethren reach that land! But, he continued, 'the priesthood shall prevail over its enemies, triumph over the devil, and be established upon the earth, never more to be thrown down.'" Hist. Ch. Vol. 5, pp. 85, 86. Note.

4 . The journey of the Pioneers began at Winter Quarters (now Florence, Nebraska) about the middle of April, 1847. It

ended on the shores of the Great Salt Lake, July 24th of the same year. The company, led by President Brigham Young in person, consisted originally of 143 men, three women, and two children. The men were well armed and equipped, and the company traveled mostly in covered wagons, drawn by horses, mules and oxen. Four large companies of emigrants followed immediately after the Pioneers, arriving in Salt Lake Valley during the autumn.

5. See Apostle Snow's discourse of July 25, 1880, reproduced in the "Improvement Era" for June, 1913.

ARTICLE NINE
THE PLACE OF SAFETY

An Inspired Choice.—Who can doubt the wisdom of the choice that made the Rocky Mountains, in lieu of the Pacific Coast, a permanent home for the once homeless Latter-day Saints? Had they gone to California, as Elder Brannan advised, it would have meant, in all probability, their disruption and dispersion as a community, or at all events another painful exodus in quest of peace and freedom. It would have been to invite, from the inhabitants of that region—fast filling up with immigrants from those very States where the persecuted people had experienced their sorest troubles—a repetition of the woes from which they were fleeing. Here in these mountain fastnesses, a thousand miles from the frontiers of civilization, they were safe from mobs and molestation.

Better Than Elsewhere.—Better for them, in every way, that they should bide where Providence placed them. The coast country, with all its attractions—and they are many—has no such rare climate as can be found in this more highly favored region. The land once supposed to be worthless, and to redeem which even in part from its ancient barrenness, has required years on years of toil and privation, turns out to be a veritable treasure-house of natural resources, a self-sustaining empire; and in periods of strife and turmoil, when war rocks the world, it is probably the safest place beneath the sun.

The Great War.—This mention again brings to the fore Joseph Smith's great "Prophecy on War." It has been seen how the Southern States, when they endeavored to withdraw from the Union, "called on Great Britain" for recognition and assistance, thus making good a portion of the Prophet's prediction. But when did Great Britain "call upon other nations," fulfilling in her own case the terms of the "Mormon" leader's fateful forecast? Certainly not during the stormy period of the "sixties," nor for many decades thereafter.

But the time came eventually. After the outbreak of the World War, when the German hosts were overrunning Belgium and Northern France, threatening even England herself, Great Britain did call upon the nations with which she had made treaties, for the help that she so sorely needed. The visit to America, before and after the United States declared war against Germany, of representatives of Great Britain and others of the Allied nations, appealing for military aid, was a potent factor in inducing our Government to send ships and troops across the Atlantic, to help beat back the Teutonic invader.

Only The Beginning.—Very evident is it that the tempest of war foretold by Joseph Smith did not cease with the close of the conflict between the Northern and the Southern States. The storm has continued intermittently to this time. Lulls there have been, but no lasting cessation of the strife. Five years after the collapse of the Southern Confederacy, came the Franco-Prussian War, foreshadowing Germany's mad attempt to conquer the world. The American Civil War, the Franco-Prussian War, and the more recent World War, were all parts of the great "outpouring" predicted on that ominous Christmas day. And the same may be said of other conflicts that have since taken place. Equally true will it be of any future strife that may be necessary to help free the world from oppression and iniquity. Unless the wicked repent, there is more—much more to come. [1]

But in what way did the revolt of South Carolina, which began the Civil War, prove a "beginning" of wars for "all nations"? This question is intelligently discussed in a pamphlet recently put forth by Elder James H. Anderson, of Salt Lake City. That writer shows that with the outbreak of the Southern-Northern conflict, the whole system of modern warfare underwent a change, and that since then it has experienced a complete revolution, through the invention and use of machine guns, airships, submarines, and other death-dealing instrumentalities, absolutely unknown in previous military history, and marking a distinct beginning, such as the Prophet indicated. [2]

Dangers Upon the Deep.—One frightful feature of the unparalleled struggle that ended with the signing of the armistice (November 11, 1918), was the havoc wrought by the German U-boats, otherwise known as submarines. There had been, before the coming of the U-boat, dreadful dangers upon the waters, as the fate of the ill-starred "Titanic"—ripped open by an iceberg—testifies. But the submarine, the assassin of the "Lusitania," multiplied those dangers a hundred fold. Did the proud world know that a prophet of God had foreseen these fearful happenings, and had sounded a warning of their approach?

In August, 1831, Joseph Smith, with a party of friends, returning from their first visit to Zion in Jackson County, encamped on the bank of the Missouri River, at a place called McIlwair's (or McIlwaine's) Bend. There, one of the party, William W. Phelps, saw in vision the Destroyer riding in awful fury upon the river, and the incident called forth a revelation in which the Lord says:

"Behold, there are many dangers upon the waters, and more especially hereafter;

"For I, the Lord, have decreed in mine anger many destructions upon the waters; yea, and especially upon these waters;

"Nevertheless, all flesh is in mine hand, and he that is faithful among you shall not perish by the waters.

* * * * * *

"Behold, I, the Lord, in the beginning blessed the waters, but in the last days, by the mouth of my servant John, I cursed the waters.

"Wherefore, the days will come that no flesh shall be safe upon the waters,

"And it shall be said in days to come that none is able to go up to the land of Zion upon the waters, but he that is upright in heart. . . . .

"I, the Lord, have decreed, and the destroyer rideth upon the face thereof, and I revoke not the decree." [3]

No Flesh Safe Upon the Waters.—Was not this condition almost realized during the darkest days of the Great War? Perils undreamed of developed; disasters without precedent, unexampled in history, were of frequent occurrence. Even upon the calm Pacific no ship pursued consecutively the same track twice. Companies operating the great ocean-liners no longer announced the dates of departure from one port or of expected arrival at another. They dared not; the destroyer was abroad, death was in the depths, and the spirit of dread brooded upon the bosom of the waters. And this upon the comparatively peaceful Western Ocean; while upon the Atlantic, in the Mediterranean, and in the North Sea, the terrible submarine told the tale of danger and disaster.

The Food Question.—Another phase of the Titanic struggle was the food question. Joseph Smith had predicted famine; [4] and the famine came. As early as October, 1876, the Prophet's successor, President Brigham Young, placed upon the members of the Relief Society a special mission—that of gathering and storing grain against a day of scarcity; and from that time the activities of the Society were put forth largely in this direction. Some made light of the labors of these devoted women, declaring that another famine could not be. Too vast an area of the earth's surface was under cultivation, and the means of rapid transit and communication were too plentiful, to permit of such a misfortune. If famine threatened any part of the world, word of it could come in the twinkling of an eye, and millions on millions of tons of food-stuffs, speedily transported to the scene, would stave off the straitness and render the calamity impossible.

The Spectre of Famine..—Alas for those who put their trust in the arm of flesh! In spite of the vast and ever-increasing productivity of the soil; in spite of railroads, steamships, and telegraphs, spreading a network of steel and electricity over the face of the planet, this was, and is still, a famine-threatened world. Europe calls upon America for food; America generously responds; but as fast as she consigns her cargoes of foodstuffs to the needy nations, the merciless and devouring submarine sends them to the bottom of the sea. Such indeed was the situation. The floor of the ocean is strewn with the wrecks of transports whose mission was to carry bread to the starving millions of other lands. And where was the man, uninspired of Heaven, who could have anticipated such a catastrophe?

Our nation became aroused to the necessity existing for the avoidance of Waste and the conservation of food stuffs. All civilized countries awakened to the same urgent call. The "Mormon" grain-storing movement was no longer a joke—a target for ridicule. The gaunt spectre of Famine had shown a glimpse of his face, and the whole world trembled at the prospect. The God of Joseph and of Brigham had vindicated the patient labors of His faithful handsmaids, and fulfilled in part the solemn forebodings of prophecy.

"Mormon" Grain for the Government.—Not the least item of interest connected with this subject, is the fact that the United States Government, through its Food Administrator, in May, 1918, made request upon the authorities of the Church of Jesus Christ of Latter-day Saints, for the turning in of all the Relief Society wheat then on hand, for use in the war. The request was cheerfully complied with, 225,000 bushels of wheat being promptly furnished by the Church to the Federal Government.

The Drought of 1919.—How easily a famine could come, was shown during the prolonged drought in the summer of 1919, when throughout the Intermountain West and in regions beyond, lands usually productive lay parching for many weeks under the torrid rays of the sun. As a result, millions of acres of growing grain, especially in the dry-farming districts, perished for want of moisture. And yet there are men who deem human powers and earthly resources all-sufficient, and who declare, in the face of prophecy, that famine and war are obsolete and never again can be.

A Scholar's Opinion.—Such a pronouncement, as to war, was made repeatedly, in public, only a short while before the World War broke out. That splendid scholar and publicist, David Starr Jordan, expressed by tongue and pen his positive conviction that another great conflict, in this advanced and cultured age, was humanly impossible—it simply could not come. [5] But Another had said, two thousand years before: "Such things must come." [6] And not long after the delivery of Doctor Jordan's optimistic, well-meant prediction, the greatest hell of conflict that this world has ever known burst forth and well-nigh wrapt the globe in a mantle of smoke and flame.

The One Safe Guide.—"Men may come and men may go," but God and Truth "go on forever." Heaven and Earth may pass, but the divine word, by whomsoever spoken, will endure unshaken "amid the wreck of matter and the crash of worlds." The sure word of prophecy, flowing from the fountain of the Spirit, is the one safe guide through the chaos of the present and the mystical mazes of the future.

A Prophet's Voice.—More firmly founded than the scholarly utterance in question, was a prediction made by President Wilford Woodruff, at Brigham City, Utah, in the summer of 1894. In the course of a public address, referring to the near approach of the judgments of the last days, the venerable leader said: "Great changes are at our doors. The next twenty years will see mighty changes among the nations of the earth." And it was just twenty years, or in the summer of 1914, when the terrible strife that has wrought so many mighty changes swept like a whirlwind over the nations.

Other Prophetic Warnings.—One could almost believe that President Woodruff's fellow Apostle, Orson Pratt, was gazing with seeric vision upon the same dreadful picture, when he thundered into the ears of the world this solemn admonition: "A voice is heard unto the ends of the Earth! A sound of terror and dismay! A sound of nations rushing to battle! Fierce and dreadful is the contest! *Mighty kingdoms and empires melt away!* The destroyer has gone forth; the pestilence that walketh in darkness; the plagues of the last days are at hand; and who shall be able to escape? None but the righteous; none but the upright in heart." [7]

Eight years later this same Apostle, then at Liverpool, about to embark for America, issued to the inhabitants of Great Britain this "Prophetic Warning":

"If you will not repent and unite yourselves with God's Kingdom, then the days are near at hand when the righteous shall be gathered out of your midst. And woe unto you when that day shall come, for it shall be a day of vengeance upon the British nation! . . . . Your armies shall perish; your maritime forces shall cease; your cities shall be ravaged, burned and made desolate, and your strongholds shall be thrown down; the poor shall rise against the rich, and their storehouses and their fine mansions shall be pillaged, their merchandise and their gold and their silver and their rich treasures shall be plundered. Then shall the lords and nobles and the merchants of the land, and all in high places, be brought down and shall sit in the dust and howl for the miseries that shall be upon them. And they that trade by sea shall lament and mourn; for their traffic shall cease." [8]

Saviors of the Nation.—To escape the judgments hanging over the wicked, and find a place where they might worship God unmolested, the Latter-day Saints fled to the Rocky Mountains. Here, and here only, during the temporary isolation sought and found by them in the chambers of "the everlasting hills," could they hope to be let alone long enough to become strong enough to accomplish their greater destiny. For there was more in that enforced exodus and the founding of this mountain-girl empire than the surface facts reveal. If tradition can be relied upon, Joseph Smith prophesied that the Elders of Israel would save this Nation in the hour of its extremest peril. At a time when anarchy would threaten the life of the Government, and the Constitution would be hanging as by a thread, the maligned and misunderstood "Mormons"—always patriotic, and necessarily so from the very genius of their religion—would stand firm upon Freedom's rocky ramparts, and as champions of law and order, of liberty and justice, call to their aid in the same grand cause kindred spirits from every part of the nation and from every corner of the world. All this preparatory to a mighty movement that would sweep every form of evil from off the face of the land, and rear the Zion of God upon the spot consecrated for that purpose. This traditional utterance of their martyred Seer is deeply imbedded in the heart and hope of the "Mormon" people.

"Mormonism's" Monument.—The State of Utah with its fringe of offspring settlements, is no adequate monument to Latter-day Israel. Zion is their monument, and it will stand in Jackson County, Missouri. Ephraim is but getting ready for his mighty mission—the Lion crouching before he springs.

Footnotes

1 . D. and C. 5:19; 45:31, 68, 69; 63:33; 88:87-91; 97:22, 23; 115:6.

2 . See "Prophecies of Joseph Smith and their Fulfillment," by Nephi L. Morris, p. 20.

3 . D. and C. 61:4-6, 14-16, 19. Compare Moses 7:66 and Rev. 16:3, 4.

4 . D. and C. 87:6.

5 . "There is no war coming," said Doctor Jordan to the press representatives who flocked to interview him on his return, in 1910, from Europe, where he had been lecturing on "Universal Peace." "The only battle between England and Germany will be on paper." In his book, "War and Waste," published a few years later, he said of the "Great War of Europe which never comes": "The bankers will not find the money for such a fight, the industries of Europe will not maintain it, the statesmen cannot. . . . . There will be no general war until the masters direct the fighters to fight. The masters have much to gain, but vastly more to lose, and their signal will not be given." In August, 1912, the Doctor delivered a spoken address to the same effect in the Salt Lake Tabernacle. This was just two years before the war that "could not come"—came.

6 . Matt. 24:6.

7 . "The Kingdom of God," July, 1849.

8 . "Mill. Star" Oct. 24, 1857. Orson Pratt, then presiding over the European Mission, had been called home, owing to a prospect of serious trouble between Utah and the United States Government. A false report that the "Mormons" were in rebellion against the Federal authority had caused the Government to send an army, under General Albert Sidney Johnston, to put down the alleged insurrection. Brigham Young, Governor of the Territory (now State) of Utah, proclaimed martial law and made preparation to resist the "invaders." A part of the preparation was the withdrawal of all "Mormon" missionaries from the outside world. It remains but to say that "The Utah War" ended by peaceable adjustment and without bloodshed.

PART THREE
A MARVEL AND A WONDER

ARTICLE TEN
THE WISDOM THAT PERISHES

The wisdom of their wise men shall perish, and the understanding of their prudent men shall be hid.—Isaiah 29:14.

The Wise and Prudent.—Most strikingly have these prophetic words been realized by "Mormonism," in its relations to the lofty and the learned who have endeavored in a worldly way and by means of human wisdom, to account for and dispose of it. Strange it is that men and women, intelligent, educated and profound, do not see in this great religious phenomenon something more than a topic to be treated lightly, or in a spirit of harshness and intolerance. Giants in intellect as to other themes, when they deal with the doctrines, aims and attitude of the Latter-day Saints, they seem suddenly changed into dwarfs, mere children, as powerless to cope with the mighty problem as were the learned Rabbis in the Temple with the youthful and divine Son of God.

Especially is this the case when they approach the question in a captious mood, determined to find fault, to berate and ridicule, rather than to fairly investigate. They cannot analyze, cannot even grasp it, and appear incapable of forming any just or adequate conception regarding it. To reply to all the bitter assaults made upon my religion and my people would be impossible, even were it worth while. I shall not attempt the hopeless task. It will suffice my purpose to consider here some of the more temperate judgments passed upon the subject, giving to each such comment as may be deemed necessary.

A Catholic Opinion.—Many years ago there came to Utah a learned doctor of divinity, a member of the Roman Catholic Church. I became well acquainted with him, and we conversed freely and frankly. A great scholar, with perhaps a dozen languages at his tongue's end, he seemed to know all about theology, law, literature, science and philosophy, and was never weary of displaying his vast eruditon. One day he said to me: "You Mormons are all ignoramuses. You don't even know the strength of your own position. It is so strong that there is only one other tenable in the whole Christian world, and that is the position of the Catholic Church. The issue is between Catholicism and Mormonism. If we are right, you are wrong; if you are right, we are wrong; and that's all there is to it. The Protestants haven't a leg to stand on. If we are wrong, they are wrong with us, for they were a part of us and went out from us; while if we are right, they are apostates whom we cut off long ago. If we really have, as we claim, the apostolic succession from St. Peter, there was no need for Joseph Smith and Mormonism; but if we have not that succession, then such a man as Joseph Smith was necessary, and Mormonism's attitude is the only consistent one. It is either the perpetuation of the Gospel from ancient times, or the restoration of the Gospel in latter days."

My reply was substantially as follows: "I agree with you, Doctor, in nearly all that you have said, but don't deceive yourself with the notion that we "Mormons" are not aware of the strength of our position. We are better aware of it than anyone else. We have not all been to college; we cannot all speak the dead languages; we may be 'ignoramuses,' as you say; but we know that we are right, and we know that you are wrong." I was just as frank with him as he had been with me.

An Episcopal View.—At a later period I conversed with another man of culture, a bishop of the Episcopal Church. He affirmed that if Joseph Smith, at the beginning, had become acquainted with that religious organization, he would have been content, and would have looked no further for spiritual light. "But," said the Bishop, "Joseph encountered the Methodists, the Baptists, the Presbyterians, and other sects; and their creeds failing to satisfy him, he sought elsewhere. Now the Episcopalians have an unbroken succession of authority all down the centuries, and if Joseph Smith had only formed their acquaintance, he would never have gone to the trouble of organizing another church."

A Psychological Notion.—Still another scholar, a student of psychology and an applicant for a doctor's degree at Yale University, presented, in a thesis forming the basis for the degree, the theory that Joseph Smith was an epileptic, and that this accounted for his mental attitude and marvelous assertions. That is to say, the Seer did not actually behold the wonderful manifestations described by him, but only imagined that he beheld them. A distinct departure, this, from the charge of conscious duplicity, usually flung at the founder of "Mormonism." He was sincere, then, however much mistaken, and was not guilty of intent to defraud. So far, so good. But in the mind of the author of this remarkable hypothesis, the magnificent organization of the "Mormon" Church, conceded by intelligent observers of all creeds and parties to be one of the most perfect systems of government in existence, to say nothing of its sublime doctrines, replete with poetry and philosophy, couched in logical and majestic phrasing—all this sprang from the diseased brain of a fourteen-year-old boy who had fallen in an epileptic fit! Self-evident absurdities need no argument. They have only to be stated, and they confute themselves. [1]

Learning's Lack of Knowledge.—And these are some of the views that learned men take of "Mormonism." With all their learning, they are not able to come to a knowledge of the Truth. They do not begin to dream of the greatness of God's work, the grandeur of Christ's cause. They comprehend but in part its real aims and attitude. Even the most conservative assume that Joseph Smith stumbled upon something of which he did not know the true value, and that it was sheer luck which gave to this religion its vantage ground, its recognized strength of position. Never was there a grosser error. There are concepts as much higher than these, as the heavens are higher than the earth. The "Mormons" are not the "ignoramuses," when it comes to a consideration of the Gospel's mighty themes.

Spiritual Illumination.—Yet it is not because of native "smartness"— not because the followers of Joseph Smith are brainier than other people, that they have a greater knowledge of God and are capable of loftier ideals in religion. It is because they have received, through the gift of the Holy Ghost, a perceptive power, a spiritual illumination, which the world, with all its learning, does not possess, and without which no man can comprehend Divinity or divine purposes. It cannot be had from books or schools. Colleges and universities cannot impart it. It comes only in one way—God's way, not man's. The Latter-day Saints possess it because they have bowed to the will of Heaven and rendered obedience to its laws, thus making themselves worthy of the inestimable boon. All men may have it upon precisely the same conditions.

Still Another Misconception.—My Episcopalian friend said to me on another occasion: "My main objection to Mormonism is its narrowness, its illiberality. You Mormons are not interested in anything going on outside of your own social and religious system. You are insulated, wrapped up in yourselves, you take no note of what other peoples are doing, and you give them no credit for the good they accomplish. For instance"—he went on—"the Bible is retranslated, with a view to making it plainer and more intelligible; but you attach no importance to work of that kind. Ancient ruins are uncovered, buried civilizations brought to light, mystical inscriptions on old-time obelisks deciphered and interpreted, in order to acquaint the present with the past; but you put no value upon such enterprise. Hospitals are founded; missions maintained; Christ's name is carried to the heathen; the Bible is published by millions of copies, and persistent efforts are made to place one in every home. But you take no account of these things; you do not commend such labors—you deem them all vain and of no worth."

Not Narrow and Illiberal.—The Bishop's remark surprised me. I was astonished that one so well informed in other ways could entertain such an opinion of the Latter-day Saints. There may be such a thing as a narrow "Mormon;" there may be such a thing as a narrow notion in the mind of some "Mormon;" but there never has been and never will be such a thing as a narrow "Mormonism." To those who know it best, it is a synonym for largeness and liberality, another name for all that is generous charitable and sublime.

Takes Note of All.—So far from ignoring what other peoples and other systems are doing, the typical "Mormon" takes careful note of all that happens; and the spirit of his religion, "the Spirit that searcheth all things," enables him to assign events and achievements to their proper place in the universal scheme. He appreciates and applauds every step in the march of progress. "If there is anything virtuous, lovely, or of good report, or praiseworthy, we seek after these things." So says the Church in its Articles of Faith.

The Fruit of Falsehood.—How, then, do such gross misunderstandings arise? They spring from prejudice and faulty inference. They are the fruit of falsehood, and of that propensity in most people for allowing themselves to be influenced by a one-sided statement—too often by mere rumor and hearsay. Confounding principle with practice, they mistake the conduct and expressions of individuals connected with a cause, for the cause itself, its character, its spirit, and the ends at which it aims.

Translation and Discovery.—Contrary to my Christian friend's erroneous deduction, the Latter-day Saints *are* interested in the retranslation of the Scriptures. And why should they not be? Joseph Smith was a translator. Did he not translate the Book of Mormon and the Book of Abraham? We believe the Bible to be the word of God only so far as it has been translated correctly. Our Prophet also revised, by the Spirit of Revelation, the English version of the Hebrew Scriptures, making it in many respects more comprehensible, and at the same time restoring to it many "plain and precious things" that had been taken away. [2] Why should we not attach importance to work of that kind?

As for archaeological discoveries, we hail them with joy, especially those that throw any light upon the Book of Mormon, that silent witness "whispering from the dust" [3] of America's "buried civilizations."

Christian Endeavor and "Mormon" Propaganda.—Go on, good Christian brother! Build as many hospitals and found as many missions as you like. Spread the glad tidings over the world, and sound the Savior's name from pole to pole. You cannot blazon the fame of Jesus Christ too far or too widely to suit us. You cannot publish too many Bibles, nor place them in too many homes. Such enterprise makes the follow-up work of the "Mormon" missionary just that much less difficult. It virtually introduces the message that he comes to proclaim. The Stick of Joseph and the Stick of Judah are "one in the hand of Ephraim," [4] Latter-day Israel, chosen and commissioned to prepare the way before Messiah's coming.

Footnotes

1 . For further particulars of the epileptic theory, see Woodbridge Riley's book, "The Founder of Mormonism," and Robert C. Webb's admirable answer thereto in Chapter 26 of "The Real Mormonism."

2 . Hist. Ch. Vol. 1, p. 132. 1 Nephi 13:35, 40.

3 . Isa. 29:4.

4 . Ezek. 37:16-19.

ARTICLE ELEVEN
THE GOD STORY

Greater than it Appears.—"Mormonism" is a much bigger thing than Catholic scholars or Episcopal bishops imagine. It is only a nickname for the Everlasting Gospel, restored to earth in the nineteenth century, that it might be preached "to every nation and kindred and tongue and people," [1] as a warning to the world that the end of wickedness is nigh, that the Kingdom of Heaven is at hand, and that the Lord whom the righteous seek is about to "come suddenly to his Temple." [2]

The Antiquity of the Gospel.—The Gospel originated in the heavens before this earth was formed, and was revealed from God out of Eternity at the very beginning of Time. It was the means whereby our great ancestor, Adam, after his expulsion from Eden, regained the Divine Presence from which he had been banished; and it is the means whereby his posterity, such as are obedient to the Gospel's requirements, may follow him into the Celestial Kingdom. The same ladder that he climbed, until beyond the reach of the fatal consequences of his transgression, the whole human race, inheriting from him the effects of the fall, must also climb, or they will never see the face of God in eternal glory.

The Path to Perfection.—But the Gospel is more than a means of escape from impending ills. To all good Christians it is as a life-boat, or a fire-escape, a way out of a perilous situation. To the Latter-day Saints, it is all this and more. A divine plan for human progress, the foreordained Pathway to Perfection—such is Christ's Gospel, as revealed to and proclaimed by Joseph the Seer.

The Word Made Flesh.—The English word "Gospel" comes from the Anglo-Saxon "Godspell" or God-story—the Story of God. It derives its significance from that great central idea of the Christian faith, the coming of God as the Son of God to redeem and save mankind. "God himself shall come down among the children of men, and shall redeem his people; and because he dwelleth in flesh, he shall be called the Son of God." [3] The fulfillment of this and similar foretellings is recorded in the opening verses of the Gospel according to St. John, referring to "The Word" that was in the beginning "with God"—the Word that "was God," and was "made flesh." In Him, as Paul affirms, "dwelleth all the fulness of the Godhead bodily." [4]

Basic Principles.—When we consider the Gospel, therefore, we should bear in mind that the term means something more than faith, repentance, baptism, and the laying on of hands for the gift (giving) of the Holy Ghost, with other rituals and requirements in the Church of Christ. We cannot separate "the laws and ordinances of the Gospel" from the basic principles upon which they rest-the mighty foundation stones of Sacrifice and Redemption, without which all this sacred legislation would be of no effect. Nor can the basic principles and powers that vitalize and make operative these laws and ordinances be dissociated from the idea of Eternal Progression, the great and paramount purpose for which the Gospel code was framed, the Gospel in its fulness instituted. [5]

The Complete Story.—The Gospel, in its fullest scope of meaning, signifies everything connected with the wondrous career of that Divine Being who was known among men as Jesus of Nazareth, but who was and is no other than Jehovah, the God of Israel, who "came unto his own," and was rejected by them, crucified at their instigation, and died to redeem the world. [6] The accounts given by Matthew, Mark, Luke and John are properly termed "gospels," for they are narratives of the personal ministry of our Lord. But they are only parts of the complete God-Story. [7] The Savior's life, death, resurrection and ascension, with the conditions prescribed by him upon which fallen man might profit further from his sacrifice for human redemption—these are all gospel features, but not the Gospel in its entirety. The full "Story" of the God who died that man might live, involves events both past and future, events pre-mortal and post-mortal, scenes in which He was chosen to play his mighty part in the great tragedy of human experience, and scenes yet to come in which He will make another and a more glorious appearing upon the stage of Time, enacting the illustrious role of King of Kings and reigning over the earth a thousand years.

Essentials to Eternal Progress.—Everything vitally connected with man's mortal pilgrimage was understood and arranged before that pilgrimage began. Earth's creation was but one of the pre-essentials. [8] The means of getting man down upon the earth, and the means of redeeming him from the fall, had also to be provided. The Gospel was instituted, and an Executor appointed to put it into effect; the machinery constructed, and the power then turned on. Eternal progress, endless exaltation, were the sublime objects in view, and over the glad prospect, despite the pain and sorrow that must necessarily intervene, "the morning stars sang together, and all the sons of God shouted for joy." [9]

Elect of Elohim.—In the Eternal Councils, while the creation of "an earth" was in contemplation, the question arose as to who among the Sons of Deity should redeem man from the fall. Lucifer, "an angel of God who was in authority in the presence of God," would fain have been selected for the mighty mission; but his scheme for human redemption was of a compulsory character, destructive of the free agency of man. Moreover, this "Son of the Morning" had become darkened to that degree that he demanded, in recompense for his proposed service, the honor and glory that belong only to the Highest. [10] Therefore was he rejected, and, rebelling, "was thrust down from the presence of God and the Son, and was called Perdition, for the heavens wept over him." [11] "And also a third part of the hosts of heaven turned he away . . . . because of their agency." [12]

The Chosen of the Father stood first among all the Sons of God. [13] He is the Father's first-begotten in the spirit, and his only-begotten in the flesh. To him was assigned the role of Earth's Redeemer. And while revelation is silent upon the subject, or not so specific in their cases, we have good reason to believe that the parts played by Adam and Eve and other "noble and great ones" in the mighty drama of Eternal Progression, were cast at the same time. [14]

The Perfect Plan.—The Gospel, Christ's perfect plan, unlike the defective scheme proposed by Lucifer, gives the right of choice between good and evil. It saves men, not *in* their sins, but *from* their sins—liberates them from spiritual darkness, the bondage of death and hell, and lifts them into the joy and freedom of light and life eternal. Hence that splendid phrase, that majestic synonym, used by the Apostle James in describing the Gospel— "The Perfect Law of Liberty." [15]

The Purpose Paramount.—The grand object in view when that great Law was instituted, is clearly, though briefly, outlined in the following passage from the writings of Joseph the Seer:

"The first principles of man are self-existent with God... Finding he was in the midst of spirits and glory, because he was more intelligent (he) saw proper to institute laws whereby the rest could have a privilege to advance like himself. The relationship we have with God places us in a situation to advance in knowledge. He has power to institute laws to instruct the weaker intelligences, that they may be exalted with himself, so that they may have one glory upon another." [16]

The Benevolence of Deity.—And thus is shown the benevolence as well as the power of Deity. Our Heavenly Father is no monopolist. Omnipotent and all-possessing, he is likewise altruistic, philanthropic. He employed his superior intelligence, which constitutes his glory, [17] to institute laws whereby the lesser spirits surrounding him might advance toward the lofty plane that he occupies. He proposed to lift them to his own spiritual stature, and share with them the empire of the universe.

Salvation and Exaltation.—The Gospel of Christ is termed by St. Paul "the power of God unto salvation." [18] Paul might have gone further, had he been so inclined, or had it been timely. He could have shown that the Gospel is also the power of God unto exaltation, a plan devised by omnipotent wisdom whereby the sons and daughters of Deity may advance from stage to stage of soul development, until they become like their heavenly parents, the Eternal Father and Mother, inheriting endless thrones and dominions and receiving "a fulness of joy." [19]

This is exaltation. It is more than salvation, being an extension of that idea or condition—salvation "added upon;" just as salvation is an extension of, or an addition to, the idea or condition of redemption. A soul may be redeemed—that is, raised from the dead—and yet be condemned at the Final Judgment for evil deeds done in the body. Likewise may a soul be saved, and yet come short of the glory that constitutes exaltation. To redeem, save and glorify, is the threefold mission of the Gospel of Jesus Christ.

Footnotes

1 . Rev. 14:6.

2 . Mal. 3:1.

3 . Mosiah 15:1, 2; 3:5. The joyful intelligence of the advent of the World's Redeemer, proclaimed by angels to the shepherds on the Judean hills (Luke 2:10), furnishes another name for the Gospel—"good tidings," or, as otherwise rendered, "glad tidings of great joy."

4 . Col. 2:9. Compare Ether 3:14, and Alma 11:38, 39.

5 . All fulness is relative, as pertaining to the revealed word of God. There can be no absolute fulness with man until everything is made known to him. The fulness of the Gospel, as delivered to the Nephites and other ancient peoples, was not so complete as is the fulness enjoyed by the Latter-day Saints. Truth is always the same, but more of its principles have been revealed in modern times than at any previous period. And the end is not yet; for, as our Prophet declares: "Those things which never have been revealed from the foundation of the world, but have been kept hid from the wise and prudent, shall be revealed unto babes and

sucklings in this, the dispensation of the fulness of times." (D. and C. 128:18.) Such an outpouring of truth and light can come only to a people prepared for it. "When that which is perfect is come, then that which is in part shall be done away" (I Cor. 13:10). Until then a comparative fulness, or all that the finite mind can contain of infinite wisdom, must suffice human aspiration and continue to be the lot even of the most enlightened.

6 . D. and C. 110:1-4.

7 . The book of Isaiah is sometimes called "the fifth gospel," it having so much to say about the coming Redeemer; and just as fittingly might the third book of Nephi be termed a "gospel," narrating as it does the risen Christ's personal ministrations to the descendants of Lehi.

8 . Abr. 3:24.

9 . Job 38:7.

10 . Moses 4:1-4.

11 . D. and C. 76:25, 26.

12 . Ib. 29:36.

"Satan (it is possible) being opposed to the will of his Father, wished to avoid the responsibilities of this position. . . . . He probably intended to make men atone for their own acts by an act of coercion and the shedding of their own blood as an atonement for their sins."—"The Mediation and Atonement," by President John Taylor, pp. 96, 97.

13 . Rom. 8:29.

14 . Abr. 3:23; Jer. 1:5, Hist. Ch. Vol. 6, p. 364.

15 . James 1:25.

16 . "Times and Seasons," Aug. 15, 1844; "Improvement Era," Jan., 1909.

Our Prophet's simple yet sublime setting forth is far more pointed and specific than the presentment made by Plato of a doctrine somewhat similar. The Greek philosopher, as quoted by Emerson, says: "Let us declare the cause which led the Supreme Ordainer to produce and compose the universe. He was good; and he who is good has no kind of envy. Exempt from envy, he wished that all things should be as much as possible like himself. Whosoever, taught by wise men, shall admit this as the prime cause of the origin and foundation of the world, will be in the truth" ("Plato," Emerson's "Representative Men"). There is a fitness, a propriety, in man's becoming like his Maker—God's child, fashioned in his image and endowed with divine attributes, developing to the fulness of the parental stature, as taught by Joseph; but how the same can be predicated of "all things," as Plato implies, is not so clear. That the lower animals, and in fact all forms of life, are to be perpetuated and glorified, is more than an inference from the teachings of the Prophet (D. and C. 29:24, 25; 77:2-4). But undoubtedly all will retain their identity in their respective orders and spheres. No creature of God's excepting man can become like God in the fullest and highest sense.

17 . D. and C. 93:36.

18 . Rom. 1:16.

19 . D. and C. 76:50-70; 93:33; Abr. 3:26.

ARTICLE TWELVE
THE GREAT VICISSITUDES

Fall and Redemption.—The Fall of Man and the Redemption from the Fall, are the great vicissitudes of human experience. One is sequel to the other, and both are steps in the march of eternal progress. The Gospel, therefore, embraces the fall as well as the redemption. Both were essential, and both were preordained. The one prepared the way before the other. Had there been no fall, there could have been no redemption; for the simple reason that there would have been nothing to redeem.

The Creation.—Preliminary to the fall, came the creation. Earth, created as an abode and a place of probation for mortal man, was not made out of nothing, as human theology asserts, but out of previously existing materials, as divine revelation affirms. Millions of earths had been created in like manner before this planet rolled into existence. [1]

To create does not mean to make something out of nothing. Such a doctrine is neither scientific nor scriptural. Nothing remains nothing, of necessity; and no power, human or divine, can make it otherwise. Creation is organization, with materials at hand for the process. Joseph Smith's position upon this point, though combatted by doctors of divinity, is confirmed by the most advanced scientists and philosophers of modern times. The dogma that earth was made out of nothing is an attempt to glorify Deity by ascribing to him the power to perform the impossible—to do that which cannot be done. As if Deity could be glorified with anything of that sort, or had need of any such glorification. It is also an effort to escape from what many religious teachers consider a dilemma, the other horn of which would commit them to what they mistakenly deem a fallacy—namely, the eternity and self-existence of matter. [2]

Eternity of Matter.—"Mormonism" stands firm-footed upon this ground. It holds matter to be uncreateable, indestructible, without beginning or end, and consequently eternal. [3] As for modern science, here are a few of its most recent conclusions upon the point at issue. Says Herbert Spencer: "The doctrine that matter is indestructible has become a commonplace. All the apparent proofs that something can come out of nothing, a wider knowledge has one by one canceled" ("First Principles"). And John Fiske confirms him in saying: "It is now inconceivable that a particle of matter should either come into existence, or lapse into non-existence" ("Cosmic Philosophy"). Robert K. Duncan clinches the argument with the emphatic pronouncement: "We cannot create something out of nothing" ("New Knowledge").

Spirit and Element.—But Joseph Smith proclaimed it first. He declared the elements eternal; [4] and even went so far as to say: "All spirit is matter, but it is more fine and pure, and can only be discerned by purer eyes." [5] Eternal spirit, eternal element, these are the "materials" out of which Earth was created—not only as a temporary abode for man, but as an eternal place of residence for the righteous.

The Value of a Body.—Man needed experience in mortality, in the midst of rudimental conditions, in order to acquire the experience that would fit him for spheres beyond. First, however, he needed a body, for purposes of increase and progression, both in time and eternity. The spirit without the body is incomplete; it cannot propagate, and it cannot go on to glory. "Spirit and element, inseparably connected, receiveth a fulness of joy; but when separated man cannot receive a fulness of joy." [6] It is a reasonable inference that our spirits advance as far as they can before they are given earthly bodies. Having received their bodies, they are in a position, by means of the Gospel and the powers of the Priesthood, to make further progress toward perfection. "We came to this earth," says Joseph Smith, "that we might have a body, and present it pure before God in the celestial kingdom. The great principle of happiness consists in having a body." [7]

Satan's Punishment.—The Prophet thus continues: "The Devil has no body, and herein is his punishment. . . All beings who have bodies have power over those who have not." The reason why Satan has no body is because he rebelled in the eternal councils when the Redeemer of the World was chosen. All who followed him shared a similar fate. Two thirds of the intelligences then populating the spirit world remained loyal, and as a reward for their fidelity were permitted to tabernacle in the flesh. One third, rebelling with Lucifer, were doomed with him to perdition. Pending their final fate, these unembodied fallen spirits are allowed to wander up and down the world, tempting and trying its human inhabitants, their evil activities being overruled in a way to subserve God's purpose in man's probation.

Placed in Eden.—Earth having been prepared for man, Adam and Eve were placed in the Garden of Eden—placed there to become mortal, that the

Lord's purpose might be accomplished. The fall, though planned, was not compelled. [8] Man still had his agency, the right and power of choice.

Innocent in the Beginning.—The Great Creator, on the morning of creation, pronounced "good" all that He had made. [9] In perfect keeping with this, modern revelation declares that "every spirit of man was innocent in the beginning." [10] Consequently, had the spirits of men remained where they were before Adam fell, they would have had no need to exercise a saving faith, no need to repent or to be baptized, having no evil practices to turn from and no uncleanness to be washed away. But they would have remained ignorant as well as innocent—ignorant of things necessary to their further progress. Without the fall, they could have advanced no further, but would have remained as they were, "having no joy, for they knew no misery; doing no good, for they knew no sin. . . . . Adam fell that men might be; and men are that they might have joy." [11]

The Woman Beguiled.—When our First Parents partook of the forbidden fruit, it was the woman who was beguiled by the Serpent (Satan) and induced to go contrary to the divine command. The man was not deceived. [12] What Adam did was done knowingly and after full deliberation. When Eve had tasted of the fruit, Adam did likewise in order to carry out another command, the first that God had given to this pair—the command to "multiply and replenish the earth." [13] Eve, by her act, had separated herself from her husband, and was now mortal, while he remained in an immortal state. It was impossible, therefore, unless he also became mortal, for them to obey the original behest. This was Adam's motive. This was his predicament. He was facing a dilemma, and must make choice between two divine commands. He disobeyed in order to obey, retrieving, so far as he could, the situation resulting from his wife's disobedience. Fully aware of what would follow, he partook of the fruit of the inhibited tree, realizing that in no other way could he become the progenitor of the human race.

Adam and Abraham. Perhaps some will see a parallel in Adam's case and Abraham's, each being directed to do a thing that could not be done unless a previous requirement were disregarded. Thus, Adam was warned not to eat of the fruit of a certain tree—the Tree of Knowledge of Good and Evil; yet that was the only way for him to reach a condition where he would be able to "replenish the earth." Abraham was forbidden to slay his son, after being commanded to "offer" him. [14] But there was this important difference in the two cases. The second command to Abraham superseded the first—canceled it. Not so with Adam. In his case the later law left unrepealed the earlier enactment. Both commandments were in force; but Adam could not obey both. What was to be done? Why, just what was done—the wisest thing possible under the circumstances.

Malum Prohibitum.—Adam's transgression, though a sin, because of the broken law, should not be stressed as an act of moral turpitude. In human law, which is based upon divine law, there are two kinds of offenses in general, described in Latin terms as *malum per se* and *malum prohibitum*. *Malum per se* means "an evil in itself," an act essentially wrong; while *malum prohibitum* signifies "that which is wrong because forbidden by law." Adam's transgression was *malum prohibitum*; and the consequent descent from an immortal to a mortal condition, was the Fall.

A Cause For Rejoicing.—Adam and Eve, with their eyes open, rejoiced over what had befallen them, [15] evidently regarding it as part of a beneficent plan to people Earth and afford to a world of waiting spirits—the loyal two-thirds who "kept their first estate" when Lucifer fell—the long looked for opportunity of entering upon their "second estate" and beginning the great pilgrimage to perfection.

No License for Sin.—Let it not be supposed, however, that disobedience to divine requirements is or ever can be justifiable. On the contrary, obedience is the great law upon which all blessings are predicated. [16] What was done by our First Parents in an exceptional instance and for a special purpose, constitutes no license for men to commit sin. Adam and Eve, having obeyed God's command to "multiply and replenish," reaped the reward of their obedience. But they had to be punished for their disobedience in the matter of the forbidden fruit. "The wages of sin is death." The fall was necessary, but it had to be atoned for: it could not be justified. "The Lord cannot look upon sin with the least degree of allowance." He can nullify its effects, however, and bring good out of evil. Redemption was also necessary, and the Atonement preordained; but this did not make the murder of the innocent Savior any the less heinous. The perpetrators of that deed were guilty of a crime—the crime of crimes—and their punishment was inevitable. Were it otherwise, God would not be just, and would therefore cease to be God. [17]

Fruits of the Fall.—The fall had a twofold direction—downward, yet forward. It brought man into the world and set his feet upon progression's highway. But it also brought death, with all its sad concomitants. Not such a death as the righteous now contemplate, and such as both righteous and unrighteous undergo, as a change preparatory to resurrection; but eternal death—death of the spirit as well as the body. There was no resurrection when Adam fell—not upon this planet.

The World in Pawn.—Hell had seemingly triumphed over man's—or rather over woman's weakness. It was as if the world had been put in pawn. Death was the pawnbroker, with a twofold claim upon all creation. Everything pertaining to Earth was in his grasp, and there was no help for it this side of Heaven. No part of what had been pledged could be used as the means of redemption. Adam could not redeem himself, great and mighty though he was, in the spirit; for he was no other than Michael the Archangel, leader of the heavenly host when Lucifer and his legions were overthrown. But that same puissant Michael was now a weak mortal man, under the penalty of a broken law, powerless to repair the ruin he had wrought. He and the race that was to spring from him were eternally lost, unless Omnipotence would intervene, and do for them what they could not do for themselves.

Where was Redemption?—Redemption must come, if at all, through some being great enough and powerful enough to make an infinite atonement; one completely covering the far-reaching effects of the original transgression. The scales of Eternal Justice, unbalanced by Adam's act, had to be repoised, and the equilibrium of right restored. Who could do this? Who was able to mend the broken law, bring good out of evil, mould failure into success, and "snatch victory from the jaws of defeat?" Where was the Moses for such an Exodus? Where the deliverance from this worse than Egyptian bondage—a bondage of which Egypt's slavery was typical?

The Price Paid.—The life of a God was the price of the world's freedom; and that price was paid by the God of Israel (Jesus on Earth, Jehovah in Heaven) who descended from his glorious throne, became mortal, and by submitting to death, broke the bands of death, and made it possible for man to go on to his eternal destiny. This spotless Lamb, the great Antitype of the Passover, gave himself as an offering for sin, and by the shedding of his own blood, paid the debt of the universe, took the world out of pawn, and became the Author of Salvation for all mankind. Christ's atonement, offsetting Adam's transgression, brought redemption from the fall, nullifying its evil results, conserving its good results, and making them effectual for man's eternal welfare.

"We Know in Part."—Why the Fall and the Redemption had to be, we, know in part, for God has revealed it. But we do not know all. That a divine law was broken, in order that "men might be;" and that reparation had to be made, in order that men "might have joy"—this much is known. But the great why and wherefore of it all is a deep that remains unfathomed. Why it was necessary to place Adam and Eve in a position so contradictory, where they were commanded not to do the very thing that had to be done—why the divine purpose had to be carried out in just that way, is one of those infinite problems that must remain to finite minds a mystery until the All-wise shall will to make it plain. Man cannot sit in judgment upon his Maker, nor measure by human standards divine dispensations. "All things have been done in the wisdom of Him who knoweth all things."

God's Greatest Gift.—The Fall, though essential to human progress, dug man's grave and opened the portal to Hades. Redemption unsealed the tomb and swung wide the gates to Endless Glory. Adam gave us mortal life. Eternal life, our greatest boon, is the gift of the Redeemer and Savior.

Footnotes

1 . Moses 1:4, 38; 7:30.

2 . The Reverend Baden Powell, of Oxford University, quoted in Kitto's "Cyclopedia of Biblical Literature," says: "The idea of 'creation,' as meaning absolutely 'making out of nothing,' or calling into existence that which did not exist before, in the strictest sense of the term, is not a doctrine of scripture; but it has been held by many on the grounds of natural theology, as enhancing the ideas we form of the divine power, and more especially since the contrary must imply the belief in the eternity and self-existence of matter."

3 . The author of the Epistle to the Hebrews asserts nothing to the contrary when he says: "Things which are seen were not made of things which do appear" (Heb. 11:3). The "things" referred to ("the worlds" that were "framed by the word of God") had existed before, in other forms, invisible to mortal eye and intangible to human touch.

4 . D. and C. 93:33.

5 . D. and C. 131:7.

6 . Ib. 93:33, 34.

7 . "Compendium" p. 288; Hist. Ch. Vol. 5, p. 403.

8 . Moses 3:17.

9 . Gen. 1:31.

10 . D. and C. 93:38.

11 . 2 Nephi 2:22-25.

12 . 1 Tim. 2:14.

13 . Gen. 1:28.

14 . Some commentators hold that Abraham misunderstood the Lord's command to "offer" Isaac, and that the second command, "lay not thine hand upon the lad," was given

in explanation. That the Lord did not intend Isaac to be slain, is evidenced from what ensued; but that Abraham misunderstood the original behest does not follow. In order to make the sacrifice of "a broken heart and a contrite spirit," and merit the reward of his obedience, it was necessary that Abraham should interpret the command just as he did—as a commandment to slay. "The sacrifice required of Abraham in the offering of Isaac," says Joseph Smith, "shows that if a man would attain to the keys of the kingdom of an endless life, he must sacrifice all things" (Hist. Ch. Vol. 5, p. 555). This was the principle that Abraham was showing forth, and it must have involved a real and terrible trial of his faith.

15 . Moses 5:10, 11.

16 . D. and C. 130:20, 21.

17 . The principle involved in this discussion, is tersely put in two lines of a well known hymn, frequently sung in the religious assemblies of the Latter-day Saints:

"Sacrifice brings forth the blessings of heaven."

"Earth must atone for the blood of that man."

ARTICLE THIRTEEN
THE GOSPEL DISPENSATIONS

Only One Gospel.—There is but one Gospel. There never has been, and there never will be, another. [1] It is the Everlasting Gospel, [2] the same yesterday, today and forever. In order to comprehend it, one must not limit his survey of the subject to the nineteenth and twentieth centuries—must not confine his calculations to any one Gospel dispensation. He must grasp the idea of a series of such dispensations, inter-related and connected, like the links of a mighty chain, extending from the morning of Creation down to the end of Time. "Mormonism" stands for the Gospel's restoration in the Dispensation of the Fulness of Times; but that is not all. It stands for the Gospel itself in *all* the dispensations, as those periods are termed during which God, from the beginning, has spoken to man and revealed from heaven these saving principles and powers.

For All Time and for All Men.—The Everlasting Gospel does not belie its name. It is not of any one time nor of any one place. Stretching from eternity to eternity, it encompasses past, present and future in its all-embracing fold. Neither is it for the benefit of any particular class, to the exclusion of other classes. It is for all men, and was made simple and plain that all might understand it, that its appeal might be universal. No creed comprehensible only to a few, no religion that mystifies the many, can by any possibility represent Him who died that the whole world might live. There is but one Savior, and but one Plan of Salvation; yet that Savior has many servants, saviors in a subordinate sense, [3] and His saving plan encompasses many truths, apportioned to the several branches of the human family, in measure large or small, according to their capacity to receive, and their ability to wisely use the knowledge meted out to them.

Sublimest Things are always the simplest. This is preeminently true of the Gospel—the simple, sublime Story of God. A child can comprehend it; and at the same time it is capable of taxing to the limit the powers of the highest human intellect. It is the profoundest system of philosophy that the world has ever known. All true principles of science are parts of it, broken-off fragments of this grand Rock of Ages—or, to change the figure, pools caught in the hollows and clefts of Time, when the great flood of Truth, during one or more of its earthly visitations, swept by on its way back to the Eternal Ocean. All that is precious and exalting in religion springs from this ancient source of divine wisdom and intelligence. Who knows not this, knows not the Gospel.

Why Man-Made Systems Endure.—Every form of faith that has benefited its believers, must have possessed at some time a portion of Divine Truth. That is what perpetuated it—not the errors associated therewith. These are as cobwebs and dust, the accumulated rubbish of false tradition, in which the jewel was wholly or in part hidden. Every creed, Christian or Pagan, that has proved a real blessing to its votaries, is as a cistern holding within it waters once wholesome and pure, waters that fell originally from Heaven in one of those grand spiritual showers called dispensations of the Gospel, when the flood-gates of Eternity were lifted, that the world might be refreshed.

God's Word Apportioned.—The Book of Mormon throws light upon this theme. A Nephite prophet says:

"Oh, that I were an angel, and could have the wish of mine heart, that I might go forth and speak with the trump of God, with a voice to shake the earth, and cry repentance unto every people; . . . .

"But behold, I am a man, and do sin in my wish; for I ought to be content with the things which the Lord hath allotted unto me. . . . .

"I know that he granteth unto men according to their desires, whether it be unto death or unto life; yea, I know that he allotteth unto men according to their wills; whether they be unto salvation or unto destruction.

"Yea, and I know that good and evil have come before all men; he that knoweth not good from evil is blameless; but he that knoweth good and evil, to him it is given according to his desires; whether he desireth good or evil, life or death, joy or remorse of conscience.

"Now seeing that I know these things, why should I desire more than to perform the work to which I have been called?

"Why should I desire that I were an angel, that I could speak unto all the ends of the earth?

"For behold, the Lord doth grant unto all nations, of their own nation and tongue, to teach his word; yea, in wisdom, all that he seeth fit that they should have." [4]

Does that sound as if "Mormonism" takes no cognizance of what is going on in the outside world? How can any intelligent reader arise from a study of the "Mormon" faith, convinced that the Latter-day Saints are not interested in anything beyond the bounds of their own social and religious system? That one selection from the Book of Mormon suffices to refute the false notion.

Of Their Own Nation and Tongue.—All down the ages, men bearing the Priesthood, the authority to represent God, have officiated for him and ministered in behalf of mankind. And other good and great spirits, not holding that authority, but imbued with a desire to benefit and uplift their fellows, have been sent into different nations, to give them, not the fulness of the Gospel, but that measure of truth and light that they had the power to appreciate and put to worthy use.

> Why came Socrates, Confucius,
> Zoroaster and Gautama?
> Why not Christ alone?
> Truth answers:
> Graded are the Master's teachings,
> Lest come wasteful overflowing,
> With a swifter condemnation
> For indifference or rejection.
> Milk, not meat, for infant palates,
> Spirit babes, though mental giants,
> Unprepared for strong nutrition,
> Ministered by agents mightier. [5]

The Arab and the Caliph.—But spirit waters, like the waters of earth, will lose their sweetness and purity, if separated too far or too long from their Fountain-head. They will become stagnant and unwholesome, like the drink carried by the poor Arab in his leathern bottle, from the sparkling spring in the desert to the distant palace of the Caliph, who magnanimously rewarded the giver, not for the rank draught presented for his acceptance, but for the goodness of his motive, the sincerity of his soul.

An Oft-restored Religion.—Man's proneness to depart from God and to mix with the clear precepts of divine truth his own muddy imaginings, has made necessary more than one restoration of the primal and pure religion. The Gospel of Christ did not make its first appearance upon this planet at the time of the Savior's crucifixion. While it seemed a new thing to that generation, who were "astonished at his doctrine," in reality it was older than all the ages, older than Earth itself. Originating in the heavens before this world was framed, it had been revealed to man in a series of dispensations, beginning with Adam and extending down to Christ.

The Book with Seven Seals.—Revelation is silent as to the number of the Gospel dispensations. But there are those—and the present writer is among them—who incline to the belief that seven is the correct figure; a belief partly founded upon the Scriptural or symbolical character of that number, and partly upon Joseph Smith's teachings relative to the seven great periods corresponding to the seven seals of the mystical book seen by John the Revelator in his vision on Patmos. [6]

The World's Hidden History.—According to the Prophet's exegesis, the book mentioned in the Apocalypse "contains the revealed will, mysteries and works of God—the hidden things of his economy concerning this earth during the seven thousand years of its continuance or its temporal existence." Each thousand years is represented by one of the seals upon the book—the first seal containing "the things of the first thousand years, and the second also of the second thousand years, and so on until the seventh." [7] The opening of these seals by the Lamb of God signifies, as I understand, the revealing of a Heaven-kept record of God's dealings with man upon this planet. [8]

Are They Dispensations?—These seven periods—millenniums—may or may not be Gospel dispensations, periods of religious enlightenment, during which the Plan of Salvation and the powers of the Priesthood have been among men, alternating with seasons of spiritual darkness. But whether or not they be so regarded, it is interesting to think of them as covering the same ground, paralleling those dispensations, or extending through the same vast stretch of duration, and dealing with events and epochs, principles and personages, connected therewith.

Symbolical and Prophetic.—Whatever their number, or the names by which they may be properly known, it is evident that the Gospel dispensations are inter-related and progressive, each preparing the way before its successor. Altogether, they represent God's special dealings with man, from the beginning down to the end of the world. They are also symbolical and prophetic, pointing forward to a great and wonderful Consummation, the long-heralded era of Restitution, when part will blend with perfect, when past dispensations will all be gathered into one—the Eternal Present, God's great Today, wherein is neither past nor future. [9]

Footnotes

1. Gal. 1:6-9.

2. Rev. 14:6.

3. Rev. 14:1, 4; D. and C. 77:11.

4. Alma 29:1-8.

5. "Love and the Light," pp. 74, 75

6. Rev. 5, 6, 8.

7. D. and C. 77:6, 7, 12.

8. Rev. 20:12.

9. Alma 40:8.

PART FOUR
A GLANCE DOWN THE AGES

ARTICLE FOURTEEN
THE ADAMIC AGE

"Dispensation" Defined.—What is meant by "dispensation." The term has a variety of meanings. To dispense is to deal out or distribute in portions, as when the sacrament of the Lord's Supper is dispensed to a religious congregation. "Dispensations of Providence" is a phrase used to describe the Creator's dealings with his creatures, either for joy or sorrow. In theology "dispensation" signifies the method or scheme whereby Deity has at different times developed his purposes and revealed himself to man. As I now use the term, it stands for the opening of the heavens and the sending forth of the Gospel and the Priesthood for purposes of salvation. It also denotes the period of time during which the saving and exalting principles thus sent forth, continue operative in pristine power and purity.

The Great Patriarch.—Adam, the patriarch of the human family, is over all the Gospel dispensations, including the Dispensation of the Fulness of Times, which is virtually all dispensations rolled into one. Nevertheless, each has its own immediate presiding authority, holding the keys of his particular period—holding them under Adam, the universal head. [1]

Distinctive Features.—Each Gospel Dispensation has certain distinguishing characteristics, and stands for some particular development of the Divine Purpose. Thus, the First Dispensation presents the following distinctive features:

1. The institution of the Law of Sacrifice, foreshadowing the Atonement that was to be made for the redemption of fallen man.

2. The introduction and earliest promulgation of the Gospel, for which the Law of Sacrifice had prepared the way.

3. The initial exercise of the Patriarchal Power, in behalf of the whole human race.

The Law of Sacrifice.—The Law of Sacrifice was revealed from Heaven soon after our First Parents were banished from Eden. God, from whose presence they were shut out, spoke "from the way toward the Garden," commanding them to "offer the firstlings of their flocks for an offering unto the Lord." Adam obeyed, and after many days an Angel appeared to him, saying: "Why dost thou offer sacrifices unto the Lord?" Adam replied: "I know not, save the Lord commanded me." The Angel then said: "This thing is a similitude of the sacrifice of the Only Begotten of the Father. Wherefore thou shalt do all that thou doest in the name of the Son, and thou shalt repent and call upon God in the name of the Son forevermore." So runs the sacred story, as rendered by Joseph the Seer. [2]

The Past Obscured.—It is not to be supposed, however, that this was Adam's first knowledge of the sacrificial statute, concerning which he must have known before it was revealed to him in mortal life. Adam was no ordinary man. He was a great and wonderful character, and the world has not seen the last of him. Undoubtedly he was among those who sat in the eternal councils when the Gospel plan was instituted and its mighty Executor chosen. Surely he knew about the Lamb of God, already slain in the spirit before the creation of the world, and, in Adam's time, yet to be slain literally in the world—an event symbolized by the very sacrifice that the first man was offering when the Lord's messenger appeared to him.

But Adam had lost the knowledge of his spirit past. It had been temporarily taken from him in order that his agency might be free and untrammeled, his conduct uninfluenced by any recollection of a former experience. Hence the need of the Angel's coming to enlighten him, and the further need of revelation by the Holy Spirit, bringing things past to remembrance and showing things to come.

Acceptable and Unacceptable Offerings.—Adam's worship was acceptable to God, for he was in every way obedient to the divine instruction; his offering truly symbolizing the heavenly Lamb, subsequently foretokened in the Feast of the Passover. Abel made a similar offering—of the firstlings of his flock; "and the Lord had respect unto Abel and to his offering." [3]

But Abel's elder brother, Cain, who also had been taught the Law of Sacrifice, took it upon himself to deviate from the course marked out. Instead of a lamb, he "brought of the fruit of the ground"—an offering in no way symbolical of the Savior. His offering was rejected; [4] for "the ordinances must be kept in the very way God has appointed." [5]

The Gospel Introduced.—The way was now prepared for the introduction of the great redemptive scheme that was to lift fallen man and open to him the opportunities for endless increase and progression. Instead of preaching "another gospel," or inventing some new form of ordinance, as the misguided Cain might have done, Adam adhered to the Gospel in its purity, carrying out to the letter the instructions God had given. He, by his own voice, commanded Adam to believe, to repent, and to be baptized; and, as it is written: "He was caught away by the Spirit of the Lord, and was carried down into the water, and was laid under the water, and was brought forth out of the water;" after which the Spirit descended upon him, "and he heard a voice out of heaven, saying: Thou art baptized with fire and with the Holy Ghost." [6]

"And thus the Gospel began to be preached from the beginning, being declared by holy angels sent forth from the presence of God, and by his own voice, and by the gift of the Holy Ghost. And thus all things were confirmed unto Adam by an holy ordinance, and the Gospel preached, and a decree sent forth that it should be in the world until the end thereof." [7]

Seeming Differences Reconciled.—Apropos of that ancient decree, I was once asked to reconcile the statement concerning it with the idea of a new dispensation. The question came to me in this form: "If the Gospel was to be 'in the world' from Adam's time 'until the end,' what was the need of restoring it—bringing it back again?"

I answered, in substance: "The two propositions do not really contradict each other. The Gospel has been in the world from Adam's day until now, by a series of dispensations, reaching through the entire range of human history. The gaps between, so wide to us, count for little with Deity, to whom past, present and future are one. [8] The finite mind is prone to take short and narrow views of things, tangling itself up in little quibbling details that often give a great deal of trouble. But the Eternal sweeps the whole universe with infinite gaze, and what seem mountains to men are less than mole-hills in His sight. He has found it necessary, at different times, to withdraw the Gospel and the Priesthood from the midst of mankind; and yet, by repeated restorations, forming a continuous chain of dispensations, he has kept the Gospel and the Priesthood in the world from the beginning down to the present." [9]

Seth Succeeds Abel.—Abel fell a martyr to the Truth. Slain by his envious brother [10], he was succeeded by Seth, another brother, born subsequently. Seth was typical of the Son of God, not only because he was "a perfect man," but because "his likeness was the express likeness of his father's, insomuch that he seemed to be like unto his father in all things, and could be distinguished from him only by his age." [11]

Adam-ondi-Ahman.—Says Joseph the Seer: "I saw Adam in the valley of Adam-ondi-Ahman. He called together his children and blessed them with a patriarchal blessing." [12] The vision was of course retrospective, having reference to the time when Adam dwelt on earth. The same event is more fully set forth as follows: "Three years previous to the death of Adam, he called Seth Enos Cainan Mahalaleel Jared Enoch and Methuselah, who were all High Priests, with the residue of his posterity who were righteous, into the valley of Adam-ondi-Ahman, and there bestowed upon them his last blessing.

"And the Lord appeared unto them, and they rose up and blessed Adam, and called him Michael, the Prince, the Archangel.

"And the Lord administered comfort unto Adam, and said unto him, I have set thee to be at the head—a multitude of nations shall come of thee, and thou art a prince over them forever.

"And Adam stood up in the midst of the congregation, and notwithstanding he was bowed down with age, being full of the Holy Ghost, predicted whatsoever should befall his posterity unto the latest generation." [13]

Ancient of Days.—But Adam is to come again—is to come as the Ancient of Days, fulfilling the prophecy of Daniel. [14] And he will come to the very place where, bowed with the weight of more than nine centuries, [15] he blessed his posterity before the ending of his earthy career. In the valley of Adam-ondi-Ahman [16] will sit the Ancient of Days, counseling his children—all who are worthy of that high privilege—and preparing them for the coming of the Son of God.

A Close Relationship.—I have said that the Gospel dispensations are inter-related. It need only be added that the mighty patriarchal blessing—the mightiest ever given—in which Father Adam forecast the history of the human race, taken in connection with his prospective advent into the midst of his righteous descendants, upon the precise spot where he bestowed his farewell benediction and uttered his wonderful world-covering prophecy, indicates a very close relationship between the First and the Final dispensations of the Gospel.

Footnotes

1 . Hist. Ch. Vol 4, pp. 208, 209. In this connection we are told that Adam's son Abel holds "the keys of his dispensation;" that is to say, of the First Dispensation, the one in which Abel figured (D. and C. 84:16). And yet it is called the Adamic Dispensation, for Adam also figured therein.

2 . Moses 5:4-8.

3 . Gen. 4:4.

4 . Ib. 4:5; Heb. 11:4.

5 . Hist. Ch. Vol. 4, pp. 208, 209.

6 . Moses 6:64-66.

7 . Ib. 5:58,59.

8 . Alma 40:8.

9 . It might also be argued that in the spirit World, which is a part of the planet that we inhabit, the Gospel has been preached for ages; so that the dead or the departed might have opportunity to embrace it (I Peter 4:6). And the withdrawal of the Gospel from this temporal sphere would not necessarily involve its withdrawal from that spiritual sphere. Thus, the divine edict, that the Gospel "should be in the world until the end thereof," receives additional vindication.

10 . Gen. 4:8.

11 . D. and C. 107:43.

12 . Hist. Ch. Vol. 3, p.388.

13 . D. and C. 107:53-56.

14 . Dan. 7:9, 13, 22; Hist. Ch. Vol. 3, p. 386.

15 . Gen. 5:5.

16 . D. and C. 116.

ARTICLE FIFTEEN
ENOCH AND HIS CITY

"Glorious things are sung of Zion,
Enoch's city seen of old,
Where the righteous, being perfect,
Walked with God in streets of gold.
Love and virtue, faith and wisdom,
Grace and gifts were all combined;
As himself each loved his neighbor,
All were of one heart and mind."

"The Seventh from Adam."—Enoch, "the seventh from Adam" in patriarchal succession, was contemporaneous with the father of the human family. Indeed, he was ordained and blessed by Adam, and was with him in the historic Valley where the future of the race was foretold by its venerable founder, [1] Enoch's period was prolific of wonderful events, but the two standing out most prominently are:

First:—The successful practice of the Law of Consecration, resulting in the founding of Zion, City of Holiness, which was sanctified through obedience to that high and holy principle, and translated or taken into Heaven without tasting of death. [2]

Second:—Enoch's vision of the future, extending past the Deluge, past the Crucifixion, down even to the Last Days and the glorious coming of the Christ.

The Power of Godliness.—Did the Zion-builder of the Adamic age stand at the head of a Gospel dispensation? Whether he did or did not, it is evident, from what has been revealed concerning him and his ministry, that the message of salvation was preached by him in mighty power and with marvelous success. The world, though young, had grown old in wickedness, and the need for repentance was urgent. [3] "So great was the faith of Enoch," and so powerful the language that God had given him, "the earth trembled and the mountains fled, even according to his command; and the rivers of water were turned out of their course; and the roar of the lions was heard out of the wilderness; and all nations feared greatly, so powerful was the word of Enoch." [4]

The Law of Consecration.—Among warring nations and in the midst of sanguinary strife, Enoch, inspired and directed by the Almighty, introduced and established a social order which cannot be better described than in the simple, sublime phrasing of the Book of Moses, the sacred volume just cited:

"And the Lord called his people Zion, because they were of one heart and one mind and dwelt in righteousness; and there was no poor among them." [5]

"Zion is Fled."—"In process of time" consecration brought sanctification, and eventually translation, to the City of Enoch, regarding which, after its ascension, went forth the saying: "Zion is fled." [6]

The Tower of Babel.—The people who built the Tower of Babel are said to have done so in order that its top might "reach unto heaven." It was to prevent them from accomplishing this purpose, that the Lord confounded their language. [7] Tradition credits Joseph Smith with the statement that the "heaven" they had in view was the translated city.

The Jaredites.—A righteous remnant of the people, namely, the Jaredites, had been exempted from the general curse of tongue confusion; [8] and through them the pure Adamic language was preserved on earth. [9] The Jaredites, divinely led, separated themselves from the other inhabitants of the land, and migrated to North America. Here they flourished for many centuries, and then fell, a slaughtered race, ruined by internal dissension. [10]

Translation and Resurrection.—Translation, says the Prophet Joseph, does not take men "immediately into the presence of God." For translated beings there is a terrestrial "place of habitation," where they are "held in reserve to be ministering angels unto many planets," and "have not yet entered into so great a fulness as those who are resurrected from the dead." Enoch received from God an appointment to minister to beings of this character. [11]

The Future Unveiled.—Enoch walked with God, and was shown "the world for the space of many generations." [12] He beheld the Millennial Dawn, and the darkest hour before the dawn. "He saw great tribulations among the wicked, and he also saw the sea, that it was troubled." [13] In a splendid outburst of epic poetry, the inspired oracle tells how Zion was taken up into heaven; how Satan "veiled the whole face of the earth with darkness;" how he and his angels rejoiced; how "the God of heaven looked upon the residue of the people and wept;" and how the heavens wept also, shedding "their tears as the rain upon the mountains." [14]

Enoch, addressing the compassionate Creator, inquires: "How is it that thou canst weep, seeing thou art holy, and from all eternity to all eternity? And were it possible that man could number the particles of the earth, yea millions of earths like this, it would not be a beginning to the number of thy creations, and thy curtains are stretched out still. . . . . And thou hast taken Zion to thine own bosom from all thy creations, from all eternity to all eternity; and naught but peace, justice and truth is the habitation of thy throne; and mercy shall go before thy face and have no end; how is it thou canst weep?" [15]

The Holy One answers, portraying the impending doom, the destruction of the wicked by the Flood, and their imprisonment in spirit dungeons until the coming of the Christ, bringing deliverance to the penitent. [16]

The Mother of Men.—Enoch hears a voice from the depths of the Earth:

"Wo, wo is me, the mother of men; I am pained, I am weary, because of the wickedness of my children. When shall I rest . . . . when shall my Creator sanctify me, and righteousness for a season abide upon my face?" [17]

The Creator's Covenant.—"And the Lord said unto Enoch: As I live, even so will I come in the last days, in the days of wickedness and vengeance, to fulfill the oath which I have made unto you concerning the children of Noah. And the day shall come that the earth shall rest.

"But before that day the heavens shall be darkened, and a veil of darkness shall cover the earth; and the heavens shall shake, and also the earth; and great tribulations shall be among the children of men. But my people will I preserve." [18]

Another Zion Promised.—"And righteousness will I send down out of heaven, and truth will I send forth out of the earth, to bear testimony of mine Only Begotten; his resurrection from the dead; yea, and also the resurrection of all men; and righteousness and truth will I cause to sweep the earth as with a flood, to gather out mine elect from the four quarters of the earth, unto a place which I shall prepare, an Holy City, that my people may gird up their loins, and be looking forth for the time of my coming; for there shall be my tabernacle, and it shall be called Zion, a New Jerusalem.

"And the Lord said unto Enoch: Then shalt thou and all thy city meet them there, and we will receive them into our bosom, and they shall see us; and we will fall upon their necks, and they shall fall upon our necks, and we will kiss each other:

"And there shall be mine abode, and it shall be Zion, which shall come forth out of all the creations which I have made; and for the space of a thousand years the earth shall rest." [19]

Awaiting its Return.—According to these teachings, the City of Enoch is now on a terrestrial plane, awaiting its return to Earth, when the season shall be ripe and the preparation complete for its reception. The change wrought upon its inhabitants by translation not being equivalent to resurrection, they will undergo a further change to prepare them for celestial glory. The Saints remaining on earth to meet the Lord will likewise be changed, not by the "sleep" of death, but "in a moment, in the twinkling of an eye," at the time of the Savior's coming. [20] When he comes, Enoch's City will come with him, Zion from above blending with Zion from below, as spirit and body in the resurrection.

The Ancient Types the Modern.—The Ancient Zion foreshadowed the Zion of the Last Days, with which it is destined to blend. [21] In Enoch's day the Lord's people, consecrating to Him their all, became equal in earthly as in heavenly things; and the righteous unity resulting from that blest condition brought forth the peace and power of sanctity. So shall it be and more when the Lord brings again Zion.

Footnotes

1. D. and C. 107:48, 53-56.

2. Heb. 11:5.

3. Moses 6:27, 8.

4. Ib. 7:13.

5. Ib. 7:18. Compare Acts 4:32, 34, 35; 4 Nephi 1:2, 3.

6. Moses 7:69.

7. Gen. 11:1-9.

8. Ether 1:33-37.

9. Orson Pratt, citing an unpublished revelation, says"What is the name of God in the pure language? The answer says: 'Ahman.' What is the name of the Son of God? Answer, 'Son Ahman, the greatest of all the parts of God, excepting Ahman.' What is the name of men? 'Sons Ahman' is the answer."—Journal of Discourses, Vol. 2, p. 342.

10. Omni 1:21, 2; Mosiah 8:6-12; 28:17. See also Article Five.

11 . Hist. Ch. Vol. 4, pp. 209, 210.

Commenting upon that passage of scripture, "Others were tortured, not accepting deliverance, that they might obtain a better resurrection" (Heb. 11:35) the Prophet says: "Translation obtains deliverance from the tortures and sufferings of the body; but their existence will prolong as to the labors and toils of the ministry, before they can enter into so great a rest and glory. On the other hand those who were tortured not accepting deliverance, received an immediate rest from their labors." He also explains the difference between an angel and a ministering spirit—"the one a resurrected or translated body, with its spirit, ministering to embodied spirits; the other a disembodied spirit, visiting or ministering to disembodied spirits." . . . . Translated beings, "designed for future missions," "cannot enter into rest until they have undergone a change equivalent to death."—"The Mediation and Atonement." pp. 75, 76.

12 . Moses 7:4.

13 . Ib. v. 66. Compare D. and C. 61:4-6, 14-19.

14 . Moses 7:26, 28.

15 . Ib. vv. 29-31.

16 . I Peter 3:18-20; 4:6.

17 . Moses 7:48.

18 . Ib. vv. 60, 61.

19 . Moses 7:62-64.

20 . I Cor. 15:51. 52.

21 . D. and C. 84:99-102.

ARTICLE SIXTEEN
NOAH AND THE DELUGE

Methuselah, Son of Promise.—God, having shown to Enoch the approaching utter destruction of Earth's wicked inhabitants, covenanted with the founder of the Sacred City that the repeopler of the devastated globe should be of his lineage. In order that this promise might not fail, Enoch's son, Methuselah, distinguished among men as the one who attained to the greatest age in mortality, [1] "was not taken" when Zion was translated, but remained to become the father of Lamech and grandfather of Noah. [2]

Earth's Baptism.—The Deluge was Earth's baptism. Baptism symbolizes birth or creation. In a certain sense, our planet was "born of water and of the Spirit" at the very beginning. [3] In Noah's day, which was reminiscent of that beginning, it experienced a rebirth, "a washing of regeneration," typical of a spiritual and fiery immersion yet to come.

Like Unto Adam.—It devolved upon Noah to recommence, after the Flood, the work begun by the great sire of the race under God's original command—the command to "multiply and replenish the earth." Noah's time, therefore, typified the period of the Creation. He, like Adam, "was the father of all living in his day, and to him was given the dominion." [4]

The Flood Foretold.—Blest and ordained by Methusaleh when but ten years old, Noah, like his predecessors in the patriarchal line, was a prophet and a preacher of righteousness. The word of the Lord came to him, saying:

"My spirit shall not always strive with man; . . . . yet his days shall be an hundred and twenty years; and if men do not repent, I will send in the floods upon them." They hearkened not, and God then decreed: "The end of all flesh is come before me, for the earth is filled with violence, and behold I will destroy all flesh from off the earth." [5]

Shem, Ham and Japheth.—Noah had three sons, Shem, Ham and Japheth—naming them in the order usually given. Japheth, however, was the eldest, and Ham the youngest, of these brothers. [6] They were among the eight survivors of the Deluge; [7] "and of them was the whole earth overspread." [8] Japheth peopled Europe, Shem Asia, and Ham Africa.

Noah's blessing upon Shem and Japheth, and his curse upon Canaan, son of Ham, are thus recorded:

"Cursed be Canaan; a servant of servants shall he be unto his brethren.

"Blessed be the Lord God of Shem; and Canaan shall be his servant.

"God shall enlarge Japheth, and he shall dwell in the tents of Shem; and Canaan shall be his servant." [9]

The Curse upon Canaan.—Part of the curse upon Canaan was "a blackness," similar to that which had been placed upon "the seed of Cain." [10] The curse also deprived the Canaanites of the Priesthood; though they were blessed "with the blessings of the earth and with the blessings of wisdom." [11]

Ham's sin, which brought the curse upon Canaan—a sin vaguely hinted at in the sacred narrative—may not be fully known; but even if it were, there would still remain the unsolved problem of the punishment of a whole race for an offense committed by one of its ancestors. It seems reasonable to infer that there was a larger cause, that the sin in question was not the main issue. Tradition has handed down something to that effect, but nothing conclusive of the question is to be found in the standard works of the Church. Of one thing we may rest assured: Canaan was not unjustly cursed, nor were the spirits who came through his lineage wrongly assigned. "Whatsoever a man soweth, that shall he also reap." Or, putting it inversely: Whatsoever a man reaps, that hath he sown. This rule applies to spirit life, as well as to life in the flesh.

Israel and the Gentiles.—From Shem came Abraham and the House of Israel; from Japheth, the Gentiles, founders of the most civilized and enlightened nations of modern times, including Great Britain, France, and the United States of America. How wonderfully God has "enlarged Japheth," the original Gentile!

Israel wields the powers of the Priesthood, and administers the laws and ordinances of the Gospel. These are his prerogatives. But the children of Japheth also have their mission—a mission in statecraft and commerce, in science and art, in discovery, invention, and kindred activities.

It was the Gentiles who discovered and peopled America; who fought for and won the freedom and independence of this chosen land, an event preparatory—though they knew it not—to the founding of a government under which Christ's work might come forth and not be crushed out by the tyranny of man. The God of Israel was with Columbus, with Washington, with the Pilgrim Fathers, with the patriots who founded this republic [12] —Gentiles all, though probably of a mixed lineage, having much of the blood of Israel in their veins. [13] He is with all good and great men whose hearts are set to do right and to uplift humanity—is with them, whether they recognize it or not, and he uses them as seemeth him good, to effect his beneficent designs.

Ham's Descendants.—The descendants of Ham became eminent, wealthy, wise and powerful in Egypt, "the cradle of civilization;" reaping "the blessings of the earth" and the blessings "of wisdom," richly realizing the heaven-inspired promises made to their forbears. They have prospered also in other African countries. But in Europe, America, and other lands, they were long held in slavery. Nor are the days of their bondage even now at end in Africa and some parts of Asia. The Ethiopian has served the Gentile and the Semite, just as Noah predicted.

Japheth and "The Tents of Shem."—What are "the tents of Shem?" In the Scriptures "tent" is a term used figuratively as well as literally. The canopy of heaven is compared to a tent; as is also the Church of Christ and the city of Jerusalem. [14] The word may therefore be applied to a country or a place of sojourn. How Japheth has dwelt "in the tents of Shem," is partly shown by the history of Palestine, Israel's original homeland, long dominated by the Saracens and Turks—both Gentile peoples—and only recently delivered from the Moslem yoke by the military power of the British, a racial blending of Japheth and Shem. [15]

Japheth's remarkable blessing has also been realized in America, the Land of Joseph, which the Gentiles now possess, and where, according to the Book of Mormon, they are to assist in gathering Israel and in building the New Jerusalem. It is their privilege to share, if they will, in all the blessings of the chosen people, and to be even as the seed of Abraham. [16]

The Asiatic, and especially the Israelitish countries, with North and South America—homes of God's people, ancient and modern, now inhabited by the children of Japheth—these I think, may be properly regarded as among "the tents of Shem."

As it Was, So it Shall Be.—Noah's period had a twofold significance. Pointing backward as well as forward, it symbolized both the Beginning and the End. The reminiscent pointing has already been indicated. The prophetic import is made plain by the words of the Savior, when weeping over Jerusalem and predicting the downfall of the Jewish commonwealth, an event also typical of the final destruction of the wicked: "As the days of Noe were, so shall also the coming of the Son of Man be." [17]

In Noah's day "a veil of darkness" covered the earth. A like condition is to characterize the Last Day, thus foretokened. [18] The disaster that overwhelmed the Antediluvians, destroying the wicked with water, is to have as its sequel a more fearful calamity, in which the unrighteous will be consumed by fire from Heaven. And as unexpectedly as came the regenerating Flood wherein our planet was once immersed, will come the purifying Flame that shall cleanse it from all iniquity and prepare it for eternal glory.

Footnotes

1. Gen. 5:27.

2. Moses 8:2-9.

3. Gen. 1:2, 9.

4. Hist. Ch. Vol. 3, p. 386.

5. Moses 8:17, 30; Gen. 6:3, 3.

6. Ib. 8:12; Gen. 10:21.

7. I Peter 3:20.

8. Gen. 9:19.

9. Ib. 9:22-27.

10. Ib. 4:15; Moses 7:8, 2.

11. Abr. 1:26.

12. I Nephi 13:12-19.

13. The word "Gentile," as used in "Mormon" writings, is not a term of reproach. It comes from "Gentilis," meaning of "of a nation," and is used in sacred history to designate the nations not of Israel. The Latter-day Saints themselves, are Gentiles in part; for while they claim lineal descent from the Hebrew patriarchs, it is mostly through Ephraim,

who "mixed himself among the people" (Hosea 7:8)—that is, among the peoples that have furnished proselytes to "Mormonism." As a result of that racial mixture, they also are of Japheth's blood.

14 . Isa. 40:22; 54:2; 33:20.

15 . The delivery of the Holy Land from the Turks dates from December 11, 1917, when General Allenby, at the head of a British army, entered and took possession of the City of Jerusalem. Subsequently Herbert Samuel, an English Jew, was made Governor of Palestine by the British Government.

16 . Abr. 2:10.

17 . Matt. 24:37-39.

18 . Moses 7:26,

ARTICLE SEVENTEEN
ABRAHAM AND THE HOUSE OF ISRAEL

The Lord's Lineage.—The House of Israel was established in order that the God of Israel, who became the Savior of the World, might have a proper lineage through which to come, and a worthy medium whereby to promote His great and benevolent designs toward the human family.

"Prince of God."—The name "Israel" means "Prince of God," and is first used in the Scriptures as the surname of Jacob, from whom sprang the Hebrew nation or the Twelve Tribes of Israel. Jacob, returning from Padan-Aram, whither he had fled from the jealous wrath of his brother Esau, came to the ford Jabbok, where "there wrestled a man with him until the breaking of day." We are left to infer that Jacob believed this "man" to be God; for he "called the name of the place Peniel," saying, "I have seen God face to face."

"Let me go," demanded the heavenly visitant. "I will not let thee go," replied Jacob, "except thou bless me."

The "Man" then blessed him and changed his name from Jacob to Israel; "for," said he, "as a prince hast thou power with God and with men, and hast prevailed." [1]

Jacob's Blessing Confirmed.—Subsequently the name Israel was confirmed upon Jacob at Bethel, where the Lord appeared to him and blessed him, promising that a nation and a company of nations should be of him, and that kings should come out of his loins. [2]

The Father of the Faithful.—But while this was the origin of the name Israel as applied to Jacob, it was not the origin of the race of which he is the titular head. It is written that Jacob's wives, Rachel and Leah, "did build the House of Israel; [3] and build it they did, through their children and the children of their handmaids, Bilhah and Zilpah, whom they had given to their husband as wives. Already, however, had the foundation of that house been laid by Jacob's grandsire, Abraham, the Friend of God, the Father of the Faithful. Jehovah's promises to Jacob and to his father Isaac concerning their posterity, were virtual repetitions of promises made to their great ancestor.

"Now the Lord had said unto Abram, get thee out of thy country, and from thy kindred, and from thy father's house, unto a land that I will show thee; and I will make of thee a great nation; and I will . . . . bless them that bless thee, and curse him that curseth thee; and in thee shall all families of the earth be blessed." [4]

Definition of "Hebrew."—Abram, for so was he then, called, dwelt in Ur of the Chaldees, a city of Mesopotamia, which signifies "between the rivers." The rivers were the Tigris and the Euphrates. Abram had to cross the Euphrates in order to reach Canaan, the land that the Lord showed him. Because of this circumstance, he was called by the Canaanites a "Hebrew," meaning "one from beyond the river." The origin of the name is also traced to Heber or Eber, one of the ancestors of Abram. Mesopotamia was the fountain-head of idolatry in Western Asia; and because the Lord wished to raise up a people who would worship him and him only, Abraham was required to separate himself from his idolatrous surroundings. [5]

Meeting with Melchizedek.—Following his arrival in Canaan, and a brief sojourn in Egypt, came the episode of Abram's meeting with Melchizedek, King of Salem and Priest of the Most High God. To him Abram gave a tenth part of the spoils that he had taken in battle with certain kings. [6] And Melchizedek blessed Abram and conferred upon him the Priesthood. [7]

The Law of Tithing.—This is the first Bible mention of the ancient Law of Tithing. "Consider," says the author of the Epistle to the Hebrews, "how great this man was, unto whom even the Patriarch Abraham gave the tenth of the spoils." [8] So great indeed, that the Priesthood of the Son of God was named for him, and is now called the Priesthood of Melchizedek. [9]

Abram Renamed.—After this interview with the King of Salem, the Lord appeared to Abram, established His covenant with him, and changed his name to Abraham, which signifies, "father of a multitude." [10]

The Offering of Isaac.—Then followed the supreme trial of Abraham's life—the offering, at God's command, of his son Isaac, an act foreshowing the sacrifice of the Only Begotten of the Father, who was to be slain for the world's redemption. But Abraham was not permitted to consummate the act. [11] His integrity having been shown by his willingness to do as he had been directed, a further mark of favor was given by Jehovah to his tried and faithful Friend. The original promise, "In thee shall all families of the earth be blessed," was now expanded to: "I will multiply thy seed as the stars of heaven, and as the sand which is upon the seashore; and in thy seed shall all the nations of the earth be blessed."

Why Was Abraham Blessed?—What had Abraham done to merit this high distinction? He must have done something. God rewards men according to their works, and not even an Abraham would have received from Him an honor unmerited. It cannot be that he was chosen for so mighty a mission simply for migrating from his own to another country, nor even for his willingness to offer up his beloved son. As a matter of fact, the original promise was given before the sacrifice was demanded. Undoubtedly these acts of obedience were greatly to Abraham's credit, but how could they be placed to the credit of his posterity, the unborn millions who were to inherit the covenant and share in the great reward?

The Problem Solved.—The Patriarch himself helps us to a solution of the problem:

"Now the Lord had shown unto me, Abraham, the intelligences that were organized before the world was; and among all these there were many of the noble and great ones.

"And God saw these souls that they were good, and he stood in the midst of them, and he said: These I will make my rulers; for he stood among those that were spirits, and he saw that they were good; and he said unto me: Abraham, thou art one of them; thou wast chosen before thou wast born." [12]

The Pre-Existence.—Abraham had been shown in vision the spirits of the pre-existent human race, waiting for an earth to be made, that they might come upon it and pass through a mortal probation. Here they were to obtain bodies, thus becoming "souls," [13] capable of eternal increase and progression. Also, they were to be tested as to their willingness to do all that the Lord might require of them.

First and Second Estates.—They who "kept their first estate," manifesting fidelity in the pre-mortal life while "walking by sight," were to be "added upon"—that is to say, given bodies of flesh and blood, with opportunities for education and development. They who kept "their second estate," continuing loyal during their life on earth, where men are required to "walk by faith," with knowledge of the past temporarily obscured, would be glorified eternally. [14] All were "good," but some better than others; and all were to be "added upon," yet not all alike. Some were more deserving, some nobler and greater than others; and because of their superior merit and larger capacity, they were to be made "rulers" over the rest. Abraham was one of these.

Sowing and Reaping.—Here is exemplified the great principle enunciated by St. Paul: "Whatsoever a man soweth, that shall he also reap." [15] Rewards and punishments are not all deferred until the final judgment at the end of the world. There is a judgment passed upon the spirits of men before they tabernacle in mortality. Satan and his dupes, failing to keep their first estate, were denied bodies, [16] while all the rest, rewarded for keeping their first estate, were given bodies, with the promise of a glorious resurrection after death. Thus, in a general way, punishment and reward were both meted out before this life began.

A question put to the Savior by his disciples: "Master, who did sin, this man, or his parents, that he was born blind?" [17] —throws out a hint in the same direction. This is not to say, however, that all who suffer in the flesh have merited their sad fate. There are exceptions to the rule. The Savior's case is one of them; and righteous Job's another. Speaking generally, however, man's conduct in one life conditions him in the life that follows.

Original Excellence.—What had given to Abraham his superior standing in the Heavens? Had he always been noble and great? Was it an original or an acquired excellence, or both? That there is such a thing as original superiority, with varying degrees of intelligence among spirits, is plainly taught in the Book of Abraham; [18] and that all intelligence is capable of improvement, needs no assertion.

"I Know Abraham."—When God said of Abraham: "I know him," [19] it is hardly probable that He was referring merely to a knowledge of him in the present life. The founder of the Hebrew nation must have been one of the foreknown and predestined, mentioned by Paul [20] and by Alma [21] —must have been among those "called and prepared from the foundation of the world, on account of their exceeding faith and good works." It was "according to the foreknowledge of God;" but that foreknowledge, that divine prescience, was based upon experience, and had history as well as prophecy for a foundation. Such characters as Abraham were cast for their parts in life's drama long before the curtain rose on the first act of the play.

A Spirit Israel.—There was a House of Israel in heaven before there was a Hebrew Nation on earth. Else what does Moses mean when he tells how the Most High, in "the days of old," in "the years of many generations," "separated the sons of Adam" and "set the bounds of the people according to the number of the children of Israel?" [22] He must have had in mind, not a temporal Israel, unborn at the early period indicated, but a spirit Israel, according to whose numbers, known in heaven before they had taken bodies on earth, the boundaries of "the people" were determined.

Privileges and Requirements.—It was intended that this chosen nation should have "room to dwell." It was of the utmost consequence that a people upon whom rested so weighty a responsibility should be well placed, with every facility for the accomplishment of the sacred mission unto which they had been called. They were the oracles of God, the custodians and dispensers of heavenly wisdom. Upon them devolved the high duty of keeping alive on earthly altars the fires of Divine Truth. They were not to bow down to idols, as did the heathen nations around them, but worship the true God, the invisible Jehovah, walking by faith where others, less worthy, walked by sight, demanding to see before they would believe. They were forbidden to intermarry with other nations, lest they might worship the gods of those nations, practice their vices, and corrupt the noble lineage through which was to come the Savior of the World. The Lamb of God had to be "without blemish," and that he was so, physically and in every way, was partly due, no doubt, to the choice ancestry and parentage provided for him.

Gem and Setting.—Jesus of Nazareth, a descendant in the flesh of Abraham, Isaac and Jacob, fulfilled the divine promise made to those patriarchs, that in their Seed should all the nations of the earth be blessed. But in contemplating the central fact of the Savior's personal ministry, we must not overlook the related facts that went before or followed after. The gem has its setting. Christ redeemed mankind, "treading the wine press alone;" but the House of Israel prepared the way for his coming, and carried on the work that he began. This is especially true of the prophets who foretold his advent, and of the apostles who preached the Gospel to Jew and Gentile. There is only one Savior, but He has "many brethren," and they are preeminently "the salt of the earth," the preserving or saving element among men.

Princes and Servants.—If the name Israel means "prince of God" when applied to Jacob, may it not mean "princes of God" when applied to his posterity? He was promised that kings should come out of his loins. And have they not come?—princes and priests and kings, the nobility of Heaven, though not always known and appreciated on earth. The Greatest among them was not recognized even by "His own." The wise Solomon was never wiser than when he said: "I have seen servants upon horses, and princes walking as servants upon the earth." [23] The mighty Prince of Peace, the glorious King of Heaven, walked unknown and unhonored by his own servants in the dust of his own footstool.

Footnotes

1. Gen. 32:22-30.

2. Ib. 35:10, 11.

3. Ruth 4:11.

4. Gen. 12:1-3; Abr. 2:3-11.

5. Geike, "Hours with the Bible," Vol. 1, Ch. 13.

6. Gen. 14:18.

7. D. and C. 84:14.

8. Heb. 7:4.

9. D. and C. 107:1-4.

10. Gen. 17:3-6.

11. Ib. 22:1-18.

12. Abr. 3:22, 23. Read also verses 24-26.

13. Gen. 2:7; Moses 3:7, 9; D. and C. 88:15.

14. Manifestly, the second estate is a greater test of integrity than the first, and ought to result, as it does to those who overcome, in a far more glorious reward.

15. Gal. 6:7.

16. See Article Twelve.

17. John 9:2.

18. Abr. 3:18, 19.

19. Gen. 18:19.

20. Rom. 8:29.

21. Alma 13:3.

22. Deut. 32:7, 8.

23. Eccl. 10:7.

ARTICLE EIGHTEEN
MOSES AND AARON

Joseph in Egypt.—In the whole range of Bible literature, if we except what is told of the Redeemer and Savior, there is nothing more beautiful than the story of Joseph in Egypt. Joseph the dreamer, sold into slavery, exalted to a throne, and becoming, by God's design, a savior to his father's house. Who cannot see in this a prophetic likeness of the universal redemption wrought out by Him who descended below all, that He might rise above all, and deliver the souls of men from spiritual famine and starvation?

The Exodus.—Another foretokening of the same sublime event was Israel's exodus from Egypt, after centuries of oppression. Egypt, with its dusky population, devoid of priesthood and of gospel light, symbolized the sable bondage of sin and death. Moses, leader of the Exodus, and reputedly "the meekest of men," [1] was a type of the Great Deliverer, "like unto Moses," who led an enslaved universe out from the Egypt of Darkness into the Promised Land of Freedom and Light.

The Passover.—In commemoration of the Egyptian exodus, the Feast of the Passover was instituted, an observance designed to perpetuate, in the minds of the children of Israel, their liberation from slavery, and at the same time prepare them to comprehend in due time, the mightier Redemption thus foreshadowed.

The Passover was kept as follows: Obedient to God's command through Moses, each Israelitish household, on the eve of the departure out of Egypt, took a lamb, spotless and "without blemish," and slew it, sprinking its blood upon the posts and lintels of their doors. It was promised that the Angel of Death, sent to afflict the cruel nation for its mistreatment of the Lord's people, should, while slaying the first-born of every Egyptian family, pass over every Hebrew dwelling upon which the symbolic blood was found sprinkled in accordance with the divine command. Not a bone of the lamb was to be broken, nor a fragment of it left to decay; for it symbolized the Lamb of God, the Holy One, whose body was not to see corruption. [2] Neither was any bone of Him to be broken.

In the Paschal Feast the body of the lamb was spitted (transfixt) upon two pieces of wood placed cross-wise, indicating prophetically the manner of the Savior's death. The flesh was then roasted and partaken of with bitter herbs and unleavened bread—flour and water hastily mixed; the herbs typifying the bitterness of the bondage that was about to end, also the bitterness of death; and the hastily prepared meal the hurry of departure. [3] To further emphasize the idea of haste, the members of each Hebrew household, while partaking of the feast, were to be clad as if for a journey. This solemn ceremonial was observed in Israel until the coming of Christ, who fulfilled in his own person and experience the poetic-prophetic symbolism.

The Ten Commandments.—

Sacred Patterns.—The children of Israel, after their miraculous passage of the Red Sea, encamped at the foot of Mount Sinai. There God gave to Moses the tables of stone containing the Ten Commandments, also the pattern of the Ark or Sanctuary, the symbol of the covenant that Jehovah had made with his people. He likewise gave the pattern of the Tabernacle or holy tent where the Ark was to be deposited, where the priest would offer sacrifices and make atonement for the sins of the nation, and where the Lord would communicate by angels or by Urim and Thummim with the men chosen to represent Him in that sacred capacity.

The Priesthood Organized.—Moses was of the Tribe of Levi, and son-in-law to Jethro the Midianite. The Midianites were descended from Midian, the fourth son of Abraham by his wife Keturah. [4] It was from Jethro that Moses received the Melchizedek Priesthood. [5] Thus qualified, the Israelite leader organized, by divine direction, the Lesser Priesthood, with his brother Aaron at its head. [6] Aaron's sons, Nadab, Abihu, Eleazer and Ithamar, were associated with him in the priest's office. [7]

Idolatry and Expiation.—Just prior to their setting apart as priests, and while Moses, with faithful Joshua, was up in the Mount, receiving the Law and the Testimony, Israel lapsed temporarily into idolatry. In the golden calf, which they persuaded Aaron to make for them, they worshiped the Egyptian god Apis, or, as Dr. Geikie suggests, the ox-headed god of the Asiatics. This sin demanded and received prompt punishment. By command of Moses, the tribe of Levi—every man of which responded to his loyal appeal, "Who's on the Lord's side?"—slew with the sword three thousand males among the idolaters. The stern expiation complete, the work of organization proceeded.

The Levites—As an act coordinate with the destruction of Egypt's first-born, the Lord had chosen the first-born males of all the families of Israel, and had set them apart for a special purpose. He now took the tribe of Levi, instead, and made of them the sacerdotal class of the nation; a reward, no doubt, for the zeal they had displayed in wiping out the stain of idolatry from Israel. The laws of Moses were then promulged and codified, and the sublime system of heaven-revealed religion was set in motion.

A Nation on the March.—All being ready for the great march Zionward, the Camp of Israel struck its tents, and, guided by the Cloud and Pillar of Fire, moved majestically through the Sinaitic desert toward the Wilderness of Paran. The descendants of Jacob numbered at that time nearly three million souls, including an army of half a million. They were divided into four camps of three tribes each, exclusive of the Levites; Joseph being twice numbered in Ephraim and Manasseh, thus making up for the absence of the sacred class from the tribal count.

Foremost rose aloft the lion standard of Judah, the future kingly power, out of which was to come the Savior-King of Israel. Then followed the tribes and armies of Issachar and Zebulon, and after them the sons of Gershon and Merari (first and third sons of Levi), bearing the components of the Tabernacle, which it was their duty to set up and take down, as the Camp rested or resumed its journey. The standard of Reuben was next advanced, and immediately in his rear marched Simeon and Gad. The Ark then appeared, borne in the very center of the moving host on the shoulders of the sons of Kohath. Ephraim and Manasseh followed; then Benjamin; the tribes of Dan, Ashur and Naphtali bringing up the rear.

The Camp at Rest.—When the Cloud rested, indicating their stopping place, the tents were set surrounding the Tabernacle of the Congregation; the Levites encompassing it immediately about, to prevent the unsanctified from approaching too near, and purposely or inadvertently defiling it—an offense punishable by death. When the Ark set forward, Moses exclaimed: "Rise up, O Lord, and let thine enemies be scattered!" When it rested, he said: "Return, O Lord, unto the many thousands of Israel!"

A Period of Preparation.—The Chosen People no doubt cherished the hope of an early conquest of Canaan, the land which God had given to their forefathers; a land inhabited at the time of the Exodus by various tribes alien to Jehovah and unfriendly to Israel. It was a case of hope deferred. Had the Lord's people been ready, the carrying out of the program of conquest and occupation would not have been delayed. But they were not ready, and the event was therefore postponed. There had to be a season of waiting, a period of preparation. Forty years were to elapse before that migrant host, disciplined by inspired leaders under strict and wholesome laws, would be in a state of preparedness to thrust in the sickle and reap the glorious harvest springing from the divine promises of the past.

The Greater Priesthood Taken.—So long as Moses lived, both the Melchizedek and the Aaronic priesthoods were present and operative in Israel. But with the passing of the great leader, went likewise the authority of the higher priesthood, without which "the power of godliness is not manifest to men in the flesh." Nay, without it "no man can see the face of God, even the Father, and live." [8] Moses had taught this to his people, seeking diligently to sanctify them that they might behold God face to face. "But they hardened their hearts, and could not endure His presence. Therefore He took Moses out of their midst, and the Holy Priesthood also." [9]

John the Baptist.—The Lesser Priesthood, with the law of carnal commandments, continued "with the house of Aaron among the children of Israel" until John the Baptist, in the Meridian of Time, came to "make straight the way of the Lord." [10] This same John the Baptist, as an angel of God, came also in the Fulness of Times, restoring the Aaronic Priesthood, as a forerunner to the Priesthood of Melchizedek, that there might be a preparation for the second appearing of the Savior. [11]

An Acceptable Offering.—Moses represents the Melchizedek Priesthood; Aaron the Aaronic; and "whose is faithful unto the obtaining of these two priesthoods . . . . and the magnifying of their calling, are sanctified by the Spirit unto the renewing of their bodies. They become the sons of Moses and of Aaron, and the seed of Abraham, and the church and kingdom and the elect of God." [12] Moses and Aaron were sons of Levi, and their sons are to offer "an acceptable offering and sacrifice in the House of the Lord," which shall be built "upon the consecrated spot" "in this generation." Such is the divine promise.

Footnotes

1 . Numbers 12:3.

2 . Psalms 16:10.

3 . The observance thus described suggests Latter-day conditions, when, like the plagues sent upon Egypt, terrible judgments are to be poured out upon the wicked, so suddenly and so overwhelmingly that even "the righteous will scarcely escape," and when the Lord, in order to save some, will "cut short his work in righteousness."

4 . Gen. 25:1, 2; 1 Chr. 1:32 1 Chr. 1:32.

5 . D. and C. 84:6.

6 . Ex. 28:1-3.

7 . Aaron, Nadab and Abihu were probably Elders acting as Priests. Such an inference is warranted by the fact that they, with Moses and seventy of the Elders of Israel, "saw the God of Israel" (Ex. 24:9, 10); which they could not have done with safety had they held only the Aaronic Priesthood (D. and C. 84:22).

8 . D. and C. 84:19-22.

9 . Ib., vv. 23-25.

10 . Ib. 84:26-28.

11 . Ib. 13.

12 . Ib. 84:31-34.

ARTICLE NINETEEN
TO THE ENDS OF THE EARTH

Calamity's Compensations.—The compensations of calamity are apparent in some of the mightiest events that history chronicles. The Fall of Man, though it brought death into the world, proved the means of peopling a planet in accordance with the Creator's design. The Crucifixion of Christ, an overwhelming calamity to His terror-stricken disciples, who were disconsolate until they looked upon the tragedy in its true light, made effectual the predestined plan for man's salvation. The Dispersion of Israel, that heavy stroke and burden of affliction under which God's people have groaned for ages, has been overruled to subserve the divine purpose, fulfilling in part the ancient promise to the Hebrew Patriarchs, that in their seed should all the nations of the earth be blessed.

A Martyred Nation.—The history of the house of Israel is the history of a martyred nation, suffering for the welfare of other nations—whatever may be said of the immediate cause of their woes, the transgressions that justified the Shepherd in bringing upon his sheep troubles that were doubtless among the "offenses" that "must needs come." Adam fell that man might be; Christ died to burst the bands of death; and the chosen people were scattered over the world, in order that Gospel truth, following the red track of their martyrdom, might make its way more readily among the peoples with whom they were mingled.

Moses Predicts the Dispersion.—Prophecies of Israel's dispersion were made as early as the time of Moses, fifteen hundred years before the advent of the Savior. When the Twelve Tribes were about to possess themselves of the Promised Land, their great leader, who was soon to depart, told them that so long as they served Jehovah and honored his statutes, they should be prospered and remain an independent nation. But if they forsook Jehovah and served other gods, He would scatter them among all people, from one end of the earth even unto the other. [1]

A House Divided.—Joshua, succeeding Moses, conquered the land of Canaan and apportioned it among the Tribes of Israel. A season of prosperity and power was followed by decadence and ruin. As early as the days of the Judges the people began to depart from God and to invite by rebellious conduct the national calamity that had been predicted. The glory of the reigns of David and Solomon being past, the curse, long suspended, fell, and the Israelitish Empire hastened to decay. The tribes in the northern part of the land revolted and set up the Kingdom of Israel, distinct from the Kingdom of Judah, over which Solomon's son Rehoboam continued to reign. The tribe of Benjamin and the half tribe of Manasseh adhered to Judah.

Ahijah, Amos and Hosea.—Jeroboam, King of Israel, made idolatry the state religion. During his reign the dispersion was again predicted, Ahijah the prophet thus voicing the word of the Lord to his disobedient people: "The Lord shall smite Israel, as a reed is shaken in the water, and he shall root up Israel out of this good land, which he gave to their fathers, and shall scatter them beyond the river." [2] Another prophet who foretold the same disaster was Hosea; [3] still another, Amos, who declared that Israel should "surely go into captivity" and be "sifted among all nations." [4] Hosea's prophecy substitutes past for future, thus: "Ephraim, he hath mixed himself among the people," referring to the event in prospect as if it had already taken place. Possibly a prophetic vision—then past—had apprised this seer of what was coming, or it may have been only a figure of rhetoric, common even at the present day.

"The Wolf on the Fold."—About the year 725 B. C. these prophecies began to have their fulfillment. The Assyrians came against the Kingdom of Israel and commenced the work of its destruction. In a series of deportations they carried away the Ten Tribes—nine and a half, to be exact—and, as customary with conquerors in those days, supplied their places with colonists from other parts.

The Lost Tribes.—Concerning the deported—the famous "Lost Tribes"—very little is now known. Josephus, the Jewish historian, who wrote during the first century after Christ, states that they were then beyond the Euphrates; and Esdras, in the Apocrypha, declares that they went a journey of a year and a half into "the north country."

Scandinavian Cairns.—Missionaries returning from Scandinavia tell of rude monuments—cairns of piles of stones—yet to be seen in that northern region, and concerning which tradition asserts that they were erected many centuries ago by a migrating people. Whether or not these were the tribes of the Assyrian captivity, it is interesting to reflect that the rearing of such monuments, in commemoration of notable events, was an Israelitish custom, particularly as to the migratory movements of the nation. The miraculous passage of the Jordan by Joshua and the host led by him into the land of Canaan, was thus commemorated. [5]

Other Ancient Remains.—If it be objected that monuments built seven centuries before Christ's birth could not have lasted down to this day, it will be in order for the objector to explain the existence of the perfectly preserved monuments of Assyria, Babylon, Egypt, and other ancient empires, whose remains have been uncovered by modern archaeological enterprise. Such a theory need not stagger the faith of a Latter-day Saint, when he recalls that the ruins of Adam's altar are still to be seen in that part of the Old-New World now known as the State of Missouri, where they were identified by Joseph the Seer in 1838.

From the North Country.—At all events, it is from "the north country" that the lost tribes are to return, according to ancient and modern prophecy. [6] It is also a fact that from Scandinavia and other nations of Northern Europe, has come much of the blood of Ephraim, now to be found within the Church of Jesus Christ of Latter-day Saints.

Isaiah and Jeremiah—The Babylonian Captivity—Returning to the Kingdom of Israel. The prophecies concerning it were supplemented by other predictions foretelling the fate of the Kingdom of Judah. Those great prophets, Isaiah and Jeremiah, figured during this period, and both portrayed in fervid eloquence, unparalleled for pathos and sublimity, the impending doom of the Jewish nation. Their government was destroyed, and they were carried into captivity by the Babylonians under Nebuchadnezzar, B. C. 588.

Lehi and His Colony.—Just prior to that catastrophe, and while the Prophet Jeremiah was delivering his fateful message to king, princes, priests and people, Lehi and his companions, ancestors of the Nephites and Lamanites, [7] warned of God, left Jerusalem and crossed over to this land—America—which, by them and by Mulek's company that came later, was thus peopled with descendants of Joseph and of Judah, both represented, though in a degenerate state, by the savage red men whom Columbus, in A. D. 1492, discovered and named Indians. [8]

Jerusalem Rebuilt—Ezekiel and Zechariah.—The Babylonian captivity lasted for seventy years. At the expiration of that period, some of the Jews, under the permissive edict of Cyrus the Great, who had conquered Babylon, returned and rebuilt their City and Temple. These, however, were only a remnant, numbering fifty thousand, led by Zerubbabel and Joshua. The bulk of the nation remained in a scattered condition. The Jews who rebuilt Jerusalem were those to whose descendants the Christ came, and predicted, after their rejection of him, that their "House" should be "left unto them desolate." [9] Meanwhile Ezekiel and Zechariah—the former in exile among the Babylonians, the latter at Jerusalem after the restoration—had added their predictions to those already uttered relating to Israel's dispersion.

The Roman Conquest.—Centuries later, in Apostolic times, went forth the Epistle of James, with its greeting: "To the Twelve Tribes which are scattered abroad." But the dispersion, even then, was not complete. There were yet to be other painful experiences of the same kind. One of the most notable occurred in A. D. 70, when Titus the Roman came against Jerusalem, captured the city, and sold the inhabitants—such as had survived the horrors of the siege—into slavery, or scattered them through different parts of the Empire. To follow the fortunes of this branch of the fated nation in all its subsequent migrations and wanderings, would fill volumes.

What of the Benefits?—Let us now consider the question: In what way did these calamities upon Israel prove a blessing to the human race? How, by the scattering of the children of Abraham, Isaac and Jacob, was God's promise to those patriarchs in any degree fulfilled, that in their seed should all the nations of the earth be blessed? Already I have answered these questions in part, and will now answer them more fully.

The Blood That Believes.—Through these acts of deportation, enforced exile, and voluntary wandering, the blood of Israel, the blood that believes, with choice spirits answering to that blood, and no doubt selected for the purpose, were sent into those nations where the Gospel has since been preached—spirits capable of recognizing and appreciating the Truth, and brave enough to embrace it, regardless of consequences; thus setting an example of heroism, of obedience to the dictates of conscience, that would naturally appeal to the noble and upright surrounding them, and influence them in the same direction. Manifestly, that was of far greater consequence than the carrying by the captive Israelites of their laws, traditions and customs into those nations; though this also would help to prepare the way for the wonderful developments that were to follow.

Rapid Spread of Christianity.—And such things told in after years. One of the marvels of history is the rapid spread of Christianity in the days of the Apostles, who, unlettered as most of them were, and in the midst of the fiercest persecution, planted the Gospel standard in all the principal cities of the Roman Empire. From Jerusalem, the tidings of "Christ and him crucified" radiated to Britain on the west, to India on the east, to Scythia on the north, and to Ethiopia on the south—all within the short space of fifty years. [10]

Many Nations Sprinkled.—How could such things be, if Divine Providence had not prepared the way by sending the blood and genius of Israel into all nations, prior to pouring out upon those nations the Spirit of the Gospel and the Gathering? Others before Abraham had shown their faith by their works; but this does not disprove his claim to the title—"Father of the Faithful." Nor does it prove that the blood of faith, wherever found, is not his blood. The Moabite maiden Ruth, ancestor of Jesus of Nazareth; the Roman centurion, whose faith caused even the Savior to marvel; Cornelius and the Woman of Canaan—these were not of Israel, by recognized earthly descent; yet their spirits were well worthy of such a lineage, and in their veins was the believing blood with which God has "sprinkled many nations."

Footnotes

1 . Deut. 28:64.

2 . I Kings 14:15.

3 . Hos. 7:8.

4 . Amos 7:11; 9:9.

5 . Joshua 4:1-9.

6 . Jer. 31:8; D. and C. 110:11; 133:26.

7 . See Article Five.

8 . Mark the features of the American Indian. Are they not Jewish? Quite as strikingly so, as that many of his traditions and customs are Israelitish. Who than the savage Lamanite, better understands the Mosaic law of retaliation—"an eye for an eye and a tooth for a tooth?" Nor cares he to whom the eye or the tooth belongs, whether to the person who injured him, or to one of the latter's tribe or nation. He is too much of an Israelite to object to proxies and substitutes.

9 . Matt. 23:37, 38.

10 . Dean Farrar, in his "Life and Work of St. Paul," contributes this luminous passage as explanatory of the rapid spread of Christianity:

"(I) The immense field covered by the conquests of Alexander gave to the civilized world a unity of language, without which it would have been, humanly speaking, impossible for the earliest preachers to have made known the good tidings in every land which they traversed. (II) The rise of the Roman Empire created a political unity which reflected in every direction the doctrines of the new faith. (III) The dispersion of the Jews prepared vast multitudes of

Greeks and Romans for the unity of a pure morality and a monotheistic faith. The Gospel emanated from the capital of Judea; it was preached in the tongue of Athens; it was diffused through the empire of Rome; the feet of its earliest missionaries traversed the solid structure of undeviating roads by which the Roman legionaries—'those massive hammers of the whole earth'—had made straight in the desert a highway for our God. Semite and Aryan had been unconscious instruments in the hands of God for the spread of a religion which, in its first beginnings, both alike detested and despised."

A similar marvel is the spread of the restored Gospel through the Gentile nations of modern times, a work yet in its infancy. The proselyting success of the Latter-day Saints on both hemispheres, their great pilgrimage from the Mississippi River to the Rocky Mountains, the redemption of a wilderness, the founding of a State, and the extraordinary attention attracted by the "Mormon" people—altogether out of proportion to their numbers—these combined facts constitute a striking fulfillment of the prophetic picture drawn by the Savior: "Ye are as a city set upon a hill which cannot be hid."

PART FIVE
IN TIME'S MERIDIAN

ARTICLE TWENTY
THE LAMB OF GOD

A stranger Star, that came from far,
To fling its silver ray
Where, cradled in a lowly cave,
A lowlier infant lay;
And led by soft sidereal light,
The Orient sages bring
Rare gifts of gold and frankincense,
To greet the homeless King.

* * *

He wandered through the faithfulness world,
A Prince in shepherd guise;
He called his scattered flock, but few
The Voice did recognize;
For minds unborne by hollow pride,
Or dimmed by sordid lust,
Ne'er look for kings in beggar's garb,
For diamonds in the dust.

* * *

Transfixt he hung—O crime of crimes!—
The God whom worlds adore.
"Father forgive them!" Drained the dregs;
Immanuel—no more.
No more where thunders shook the earth,
Where lightnings, 'thwart the gloom,
Saw that unconquered Spirit spurn
The shackles of the tomb.
Far-flaming falchion, sword of light,

> Swift-flashing from its sheath,
> It cleft the realms of darkness and
> Dissolved the bands of death.
> Hell's dungeons burst! Wide open swung
> The everlasting bars,
> Whereby the ransomed soul shall win
> Those heights beyond the stars! [1]

The Crucified and Crowned.—An attempt to tell, even in brief, the sublime story of the Christ, would be foreign to my present purpose, Even if space permitted, what pen could do justice to the theme? Suffice it that the Christ came, in the Meridian of Time, as ancient seers and prophets had foretold. Surrendering himself to to death, that there might be no more death, He arose from the grave and ascended on High, glorified with that glory which the Eternal Son had with the Eternal Father before this world was formed.

The Passover Realized.—In the Savior's crucifixion, the prophetic symbolism of the Passover had a most remarkable realization. In nothing was this more strikingly manifest than in certain incidents immediately following the Death on Calvary. The commandment instituting the Paschal Feast required that no bone of the lamb should be broken, and no fragment of it be left to decay, representing as it did the body of the Holy One, which was not "to see corruption." [2] Mark now the exact fulfillment: The Savior had been crucified between two thieves, and at sundown on the day of crucifixion the Jewish Sabbath began. In order that the day might not be "desecrated," the Rabbis prevailed upon the Roman governor to have the three bodies taken down from the crosses and buried. [3] When the soldiers went to remove the bodies, finding the two thieves still alive, they put an end to them by breaking their legs; but Jesus was spared this further indignity, he being "dead already." [4] Pierced with five wounds, yet not a bone of him broken, the Lamb of God, answering in every particular to the likeness of the paschal lamb, was laid in the rocky tomb, whence He came forth on the third day, his perfectly preserved tabernacle glorified in immortality.

The Lord's Supper.—The night before the Crucifixion, Jesus, having partaken of the Passover with his disciples, instituted in its stead the sacrament of the Lord's Supper, commanding them to observe it thenceforth. [5] The Supper, like the Feast, pointed to the Atonement; but in the Passover the pointing was forward to an even that had not yet occurred, while in the Supper, for the reverse reason, the indication is backward. It is said that the paschal lamb was offered in the Temple at Jerusalem about the same hour that Christ died; the substance and the shadow thus corresponding. Thereafter the Passover was obsolete, having fulfilled its purpose, and as the type no longer typified, it should have been discontinued. The Jews, however, perpetuated the old-time observance, not recognizing in Jesus their Messiah.

"It is Finished."—The Savior's dying words, as reported by the Beloved Disciple, [6] have been the subject of much controversy. "It is finished." What did those words signify? The notion has been entertained that Christ's crucifixion completed his work, so far as personal ministrations went, and that after the opening of the so-called Christian Dispensation, there was no further need of communication between God and man. "O most lame and impotent conclusion!" Whatever construction be placed upon that final utterance of our Lord's, it is perfectly clear, from what followed, that it never was intended to convey such a meaning.

Birth and Death Incidental.—The Death on Calvary was no more the ending, than the Birth at Bethlehem was the beginning, of that Divine Career. Both were mere incidents. The Savior's work is universal, extending from Eternity into Time, and back again into Eternity. All the Gospel dispensations, from Adam down to Joseph Smith, are parts of the all-embracing mission of Jesus Christ. Not until "the beginning of the seventh thousand years," the Morning of the Resurrection, "will the Lord God sanctify the earth and complete the salvation of man." [7] Moreover, sanctification will be succeeded by glorification, still another phase of the work of Him who bringeth to pass "the immortality and eternal life of man."

The Sacrifice Complete.—What, then, was "finished" by the Death on the Cross? Simply the pain and sorrow that the Son of God had willed to undergo, that He might ransom a lost creation, and make it possible for redeemed man, by faith and good works, to lay hold upon eternal life. The Savior's self-imposed humiliation, his voluntary sacrifice, his mysterious all-comprehensive suffering, the piled up agony of the human race, endured by him vicariously, to the end that his atonement might be infinite, reaching to every son and daughter of Adam [8] —this was finished, this was at an end; not the work of God, nor the continuous revelation of his word and will to man.

In the Spirit.—While the Savior's body was lying in the tomb, his spirit entered Paradise, and there preached to the spirits of the departed, opening, or causing to be opened, the dungeons of the damned. Returning, He took up his glorified body, and appeared in it to his astonished, half-doubting disciples.

On Both Hemispheres.—Christ died for all; but all are not entitled to his personal ministrations. The sheep, however, have the right to see their Shepherd and to hear his voice. Accordingly, after he had confirmed the faith of his Jewish disciples, had chosen twelve apostles, and sent them forth to preach the Gospel in the power and demonstration of the Holy Spirit, he visited the Nephites, in America, for a similar purpose. They, in common with all Israel, had been warned by prophets to prepare for his coming; and the righteous were ready to receive him. Already they had the Gospel and the Priesthood, and now the Savior organized his Church among them. This done, He visited other broken-off branches of the "tame olive tree," [9] their whereabouts as unknown to Lehi's descendants in the Land Bountiful, as was the existence of the Nephites to the inhabitants of Judea.

The "Other Sheep."—Jesus had said to his Jewish followers: "Other sheep I have, which are not of this fold: them also I must bring, and they shall hear my voice." [10] They inferred that He meant the Gentiles; but such was not his meaning. His direct, special errand was to "the lost sheep of the house of Israel." [11] The Gentiles were to be converted through the preaching of Jewish-Christian evangels. [12]

The "other sheep" were the Nephites, to whom the Savior explained his half-veiled utterance; [13] also declaring that He had still "other sheep," not of the Nephite fold nor of the Jewish fold, and that they likewise should see him and hear his voice. [14] Undoubtedly this allusion was to the "Lost Tribes;" but not to them alone. It included other Hebrew remnants, unknown to man, but known to Jehovah, "keeping watch above his own" in the mystical and remote regions whither his judgments had driven them.

In Remembrance of Him.—Both in Judea and in the Land Bountiful, the Savior instituted, among those who had received the Gospel, the sacrament of the Lord's Supper, that memorial of his sacrifice, once prospective, now retrospective; once a prophecy, now a fulfillment. But its institution among the Nephites, unlike its introduction among the Jews, was after his resurrection. Concerning the earlier incident, the New Testament says:

"As they were eating, Jesus took bread and blessed it, and brake it, and gave it to the disciples, and said, Take, eat; this is my body.

"And he took the cup, and gave thanks, and gave it to them, saying, Drink ye all of it:

"For this is my blood of the new testament, which is shed for many for the remission of sins." [15]

"The Real Presence."—After the living oracles had departed, and only the dead letter of the Scriptures remained, uninspired "private interpretation" [16] conceived the notion that Jesus, when he said, "This is my body" and "my blood," meant the words to be taken literally. From that erroneous inference sprang the doctrine of transubstantiation, with its twin heresy, consubstantiation; the former a Roman Catholic tenet, the latter an unorthodox Protestant tenet relating to the Eucharist. So insistent was the Catholic Church upon this point, that men and women were condemned and punished as heretics, for denying "the real presence," the actual flesh and blood of Christ, in the elements of the Lord's Supper. [17]

Figurative, not Literal.—The language of Jesus, when he instituted the Lord's Supper at Jerusalem, was undoubtedly figurative. When He said, of the bread and wine, "This is my body" and "my blood," his body was intact, his spirit in his body, and his blood yet unsplit. He was there in person, whole, complete. This being the case, how could he have meant to identify the bread and wine with the constituents of his mortal tabernacle? "These are the emblems of my body and blood"—that was his meaning. He made this clear to the Nephites, in saying: "This shall ye do in remembrance of my body." Remembrance presupposes absence. Because he would be absent in body thereafter, they were to do this "in remembrance of" his body. What need to remember him, if he were present in person? As well require faith from one having a perfect knowledge. [18]

Use of Wine Forbidden.—The Latter-day Saints have been criticized for using water in the Sacrament; the Savior having sanctioned the use of wine both among the Jews and the Nephites. The explanation for the change is simple. The Church of Christ is not dependent upon books, nor upon tradition. It has an inspired Priesthood, led by immediate, continuous and direct revelation. The Lord has commanded his people in these days not to use wine in the Sacrament under existing conditions. This is the word they are under obligation to obey—not the word given to other peoples in former dispensations. [19]

Christ to Come Again.—Neither the Savior's resurrection, nor his ascension into Heaven [20] signalized the end of his personal ministry, the cessation of his labors in behalf of mankind. After his resurrection, He "went in body to minister to translated and resurrected bodies;" [21] and with these He will return when Enoch's City descends and all is ready for his glorious advent.

Footnotes

1 . "Elias," Canto 3, Part 2.

2 . Psalms 16:10.

3 . The hypocrites! They could commit murder, could cause the death of the innocent, and feel no compunction: but they were horrified at the thought of a technical Sabbath-day desecration. Could there be a more glaring instance of "straining at a gnat and swallowing a camel"?

4 . John 19:33.

5 . Matt. 26:17-20; Mark 14:12-25; Luke 22:7-20.

6 . John 19:30.

7 . D. & C. 77:12.

8 . Ib. 19:16-19.

Such was the mission of him concerning whom Nephi of old prophesied: "And he cometh into the world that he may save all men if they will hearken unto his voice; for behold, he suffereth the pains of all men, yea, the pains of every living creature, both men, women, and children, who belong to the family of Adam. And he suffereth this that the resurrection might pass upon all men, that all might stand before him at the great and judgment day." (2 Nephi 9:21, 22.)

9 . Jacob 5:3.

10 . John 10:16.

11 . Matt. 15:24.

12 . Nevertheless, it was all the work of the Lord; for those evangels were his servants, his messengers, clothed with his authority and acting in his name and stead. The subordinate is swallowed up in the principal. It is the general of an army who wins victory or suffers defeat, though millions of soldiers may have been fighting under his direction. The Roman myrmidons who nailed Jesus to the cross were not so much to blame for the cruel deed, as were Pilate, the Procurator, who permitted, nay, ordered it to be done, and the Jewish Rabbis who instigated the "judicial murder" of the sinless Son of God.

13 . 3 Nephi 15:21-24.

14 . Ib. 16:1-3.

15 . Matt. 26:26-28. Compare 3 Nephi 18:1-7.

16 . 2 Peter 1:20.

17 . A fact sufficient, of itself, to show that the Church was in an apostate condition.

18 . Too much reliance upon either the literal or the figurative in language, is apt to be misleading. An attendant in an art gallery or other public place where statues or paintings are on exhibit, might point out one and say to the visitor: "That is Caesar" or "That is Washington;" but the one addressed would not be likely to infer that Caesar or Washington was there in actual flesh and blood, or that the attendant meant to be so understood. Nor would the visitor need to be told that the statue or the painting represented the original. Such an explanation would be superfluous. The form of the Savior's instruction on the Sacrament—assuming that the correct translation has come down to us—may be accounted for in like manner. He knew that his disciples would understand him—and they did. They were not dependent upon the letter alone; the interpreting Spirit was with them to give it life.

19 . D. & C. 27:2-5.

20 . Acts 1:10, 11.

21 . "Mediation and Atonement," p. 76.

ARTICLE TWENTY-ONE
THE SPECIAL WITNESSES

The Men Who Knew.—The Twelve Apostles were the special witnesses of Jesus Christ. As such they had to *know*, not merely believe that he had risen from the dead. And they did know, for they had seen him, and heard him, and had even been permitted to touch him, that they might be convinced beyond all question that he was indeed what he proclaimed himself—the Author of the Resurrection, the Giver of eternal life. It was their right to receive this rare evidence, owing to the unique character of their mission. But the world was required to believe what the Apostles testified concerning Him. If men desired salvation, which could come only through the Savior, they must receive in faith the message He had sent his servants to deliver.

The Case of Thomas.—One of the Twelve was absent when his brethren received their first visitation from the risen Redeemer; and when they said, "We have seen the Lord," he answered: "Except I shall see in his hands the print of the nails, and put my finger into the print of the nails, and thrust my hand into his side, I will not believe." Subsequently the Savior appeared to this Apostle (Thomas) saying: "Behold my hands; and reach hither thy hand, and thrust it into my side; and be not faithless, but believing." "My Lord and my God!" exclaimed the doubter—and was convinced. [1]

Complete Qualification.—Thomas has been censured for demanding to see and to feel before he would believe. How much blame attaches to him for doubting, I will not presume to say. But this much seems clear: He had the same right as the rest of the Twelve to a personal appearing of the Lord—the right to come in contact with Him of whose resurrection he was required to testify. The others had seen and heard—perhaps had even felt, for Jesus offered them that privilege. [2] Why should not Thomas share in the experience? What else could completely qualify him as a special witness?

A Peculiar Position.—Sign-seeking is an abomination, indicating an adulterous disposition. [3] It is blessed to believe without seeing, [4] since through the exercise of faith comes spiritual development; while knowledge, by swallowing up faith, prevents its exercise, thus hindering that development. "Knowledge is power;" and all things are to be known in due season. But premature knowledge—knowing at the wrong time—is fatal both to progress and to happiness. The case of the Apostles was exceptional. They stood in a peculiar position. It was better for them to know—nay, absolutely essential, in order to give the requisite force and power to their tremendous testimony.

The Commission of the Twelve.—"Go ye into all the world, and preach the Gospel to every creature.

"He that believeth and is baptized, shall be saved; but he that believeth not, shall be damned.

"And these signs shall follow them that believe: In my name shall they cast out devils; they shall speak with new tongues; they shall take up serpents; and if they drink any deadly thing, it shall not hurt them; they shall lay hands on the sick, and they shall recover." [5] "Go ye therefore and teach all nations, baptizing them in the name of the Father, and of the Son, and of the Holy Ghost;

"Teaching them to observe all things whatsoever I have commanded you; and lo, I am with you alway, even unto the end of the world. Amen." [6]

The Promised Signs.—Thus we see that certain miraculous "signs" were promised to "them that believe." But these signs were intended to comfort the Saints, not to encourage the sign-seeker; and they were to "follow," not precede, belief. It is not the sign, but the seeking, that the Lord deprecates, the motive being evil. [7]

Apostolic Activities.—Obedient to the divine mandate, the Apostles at Jerusalem, having been "endued with power from on high" [8] went forth with their fellows, preaching. "Christ and him crucified," calling upon men to believe, to repent, and have their sins remitted by baptism, that they might receive the gift of the Holy Ghost. Great power accompanied their ministrations. Within the next half century the glad tidings borne by them had spread over the whole Roman Empire and into barbarian realms beyond.

Equality and Unity.—The Apostles must have known of Enoch's wonderful work. Jude refers to Enoch's prophecy of the Lord's coming "with ten thousand of his saints." [9] Possibly the Twelve had access to the Book of Enoch, [10] one of the lost books of Scripture. At all events, they sought to introduce, among the earliest proselytes to the Christian faith, a similar order to that established in Enoch's day. Concerning the later attempt to "bring forth Zion," it is written:

"And the multitude of them that believed were of one heart and of one soul; neither said any of them that aught of the things which he possessed was his own; but they had all things common. . . . .

"Neither was there any among them that lacked; for as many as were possessors of lands or houses sold them and brought the prices of the things that were sold,

"And laid them down at the apostles' feet; and distribution was made unto every man according as he had need." [11]

How long this condition lasted with the Jewish Saints, we are not told. Among their contemporaries, the Nephite followers of Christ, the splendid results flowing from the practice of the Law of Consecration are thus portrayed:

"The people were all converted unto the Lord, upon all the face of the land, both Nephites and Lamanites, and there were no contentions and disputations among them, and every man did deal justly, one with another;

"And they had all things common among them, therefore they were not rich and poor, bond and free, but they were all made free, and partakers of the heavenly gift." [12]

The Apostles Taken.—One by one the Apostles were taken. James was slain with the sword at Jerusalem. Peter, if the tradition be trustworthy, was crucified at Rome, where Paul likewise suffered martyrdom, by decapitation. All were put to death, save one, concerning whom Peter had inquired of the Lord: "What shall this man do?" And the Lord had said: "If I will that he tarry till I come, what is that to thee?" "Then went this saying abroad among the brethren; that that disciple should not die." [13]

John Tarries.—Modern revelation confirms the ancient tradition that John the Beloved did not taste of death, but obtained from the Lord a promise that he should remain in the flesh, fortified against disease and dissolution, and do a wondrous work. He was to "prophesy before nations, kindred, tongues and peoples, and continue on earth until the Lord came in his glory." [14] It is traditional that an attempt was made upon John's life by throwing him into a cauldron of boiling oil; but he escaped miraculously.

A Falling-Away Foreseen.—In the ninety-sixth year of the Christian era this Apostle was on the Isle of Patmos, in the Aegean Sea. Patmos served the Romans very much as Siberia has since served the Russians. To that desolate place the Empire banished its criminals, compelling them to work in the mines. John was an exile for Truth's sake. But the Lord had not forgotten his servant, though men had rejected him and cast him out. The Heavens were opened to him, and he was shown things that would come to pass thereafter, also events that were even then taking place. He beheld the sad spectacle of a paganized Christendom, the "falling away" that St. Paul had predicted. [15]

Restoration and Judgment.—But John also looked forward to a time when the pure Christian faith would be restored; when an Angel would "fly in the midst of heaven, having the everlasting gospel to preach unto them that dwell on the earth;" [16] when Israel would be called out from the nations; [17] when the hour of God's judgment would come, and the dead, small and great, would stand before the Great White Throne, to give answer for the deeds done in the body. [18]

Among the Nephites.—The experience of the Church of Christ on the Western continents was in many respects a duplicate of its experience in Oriental lands. Here as well as there, special witnesses were chosen, [19] and to three of the Nephite Twelve, Christ gave the same promise that he had given to the Apostle John—a promise that they should remain in the body, not subject to death, and bring souls to Him. [20]

A Foretaste of the Millennium.—The Nephite Church had a marvelous career—even more marvelous than had the Jewish Church. "The people were all converted unto the Lord," and for two full centuries [21] a social condition similar to that which had characterized Enoch's ancient commonwealth, was the favored lot of this flourishing branch of the House of Israel. It was a foretaste of the Millennium, a foreshadowing of the great Day of Peace.

Japheth Smites Jacob.—Then came pride, the besetting sin of the Nephite nation, with class divisions, envyings, covetousness, strife, and— for the civilized portion of the once delightsome people—extermination. Darkened in body and in mind, the degenerate Lamanites were left to meet the on-rolling tide of over-seas immigration, and be over whelmed thereby; "a remnant of Jacob," to be smitten and driven by the children of Japheth, "until the times of the Gentiles were fulfilled." [22]

Footnotes

1 . John 20:24-28.

2 . Luke 24:39.

3 . Matt. 16:4.

4 . John 20:29.

5 . Mark 16:15-18.

6 . Matt. 28:19, 20.

7 . Says the Prophet Joseph"When I was preaching in Philadelphia, a Quaker called out for a sign. I told him to be still. After the sermon he again asked for a sign. I told the congregation that the man was an adulterer; . . . . that the Lord had said to me in a revelation that any man who wanted a sign was an adulterous person. 'It is true,' cried one, 'for I caught him in the very act,' which the man afterwards confessed when he was baptized." (Hist. Ch. Vol. 5 p. 268). More than one "Mormon" missionary, pestered by sign-seekers, has applied the test furnished by the Prophet, with invariable and complete success.

8 . Luke 24:49; Acts 2:1-4.

9 . Jude 14.

10 . D. & C. 107:57

11 . Acts 4:32, 34, 35.

12 . 4 Nephi 1:2, 3.

13 . John 21:20-23.

14 . D. & C. 7.

15 . Thess. 2:3; 1 Tim. 4:1; 2 Tim. 3:1-5; Rev. Chaps. 17, 18.

16 . Rev. 14:6.

17 . Ib. 18:4.

18 . Ib. 20:11, 12.

19 . 3 Nephi 19:4.

20 . Ib.28:4-23.

21 . 4 Ib. 1:22.

22 . Though tramped upon for many generations, the Lamanites are not a dying race, as is generally supposed. According to Doctor Lawrence W. White, of the United States Indian Bureau, the Indian population in 1870, when the first reliable census was made by the bureau, was placed at 313,712. It is now 333,702, a number not exceeded, thinks that expert, by the total of aborigines in America at the time of its discovery by Columbus.—See editorial article, "Indians Reviving," Salt Lake Tribune, February 13, 1920.

PART SIX
THE ERA OF RESTITUTION

ARTICLE TWENTY-TWO
THE CALL OF THE SHEPHERD

"Come Out of Her, My People."—The Dispersion of Israel has for its complement the Gathering of Israel; the prophets who predicted the one likewise foretelling the other. The Savior's personal visits to the various branches of the Israelitish race, before or after His resurrection, were prophetic of a general restoration of the Lord's people to their ancient lands, and the folding of the scattered sheep into one great flock, with him as the Shepherd over all. [1]

Prophecies of the Gathering.—The more notable of the Hebrew prophecies pertaining to the Gathering are as here given:

Isaiah.—"And He shall set up an ensign for the nations, and shall assemble the outcasts of Israel, and gather together the dispersed of Judah from the four corners of the earth." . . . .

"They shall fly upon the shoulders of the Philistines toward the West." . . . .

"And there shall be an highway for the remnant of his people, which shall be left, from Assyria; like as it was to Israel in the day that he came up out of the land of Egypt." [2]

Jeremiah.—"I will take you one of a city, and two of a family, and I will bring you to Zion." . . . .

"Therefore, behold, the days come, saith the Lord, that it shall no more be said, The Lord liveth, that brought up the children of Israel out of the land of Egypt;

"But, the Lord liveth that brought up the children of Israel from the land of the north, and from all the lands whither he had driven them; and I will bring them again into their land that I gave unto their fathers.

"Behold, I will send for many fishers, saith the Lord, and they shall fish them; and after will I send for many hunters, and they shall hunt them from every mountain, and from every hill, and out of the holes of the rocks." . . . .

"Behold, I will bring them from the north country, and gather them from the coasts of the earth. . . . .

"For I am a father to Israel, and Ephraim is my first born.

"Hear the word of the Lord, O ye nations, and declare it in the isles afar off, and say, He that scattered Israel will gather him, and keep him, as a shepherd doth his flock." [3]

Jesus Christ.—"And again this gospel of the kingdom shall be preached in all the world, for a witness unto all nations, and then shall the end come, or the destruction of the wicked." [4]

"And He shall send his angels with a great sound of a trumpet, and they shall gather together his elect from the four winds, from one end of heaven to the other." [5]

The Savior also predicted to the Nephites the gathering of the House of Israel; [6] and John the Revelator foresaw the same event in his great vision on Patmos. [7]

The Realization.—How marvelously and how rapidly these predictions are being fulfilled, the history of the past hundred years plainly tells. The Angel with the Everlasting Gospel has flown from heaven to earth, and the message borne by him is being preached "again" in all the world, as a final witness to the nations.

Isaiah's reference to the setting up of an Ensign for Israel's gathering finds its fulfilment in the restoration of the Gospel and the Priesthood, and in the organization of the Church of Christ in this dispensation. [8] Then and there was raised a rallying standard for the sons and daughters of Ephraim, the first scions of Jacob's household to be "born again," to embrace the ancient faith in modern times—the first of the broken off branches of Israel's "olive tree" to be "grafted in again" and bear good fruit. [9]

Keys of the Gathering Restored.—Before there could be a complete gathering of the chosen people, the Keys of the Gathering had to be restored. Accordingly, when the time was ripe, they were conferred upon the founder of the Latter-day Church. Moses, who held those keys at the time of the Exodus from Egypt, was the messenger who now restored them. The place of restoration was the Kirtland Temple; the time, April, 1836. Joseph Smith and Oliver Cowdery testify that "the veil" was taken from their minds, and they "saw the Lord," even Jehovah, who proclaimed to them his identity with the Savior of Mankind. The record then continues: "After this vision closed, the heavens were again opened unto us, and Moses appeared before us, and committed unto us the keys of the gathering of Israel from the four parts of the earth, and the leading of the ten tribes from the land of the north." [10]

First Latter-day Saints.—Then began the great work for which these keys had been restored. All preceding it was but preparatory. "Mormonism's" first converts had been made in the region where the Church arose—the farming districts of Western New York and Northern Pennsylvania. But Kirtland, Ohio, was the cradle of the Kingdom. There a Temple was built, and the Priesthood more perfectly organized, preliminary to the sending of the Gospel to foreign nations, and the gathering of scattered Israel to the Land of Zion. Up to the summer of 1837 the "fishers of men" were busy only in the United States and in Canada. Now they crossed over the British Isles, and later to the continent of Europe. Instant and marvelous was their success. In parts of England—notably Lancashire and Herefordshire—whole villages and congregations were swept into the Church by the unlettered yet divinely empowered Apostles of the new dispensation. [11]

Earliest Immigrants.—A small company of Latter-day Saints, numbering but forty-one—the first to "gather" from abroad—sailed on the ship "Britannia" from Liverpool for New York, in June, 1840. They were bound for Nauvoo, Illinois. Each succeeding year added its quota to the fast growing nucleus of the Savior's kingdom. Thus was set in motion the mighty tide of immigration which, swelling the numbers of the Saints in the Mississippi Valley, eventually peopled with the skilled mechanics and hardy yeomanry of Great Britain, Scandinavia and other European countries, the mountains and valleys of the Great West.

The Impelling Motive.—How different the motives impelling these people, from the motives generally imputed to them! It was not for gold and silver, flocks and herds, nor any of "the good things of this world," that they forsook home and country and "gathered" to the Land of Zion. It was not to better their temporal condition, that they abandoned comfort and in some cases affluence, crossed the stormy ocean, dragged rickety hand-carts over parching plains and snow-capt mountains, to settle in a barren wilderness and endure hardships and privations innumerable, while redeeming the waste and dotting it with cities, farms and vineyards. It was for God and his Kingdom—nothing less; and it was the love of Truth that inspired and impelled them. [12]

Character of the Saints.—Utah's early settlers were stigmatized as ignorant and malicious. It was ignorance or malice that so stigmatized them. "Scum of the earth," "offscourings of civilization," were some of the pet names bestowed upon them by their enemies. How utterly unjust these epithets, how grotesquely misapplied, everyone must know who has any knowledge of the facts. In reality, they were among the best men and women of their time. Many of them were descended from the Pilgrims and the Patriots who founded this nation, and in their veins, as Children of the Covenant, flowed the blood of priests and kings, illustrious through a thousand generations. [13]

These modern Zion-builders were not among those who wait for a cause to become popular before embracing it. Lowell little realized how admirably he was painting their portrait when he penned these lines:

> Then to side with Truth is noble,
> When we share her wretched crust,
> Ere her cause bring fame and profit,
> And 'tis prosperous to be just.
> Then it is the brave man chooses,
> While the coward stands aside,
> Doubting in his abject spirit
> Till his Lord is crucified,
> And the multitude make virtue
> Of the faith they had denied.

* * *

> They are slaves who fear to speak
> For the fallen and the weak;
> They are slaves who will not choose
> Hatred, scoffing and abuse,
> Rather than in silence shrink
> From the truth they needs must think;
> They are slaves who dare not be
> In the right with two or three.

Not slaves, but free men and free women, founded the Church of Jesus Christ of Latter-day Saints. They were of the sheep that knew the Shepherd's voice, and when put to the test, they showed "the mettle of their pasture."

"One of a City and Two of a Family."—Jeremiah's prediction was uttered at a time when families (tribes) were much larger than they now are—large enough for one tribe to fill several cities. [14] Otherwise, the prophet might have changed his wording to read: "One of a family and two of a city." Phrased either way, the forecast has been literally fulfilled in the painful and pathetic experiences of many Latter-day Saints, including women and children, turned out-of-door by parents or guardians, for daring to be "one of a city" or "two of a family," in identifying themselves with a people everywhere "spoken against." [15]

"The Shoulders of the Philistines."—This phrase translates itself into the facilities for far and rapid transportation owned and operated by the Gentiles, but utilized by the God of Jacob in bringing his people from foreign shores, and up into the tops of "the high mountains of Israel." [16] "They shall fly upon the shoulders of the Philistines toward the West." When Isaiah wrote those words, he was gazing with prophetic eye upon this very period. He beheld the ships and railroads of the Gentiles, likewise the Land of Zion, now occupied by the Gentiles, but formerly peopled by the Nephites (Joseph and Judah) and included in the lands that God gave to their forefathers. [17] Israel needs the help of the Gentiles—their wealth, their power, their wonderful insight into and command over material things, their intelligence and skill in manipulating temporalities. How, without the children of Japheth, could the children of Jacob be gathered out from the nations? [18]

The Lost Tribes.—It is maintained by some that the lost tribes of Israel—those carried into captivity about 725 B. C.—are not longer a distinct people; that they exist only in a scattered condition, mixed with the nations among which they were taken by their captors, the conquering Assyrians. If this be true, and those tribes were not intact at the time Joseph and Oliver received the keys of the gathering, why did they make so pointed a reference to "the leading of the ten tribes from the land of the north?" This, too, after a general allusion to "the gathering of Israel from the four parts of the earth." What need to particularize as to the Ten Tribes, if they were no longer a distinct people? And why do our Articles of Faith give those tribes a special mention? [19]

The "Highway."—Isaiah's reference to the "Highway" points directly to the lost tribes, respecting whose return from "The North Country," his fellow prophet, Jeremiah, promises an event that shall so far eclipse in scope and grandeur Israel's exodus from Egypt, that the latter will no more be mentioned.

Joseph the Seer must have had the same thing in mind when he wrote: "And they who are in the north countries shall come in remembrance before the Lord, and their prophets shall hear his voice, and shall no longer stay themselves, and they shall smite the rocks and the ice shall flow down at their presence, and an highway shall be cast up in the midst of the great deep." [20]

Already he had foretold the removal of the Latter-day Saints to the Rocky Mountains—then a desolate, uninhabited region—and was evidently pondering that thought when he further declared: "And in the barren deserts there shall come forth pools of living water; and the parched ground shall no longer be a thirsty land." [21]

Ephraim and the Returning Tribes.—It was Ephraim who lifted the Ensign for the Gathering. It is to Ephraim that the returning tribes will "bring forth their rich treasures," receiving from him their spiritual blessings. "And the boundaries of the everlasting hills shall tremble at their presence." [22]

Judah and Jerusalem.—The same prophecy mentions the tribe of Judah, whose gathering place, however, is not the Land of Zion, not the New Jerusalem, but Jerusalem of old, yet to be rebuilt upon a scale of magnificence paralleled only by the splendor of her sister city and twin capital of Christ's Kingdom. [23]

Even as the Waters.—Hear, O Israel! Children of Jacob! The night of dispersion is past. The day of gathering has dawned. The tempests that broke above the heads of your ancestors have spent their fury, and the clouds have parted and are rolling away. The barren ground, refreshed by the fearful visitation, has brought forth abundantly, and a ripened harvest awaits the reaper's cycle. The revivifying rains, having fulfilled their mission, must now return to the ocean whence they were taken. Such is the meaning, the symbolism, of the scattering and gathering of Israel.

Footnotes

1 . John 10:16; 3 Nephi 15:21; 16:1-3; 21.

2 . Isa. 11:12, 14, 16. See also 5:26; 35:10; 43:5, 6. The same Prophet declares:

"And it shall come to pass in the last days, that the mountain of the Lord's house shall be established in the top of the mountains and shall be exalted above the hills; and all nations shall flow unto it.

"And many people shall go and say, Come ye, and let us go up to the mountain of the Lord, to the house of the God of Jacob; and he will teach us of his ways, and we will walk in his paths: for out of Zion shall go forth the law, and the word of the Lord from Jerusalem." (Isa. 2:2, 3.)

This prophecy, however; seems to refer, not so much to a gathering of Israel, as to an Israel already gathered, unto whom the nations will come to learn the ways of the Lord.

3 . Jer. 3:14; 16:14-16; 31:8-10.

4 . Matt. 24:31, as rendered by Joseph the Seer, Pearl of Great Price, p.78.

5 . Ib. Bible, King James' version.

6 . 3 Nephi 21.

7 . Rev. 14:16; 18:4. See also Deut. 33:17; Psalms 50:5; Ezek. 34:12-14.

8 . D. & C. 115:4, 5; 45:9; 64:42.

9 . Jacob 5 and 6.

10 . D. & C. 110:1-4, 11.

11 . Heber C. Kimball, one of the Twelve, was placed at the head of the first foreign mission. He was accompanied by Orson Hyde, Willard Richards, and other Elders. Subsequently another apostolic mission, headed by Brigham Young and including a majority of the Twelve, carried the Gospel to all parts of the British Isles.

12 . I was once asked by a gentleman, friendly to the Latter-day Saints, why they did not co-operate with the millionaire philanthropists who have endeavored in recent years to place upon arid lands poor Jews taken out of large cities; but whose efforts, owing to inexperience in such enterprises, have been more or less futile. My questioner thought a copartnership between such capitalists and such colonists—one to furnish the money, the other the knowledge and skill necessary for the undertaking—might work a splendid result. He added with unction: "You could stipulate, you know, that every Jew thus colonized should become a Mormon—and just think how that would build up your Church!"

The intent was serious, but the effect was to amuse. It suggested the Shakespearean court scene, where the Venetian Duke decides that the Jew Shylock, as part of his punishment for seeking the life of Antonio, shall "presently become a Christian." ("Merchant of Venice," Act 4. Scene

1). As if Christians could be made by judicial decisions or "Mormons" by contracts for colonization.

13 . Talent and genius, brain and brawn, from every part of the world came in the early immigrations to Salt Lake Valley—farmers, laborers, tradesmen, mechanics, merchants, manufacturers and business men, with a liberal sprinkling of artists, musicians, writers and other professional people. "In their degree the pick and flower of England," was the comment passed upon a ship's company of "Mormon" emigrants, by Charles Dickens, the great English author, in his sketch "The Uncommercial Traveler," published in 1863.

14 . Joshua 21:41

15 . Acts 28:22

16 . Ezek. 34:14

17 . Jer. 16:15; Deut. 33:13-16; Gen. 49:22-26.

18 . The work is too vast, too arduous, for any one people to accomplish, particularly a people who are a mere handful among earth's teeming millions. God, not man, is doing this work, and He is not limited in his choice of instruments to his own covenant people. All men, all nations, knowingly or unknowingly, are playing into his hands.

19 . The fact that Arctic explorers have found no such people at the North Pole—where some theorists have persisted in placing them—does not prove that the "Ten Tribes" have lost their identity. It was tradition, not revelation, that located them at the North Pole. "The north country," "The land of the north," these are the scriptural designations of their unknown abode. All the rest is inference. Those tribes could still be intact, and yet much of their blood be found among the northern nations. Some of the pilgrims might easily have mixed with the people encountered by them while journeying toward their ultimate destination; and that Ephraim did so mix, Hosea the Prophet (7:8) declares.

20 . D. & C. 133:26, 27.

21 . Ib. 133:29.

22 . Ib. vv. 30,32.

23 . Isa. 2:3.

In April 1840, Orson Hyde and John E. Page, both Apostles, were sent from Illinois on a mission to Palestine, to bless the soil, that its barrenness might depart and the way be opened for the restoration of the Jews to their ancient homeland. John E. Page faltered and fell by the way, but Orson Hyde accomplished his mission. On the 24th of October, 1841, from the summit of the Mount of Olives, overlooking Jerusalem, he offered to the God of Israel, a fervent and eloquent prayer in behalf of his down-trodden people. He blessed the sterile land that in might once more become fruitful, and that Judah might repossess his heritage. Elder Hyde afterwards predicted that the British nation would take an active part in the redemption of Palestine; a prophecy fulfilled during the World War. In 1872, President George A. Smith went with a party from Salt Lake City, and again dedicated the Holy Land for the return of the Jews and the rebuilding of Jerusalem.

ARTICLE TWENTY-THREE
THE ZION OF LATTER DAYS

A Work of Preparation.—The Church of Jesus Christ of Latter-day Saints stands for the gathering of the House of Israel and the building of the modern Zion, New Jerusalem, preparatory to the Millennial reign of righteousness. Israel must be gathered, because it is the God of Israel who is coming to reign, and the descendants of Jacob are the only people who have the right to receive him when he appears. And they must become pure in heart, in order to be worthy of that high privilege.

To His Own—The Christ is coming to "his own," as he came anciently; but it will not be said again that "his own received him not." They are even now preparing to receive him, as fast as circumstances will allow. All of "Mormonism's" varied activities—proselyting, migrational, colonizing, commercial, industrial and educational—have this as their paramount objective. The Latter-day Saints claim lineal descent from the Hebrew patriarchs. They are literally of the seed of Abraham, Isaac and Jacob—mostly through Ephraim, the "first-born" in the divine process of gathering Israel and bringing forth Zion.

The Ensign Lifted.—It developed upon Joseph Smith, a lineal descendant of Joseph of old, to begin, upon the Land of Joseph, the gathering of God's people from the nations. The organization of the Church was the setting up of the prophetic "Ensign," [1] to assemble the outcasts of Israel, and gather together the dispersed of Judah from the four corners of the earth. Joseph lived only long enough to assemble a portion of the half tribe of Ephraim, to which he belonged; but the work begun by him will go on until all the tribes of Israel are gathered, and the way is fully prepared for the blest reign of the King of Kings.

Place and Plan.—The Church, organized on the sixth of April, 1830, was less than one year old when it removed from its birth-place, Fayette, New York, to Kirtland, Ohio, where its infancy was cradled. There the Prophet announced the place for the New Jerusalem and the plan whereby the Holy City was to be established. Western Missouri was the place. [2] The plan became known as "The United Order." [3]

The Pure in Heart.—"This is Zion—the pure in heart." [4] So said Joseph Smith. For Zion is not only a place; it is also a people and a condition. "Blessed are the pure in heart; for they shall see God." [5] They are the only ones who will be permitted to see Him. Zion the place is where Zion the people will assemble for that purpose. In a general sense, the whole of America, North and South, is the Land of Zion. [6] Specially, Zion, "the place for the city," is in Jackson Country, Missouri. [7]

Consecration.—The Zion of old—Enoch's commonwealth—was sanctified and translated through obedience to the Law of Consecration, [8] a heaven-revealed principle subsequently practiced by the followers of Christ, both Jews and Nephites. [9] The modern Zion, "the perfection of beauty," "the joy of the whole earth," [10] is to be brought forth upon precisely the same principle—"every man seeking the interest of his neighbor, and doing all things with an eye single to the glory of God." [11]

Equality and Unity.—As a preliminary to the wonderful achievement in prospect, the Latter-day Saints were required to consecrate all their properties to the Lord. This was done, not to enrich any man nor any set of men, but to establish equality in material possessions, as a prerequisite to the unity and power necessary for the mighty undertaking. Equality—not of intelligence and capacity, of course, but of ownership and of opportunity to advance and achieve—this was the purpose in view. The members of the community were to be equal in earthly things, that they might be "equal in obtaining heavenly things."

A Celestial Law.—It was a law of the Celestial Kingdom—the Zion of Eternity—that the Saints were required to obey, to the end that the Lord's will might be done on earth even as it is done in heaven—that Earth might become a heaven, in fact, and they who made it so be prepared for "a place in the celestial world." [12]

Stewardships.—It was not proposed to take from the people their possessions, and demand all their time and service, without making ample provision for their support. They were not to be pauperized, but enriched, through obedience to God's law. The properties they consecrated—farms, printing offices, mills, work-shops, money, etc.—were to be returned to them as "stewardships," differing, as talents, aptitudes, and the ability to handle much or little differ, but all to be managed in the interest of the common cause. All earnings were to go into a general fund, from which each steward would derive a maintenance, "every man according to his wants and his needs, inasmuch as his wants are just." [13]

First Bishops.—The introduction of this system was the occasion for the call of the first Bishops. The men chosen to manage, under the direction of the First Presidency, the temporalities of the United Order, were Edward Partridge and Newel K. Whitney. The former, as Bishop in Zion, received consecrations, Missouri. The latter officiated in a similar capacity at Kirtland, Ohio, the headquarters of a State of Zion. [14]

Against Lawlessness.—The United Order did not encourage lawlessness. It was the very antithesis of anarchy. It stood for law and government, for wise and good government—the government of God for the benefit of man. Sounding the death-knell of monopoly, fraud, and the misuse of power and privilege, it proposed to do away with class distinctions, founded on pride, vanity and the worship of wealth. It would abolish such conditions—not by violence, but peacefully and by common consent. Doctrine, not dynamite; humility, not self-assertion; love of God and fellow man, not hatred and strife, were to effect the desired emancipation. Under the benign influence of the Holy Spirit—God's gift to all who take upon them his name—envy and greed would give way to brotherly love and mutual helpfulness.

No Drones in the Hive.—While philanthropic in the highest degree, the United Order was no mere alms-giving concern, no eleemosynary institution. Every member of the community was expected to work, to do that for which he or she might best be fitted. There were to be no drones in the hive, no idleness eating the bread of industry. Employment for all, a place for everything and everything in its place—such was the ideal of this social-religious organization. It stood, in short, for justice and fair-dealing, with every man in the secure possession and full enjoyment of his own. Out of the righteous unity resulting from this ideal condition, was to come the power to build up Zion and prepare the way of the Lord.

Why the Ideal Was Not Realized.—The United Order was not permanently established; nor did its original workings long continue. Selfishness within, and persecution without, were the two-fold cause. The Church, driven from place to place, found it impracticable, with an imperfect acceptance by its members of the Law of Consecration, to bring forth Zion at that early day. The great event, however, was only postponed. The realization of the ideal is still in prospect.

The Jackson County Expulsion—An attempt to rear the New Jerusalem was made in the summer of 1831, a colony approximating fifteen hundred men, women and children, settling for that purpose in Jackson County, Missouri, [15] upon lands purchased from the Federal Government. Ground was consecrated, and a City laid out, including the site for a Temple. But a lack of the perfect unity necessary on the part of those selected for this sacred task, prevented its accomplishment at that time. "There were jarrings and contentions, and envyings and strifes, and lustful and covetous desires among them; therefore, by these things they polluted their inheritances." [16] Forewarned by the Prophet of what would result if these evils were not corrected, the colonists did not as a whole pay sufficient heed to the admonition, and the Lord permitted their enemies to come upon them and drive them from "the goodly land."

Persecuted and Persecutors.—The Jackson County colonists, whatever their faults, were superior to the people who mobbed them and drove them from their homes, misinterpreting their motives and falsely accusing them of unfriendly acts or intentions toward the earlier settlers. The persecuted were better than the persecutors; but not good enough to completely carry out the high and holy purposes of Deity. It was in the autumn of 1833 that the "Mormon" colony was expelled from Jackson County. [17]

Zion Not Moved.—Then, and at a later period, when similar and worse mobbings and drivings had taken place, those who committed or countenanced the outrages were wont to say mockingly: "Whenever the Mormons are driven from one Zion, their Prophet gets a revelation appointing Zion somewhere else." How utterly unfounded this assertion, is best told in the language of a revelation given a few weeks after the Jackson County expulsion. Therein the Lord says:

"Zion shall not be moved out of her place, notwithstanding her children are scattered;

"They that remain, and are pure in heart, shall return, and come to their inheritances, they and their children, with songs of everlasting joy, to build up the waste places of Zion. . . . .

"And, behold there is none other place appointed than that which I have appointed; neither shall there be any other place appointed . . . . for the work of the gathering of my saints,

"Until the day cometh when there is found no more room for them; and then I have other places which I will appoint unto them, and they shall be called stakes, for the curtains or the strength of Zion." [18]

Stakes of Zion.—Hear it, ye Gentiles! Hear it, O House of Israel! Jackson County, Missouri, is the chosen site for the City of Zion. No other place has been or will be appointed for that purpose. All other gathering places for God's people are Stakes of Zion, holding the outside cords and curtains of the spiritual Tabernacle of the Lord.

Zion's first Stake was at Kirtland, Ohio; and other stakes were organized in Missouri, Illinois, and Iowa. All these have been abandoned; but many others, since established, now flourish in the region of the Rocky Mountains. There was no stake organization in Jackson County, though that part is sometimes referred to as "The Center Stake." Zion is there, or will yet be there—the very City of God; but no Stake of Zion. [19]

In Abeyance.—Zion is greater than any of her Stakes. It will require the Law of Consecration to bring forth Zion; while a lesser law suffices for the creation of stakes, When the building up of Zion was postponed, the Law of Consecration was suspended, and the United Order went into abeyance. Then was introduced the Law of Tithing, [20] a law adapted to the undeveloped condition of the Church. Since that time the work of founding and maintaining Stakes of Zion, preparatory to the coming forth of Zion proper, has engrossed the attention of the gathered children of Ephraim.

Footnotes

1 . Isa. 11:12.

2 . D. & C. 45:64-71; 57:1-4.

3 . Ib. 104:48.

4 . Ib. 97:21.

5 . Matt. 5:8.

6 . Hist. Ch. Vol. 6 pp. 318, 319.

7 . D. & C. 57:2.

8 . Moses 7:18-21.

9 . Acts 4:32-35; 4 Nephi 1:2, 3.

10 . Psalms 50:2, 48:2.

11 . D. & C. 82:19.

12 . Ib. 78:5-7.

13 . D. & C. 82:17

14 . Ib. 41:9; 72:8

15 . D. & C. 45:64-71.

16 . Ib. 101 :6.

17 . Hist. Ch. Vol. 1, pp. 390, 426.

18 . D. & C. 101:17, 18, 0, 1; 115:6.

19 . Zion, in sacred writ, is symbolized by a tent or portable tabernacle, such as the Israelites carried with them in the Wilderness. Evidently it was the custom then, as it is now,

when setting up a tent, to drive stakes and fasten cords thereto—cords stretched from the tent, to make it firm and secure. Hence the phrase: "Lengthen thy cords and strengthen thy stakes," a metaphor applied to Zion by the Prophet Isaiah. (54:2; 33:20). When a tent is erected, no center stake is driven; it would be in the way—an obstacle to stumble over. Figuratively and in a larger sense, the same would be true of a Center Stake of Zion. There is no need for such a thing, and it would spoil the symbolism of the picture.

20 . D. & C. 119.

ARTICLE TWENTY-FOUR
REDEMPTION BY POWER

To Redeem Zion.—The failure of the Latter-day Saints, through lack of unity and obedience, to build up Zion in Jackson County, has been dwelt upon. It remains to tell of an effort to "redeem Zion," to reinstate the plundered people upon the lands of which they had been unlawfully and violently dispossessed. This effort was put forth early in the year 1834, when an expedition was organized in Ohio for that purpose.

The Zion's Camp Expedition.—So was it styled. The Camp consisted of two hundred and five men, led by Joseph Smith in person, and including quite a number of Elders subsequently called to positions of high prominence in the Church. The expedition failed of its object—its avowed object—for reasons similar to those which had caused the expulsion from Jackson County. Disobedience and rebellion on the part of some members of the Camp, and the continued disregard, by many of the exiles, of the divine requirements made of them, prevented their restoration to the homes and possessions of which they had been despoiled.

A Want of Preparedness.—Zion might have been redeemed, even at that early day, had the redemptive machinery been ready and in condition to do the necessary work. [1] But such a condition did not exist. "Gather up the strength of my house," the Lord had said concerning those upon whom he proposed to lay the sacred duty of Zion's redemption. But "the strength" of his "house" did not hearken to the appeal, [2] and the few who enrolled themselves as members of that historic band were not all trained for the task nor equal to the trials that lay before them.

"The Redemption of Zion Must Needs Come by Power." [3] —So spake the Divine Oracle. But "power dwells in unity, not in discord; in humility, not in pride; in sacrifice, not selfishness; in obedience, not rebellion." [4] Had all the Jackson County colonists borne this in mind and practiced accordingly, no such catastrophe as that which occurred would have befallen them. And if all who went to their relief had acted consistently with the same righteous principle, they would have escaped the tribulation that came upon them as a chastisement.

Transgression the Cause.—The failure to build the New Jerusalem was due to transgression; [5] in other words, to a lack of preparedness on the part of those selected for the sacred undertaking. Had the players been ready, the play could have been staged and presented. But nothing could compensate for the absence of readiness on their part. There is no substitute for the qualities that men and women must possess who are chosen for so exalted an enterprise.

All Not Responsible.—All members of the Church were not responsible for the Jackson County failure; [6] but all had to share in the consequences entailed. The strength of a chain is proverbially the strength of its weakest link, and the general average of the newly-formed and inexperienced community was not high enough to justify a better outcome.

Not a Complete Failure.—The Camp of Zion did not utterly fail. Indeed, there are good reasons for believing that it accomplished everything expected of it under the circumstances. And if this be true of the members of the Camp, it is also true of those whose relief and reinstatement were the announced purpose of the expedition.

All Things Foreseen.—At all events, what occurred must have been foreseen. Divine prescience extends to all things connected with the Lord's work. When He commanded his people to build the New Jerusalem, he knew how much, or how little, they were capable of accomplishing in that direction—knew it just as well before as he did after. Such a thing as surprise or disappointment on his part is inconceivable. An all-wise, all-powerful Being who has created, peopled, redeemed and glorified "millions of earths like this," [7] is not one to be astounded by anything that happens on our little planet. [8]

The Time Not Ripe.—The All-knowing One knew in advance what those Zion-builders would do, or leave undone, and he shaped his plans accordingly. Evidently the time was not ripe for Zion's redemption. The proof is in the trespasses committed by them against the divine laws ordained for their government.

A Season of Waiting.—"In consequence of the transgression of my people, it is expedient in me that mine Elders should wait for a little season for the redemption of Zion." So came the voice of the Lord to Zion's Camp, on Fishing River, Missouri. But this word of comfort came with it: "I have heard their prayers and will accept their offerings; and it is expedient in me that they should be brought thus far for a trial of their faith." [9]

"A Trial of Their Faith."—Such then, was the real purpose of the call for that expedition. More was not expected of the members of Zion's Camp, than a manifestation of willingness to do all that the Lord might require of them.

No Endowments.—Another proof that Zion's redemption was not intended for that time, is found in another part of the same revelation: "And this cannot be brought to pass until mine elders are endowed with power from on high." [10] Take note that the Church had no "endowments" in 1834. There was no Temple that early, and the sacred ritual of the House of God, even if revealed to the Prophet, had not been made known to the people. Whether this was the endowment referred to in the revelation, or whether it meant something else, it is evident that the blessing spoken of was in the future. [11]

Zion could not be redeemed until the Elders were "endowed with power from on High." And yet these same Elders, unendowed, had been sent forth to redeem Zion! Surely, the Lord did not design it then to be. Else would He not have endowed them beforehand? This admitted, and what becomes of their "failure?" They were blameworthy for their disobedience, but surely not for their failure to do what could not be done by men unendowed and consequently not equal to the undertaking.

Left to the Future.—Zion was not redeemed in that day for precisely similar reasons to those which kept ancient Israel wandering for forty years in the Wilderness, almost within sight of their coveted Canaan, which they were not permitted in that generation to possess. [12] Like Moses, these modern pilgrims beheld, as from Pisgah's top, their promised land. Like Moses, on account of transgression, they were not permitted to "cross over." There were Calebs and Joshuas in the Camp who were worthy; but the great event, in the wisdom of the Highest, was not destined then to be. It was left for a future generation and its Joshua to go up in the might of the Lord and redeem Zion. [13]

"With a Stretched Out Arm."—The Lord made it plain to His people that they must prepare themselves for the great things awaiting them. Before they could hope to accomplish their glorious destiny, they must become mighty, not only in numbers and material influence, but morally and spiritually mighty—mighty by the power of God, descending upon them as an endowment from on High. [14] When ready to redeem Zion, the way would be prepared for them, angels and even the Divine Presence going on before. They were not to use violence to secure their rights. God would fight their battles. They were "the children of Israel, and of the seed of Abraham," and "must needs be led out of bondage by power and with a stretched out arm." [15]

Tried and Proven.—From the ranks of the survivors of Zion's Camp—decimated by cholera while on its way to Jackson County—were chosen the first Twelve Apostles and the first quorums of Seventy in this dispensation. [16] These men were deemed reliable. They had been put to the test, and had endured valiantly The trial of their faith was complete.

Nigh at Hand.—When will end the "little season" of waiting? When will the day of Zion's redemption dawn? I know not; but this I know. That day is rapidly approaching. The Order of Unity and Equality, involving the consecration, not only of properties, but also of hearts and hands, will yet be established and perpetuated. It must be, for Zion cannot be built up without it: [17] and until there is a Zion on Earth, the Lord, the King of Kings, will not come.

Footnotes

1 . D. & C. 105:2.

2 . Ib. 103:30; 105:16.

3 . D. & C. 103:15.

4 . "Life of Heber C. Kimball," p.77.

5 . D. & C. 105:2, 9.

6 . Ib. 105:7.

7 . Moses 7:30.

8 . Some may question this assertion, and point to the passage, "It repented God that he had made man" (Gen. 6:6), as an instances of divine disappointment. But it should be borne in mind that makers of Scripture, like all wise teachers, adapt their language to the comprehension of those whom they teach, speaking that they "may naturally understand" (D. & C. 29:34; 19:6-12). Whatever the dead letter may seem to say, God is not man, that He should "repent" (1 Sam. 15:29), or fail to foresee how his creatures will conduct themselves. It was Noah, not God, who "repented," in the case now under consideration.—Moses 8:25.

9 . D. & C. 105:9, 19.

10 . Ib. v. 11.

11 . Ib. v. 18.

12 . Compare Article Eighteen, paragraph "A Period of Preparation."

13 . D. & C. 103:16.

14 . Ib. 105:11.

15 . Ib. 103:17.

16 . Hist. Ch. Vol. 2, pp. 180, 201.

17 . D. & C. 105:5.

ARTICLE TWENTY-FIVE
CLEARING THE WAY

"I Will Fight Your Battles."—In a revelation, already cited, given through Joseph the Seer while Zion's Camp was resting on Fishing River, the Lord says concerning the Elders of his Church:

"I do not require at their hands to fight the battles of Zion; for, as I said in a former commandment, even so will I fulfill. I will fight your battles."

"Behold, the destroyer I have sent forth to destroy and lay waste mine enemies; and not many years hence they shall not be left to pollute mine heritage and to blaspheme my name upon the lands which I have consecrated for the gathering together of my Saints." [1]

War and Deity.—There are many good people who believe that anything of a war-like character, anything involving violence and bloodshed, is wholly incompatible with the benign disposition and benevolent purposes of Deity. According to their view, God has nothing to do with wars. From first to last they are the work of the Evil One, moving upon wicked men to stir up strife for selfish and sordid ends. Everything peaceful and pleasant comes from him who is the Prince of Peace; everything of an opposite nature, and especially war, that prolific source of misery and sorrow, is due entirely to the Adversary. It is all well meant, of course, the object being to forefend Deity against the reproach that these good people fear would lie at his door, if it were admitted that he had even a share in what they conceive to be an unmixt evil, a thing absolutely wrong and unjustifiable. But how can such views be reconciled with divine revelation and the history of God's dealings with man? If war is always wicked, and destruction ever at variance with the will and purposes of Providence, how are we to understand such passages of scripture as the foregoing, wherein Jehovah, who is no other than Jesus, the meek and merciful, assures his servants that he will fight their battles, and assumes full responsibility for sending forth the destroyer to lay waste his enemies and theirs?

Prince of Peace and Lord of Hosts.—The problem, seemingly complex, is in reality simple and easy of solution. There are two sides to the Divine Character, two distinct and differing phases of God's dealings with mortals.

The Lion as well as the Lamb plays a part in the stirring drama of human progress. The same perfect Being who counseled patience, charity, and the turning of "the other cheek," sternly rebuked hypocrisy, denounced wickedness in unmeasured terms, and with wrathful speech and thong of knotted cords, drove the thieving moneychangers from the Temple. "Blessed are the merciful," said the Author of the Beatitudes. [2] "Love your enemies," enjoined the Redeemer of the World. [3] But already He had proclaimed: "Vengeance is mine—I will repay;" [4] and that high decree has never been revoked. Jehovah is both Prince of Peace and Lord of Hosts, the God of Sabaoth. These are among the titles belonging to him. Why are they his, if he has nothing to do with war—if such things are independently and exclusively the work of Satan?

Providence Over All.—The student of this problem must not lose sight of the fact that Satan's sphere, like man's, is limited. Neither can do more than the Most High is willing should be done; and his willingness extends only to such things as contribute, ultimately if not immediately, to the carrying out of his beneficent designs. The Book of Job is very plain upon this point. Only so far as the Almighty would permit, and it was deemed wise for that righteous man to be afflicted, in order to test his integrity, further develop the excellence of his character, and endow future ages with a deathless example of godlike patience—only so far was Satan allowed to go. He seemed to be having his own way with Job, and up to a certain mark did have it; but nothing beyond. The Lord had his way. Whatever he bade Satan not to do. Satan had to leave undone.

The Uses of Adversity.—Job's case is a reminder of the fact that the wicked can be used as a means of developing and improving the righteous, or of chastising and correcting people better than themselves. The painful experiences of the Latter-day. Saints furnish many cases in point. In Missouri, for instance, they were the victims of atrocious wrongs. They had done nothing, so far as their fellow men were concerned, to justify the cruel treatment meted out to them. But the Lord, in order to chasten his people and teach them wholesome lessons that they needed to learn, allowed their enemies to drive and despoil them. [5]

Divinity Always Supreme.—Despite all appearances to the contrary, the Divine Will reigns supreme. To conclude otherwise is to mentally dethrone Deity, and allow that Evil is stronger than Good. God is above Satan, and holds him in leash. [6]

Destruction Essential.—We are not to suppose, however, that the Lord delights in war—that He prefers it to peace; or that he would have aught to do with strife and devastation, if his good and wise purposes could always be accomplished by other and milder means. But if strife becomes necessary, and destruction essential, as when an old building is torn down to make room for a new one, and if the All-wise be the doer or director of the deed, who can question its rightfulness? "Shall the axe boast itself against him that heweth therewith? Or shall the saw magnify itself against him that shaketh it?" [7]

Wars Decreed.—"I have sworn in my wrath and decreed wars upon the face of the earth, and the wicked shall slay the wicked." [8] So says the Almighty to his servant Joseph. And there lies the problem in a nutshell. God has "decreed wars"—decreed them for a purpose. Human iniquity brings down divine retribution, and the wicked are permitted to slay one another—partly as a punishment for their sins, but mainly to help clear the way for a higher and better order of things.

Just and Unjust Wars.—Michael and the Dragon.—Some wars are righteous and just; others wrong and unjust. All depends upon the purpose for which they are waged, and whether or not the Lord sanctions them. All unrighteous wars are the work of Satan and his minions. But all wars are not unrighteous. When Michael and his angels fought against the Dragon, and overcame him, [9] surely the fight was a righteous one on Michael's part. As for the provocation—that springs another question. It is undoubtedly true that there would have been no "war in heaven," if Lucifer had not rebelled; but, having rebelled, he had to be put down, and a righteous war was waged for that purpose. The conduct of those who make such wars necessary, is not to be compared with the acts of those who rise up to vindicate right and vanquish wrong.

Agnostic Arguments.—Joshua's conquest of Canaan—let us consider that. [10] Agnostic writers, taking the view that all such wars are wicked, affect to regard this event as a grave crime. They brand Joshua as a murderer, and charge Jehovah with being a violator of his own statutes—a greater murderer, in short, who, after punishing the first slayer of his fellow man, the fratricidal Cain, [11] and laying down the law to Noah, "Whoso sheddeth man's blood, by man shall his blood be shed." [12] —emphasizing it later with the commandment, "Thou shalt not kill" [13] —directed the general of his armies to commit wholesale slaughter and extermination. Therefore was he a murderer and a lawbreaker. Such is the logic of Robert G. Ingersoll and other writers of his class.

And what a wretched piece of sophistry it is. How utterly shallow and vain. As if the Giver of life could not take back what he had given—the right to it having been forfeited—without committing a crime! As if the Author and Ruler of the universe could not repeal or suspend one of his own enactments, without being a law-breaker! Think of it: Colonel Ingersoll, an experienced lawyer, a practitioner and devotee of the science of jurisprudence, denying to the great Law-Giver a right inherent in and exercised by the humblest legislative body on earth! To such illogical extremes will men go, when they presume to pass judgment upon Providence.

The Case of the Canaanites.—Joshua's war upon the Canaanites was a just war, designed to rid the earth of a corrupt generation, which had forfeited its right to longer remain, encumbering the soil, particularly that part which the Creator and Owner of the planet had given to a worthier people. Jehovah's command to clear the ground upon which he proposed erecting a national structure that should stand as a temple of wisdom and light for the welfare of all succeeding generations, did not impinge upon any command of his previously given. Neither is the Divine One amenable to human judgment. "Thou shalt not kill" was a commandment *from* God, not to him. His word is superior to all human enactments and to all man's notions of right and wrong. The war waged by Joshua and the hosts of Israel against the wicked and usurping Canaanites was in every respect justifiable, so far as it was conducted according to Jehovah's command. [14]

"The King Can Do No Wrong."—This proverb, when used by corrupt rulers to justify and cloak their crimes, is flagrantly false and pernicious. When applied to the King of Heaven, it is eminently and unquestionably true. The Author of life can send forth the destroyer and lay waste his enemies, without blood-guiltiness or even the shadow of wrong-doing. He can decree wars, and allow the wicked to slay the wicked, without partaking of their evil deeds or making himself responsible for their demon-inspired atrocities. These must all be accounted for at the bar of Eternal Justice.

The American Revolution.—It was not Satan who caused the heroic struggle of the American colonies, giving them power to win their freedom and independence, to the end that a nation might arise upon this chosen soil with a mission to foster and protect the infant and growing Church of Christ. That was a righteous war, and the divine inspiration for it rested upon the Patriot Fathers, [15] who, at the hazard of their lives, signed the immortal Declaration, and drew their swords to defend and perpetuate that sublime annunciation of liberty and equal rights.

The World War.—So with the great war that over-threw the German Kaiser, putting an end to the wicked strife that he was waging. It was a righteous against an unrighteous exertion of military force. What better motive could a nation have than that which actuated the American people in sending forth their armies and navies to check the on-rushing hordes that were bent upon crushing freedom and setting an iron heel on the neck of the world? It was a holy war, so far as America was concerned; and a just war, a war of self-defense, on the part of her associated powers. The God of Justice was in it for the welfare of humanity. Who can doubt that He upheld and sustained the arms of those who carried it to a victorious conclusion? And if the result shall be even a partial clearing of the way for the introduction or further spread of Liberty's Perfect Law among spiritually benighted nations, the mightiest and costliest of earth's conflicts will not have been in vain.

Footnotes

1 . D. & C. 105:14, 15.

2 . Matt. 5:7.

3 . Ib. 5:44; Luke 6:27, 35.

4 . Rom. 12:19; Deut. 32:35.

5 . Job saw the matter in a clear light (2:10). He did not charge Deity with the authorship of evil—evil as well as good being self-existent. He knew that God is a hater of iniquity (Psalms 45:7; Heb. 1:9); but he also knew that evil is controlled by the divine ruler and made tributary to the success of his plans. Therefore he did what all should do—he acknowledged the hand of the Lord in all things, in adversity as well as prosperity.

6 . President Woodruff, in his Brigham City address, June 24, 1894,—an address already cited in these pages—speaks thus of the Latter-day judgments: "God has held the angels of destruction for many years, lest they should reap down the wheat with the tares. But I want to tell you now, that these angels have left the portals of Heaven, and they stand over this people and this nation now, waiting to pour out the judgments."

7 . Isa. 10:15.

8 . D. & C. 63:33.

9 . Rev. 12:7-9.

10 . Joshua 1-12.

11 . Gen. 4:11, 12.

12 . Ib. 9:6.

13 . Ex. 20:13.

14 . The same may be said of Israel's war upon the Amalekites, in the days of King Saul, and of similar wars undertaken by "the armies of the living God," heaven-directed and divinely empowered. Samuel's hewing of Agag "in pieces before the Lord," was not a crime, but an act of justice, a righteous retribution upon an unrighteous ruler, whose sword had "made women childless."—1 Sam. 15:33.

15 . 1 Nephi 13:16-19.

ARTICLE TWENTY-SIX
GOD'S HAND UPON THE NATIONS

Compelling Situations.—The Lord will force no man to Heaven, nor permit Satan to force any man to Hell. Human agency remains inviolate. But while there is no such thing in the Gospel of Christ as compulsion, in the sense of fettering man's free will, there is such a thing as a compelling situation, the creating of conditions and shaping of circumstances that have often influenced men to do, of their own volition, what they would not have done if the situation had not changed, if such conditions and circumstances had not arisen.

A simple illustration is furnished in the old-time anecdote of the boy up the farmer's apple tree—refusing to come down when kindly requested; persisting in his refusal when sharply reprimanded and a handful of turf thrown; but, when pelted with stones, scrambling down in a hurry—of his own accord. That is my idea of a compelling situation; the offender retaining his freedom, exercising his right of choice, but yielding to force of circumstances, and changing his mind for his own behoof.

"There's a divinity that shapes our ends, Rough hew them as we will."

The Parable of the Supper.—Force, indirect compulsion, applied without infringing upon man's agency, is undoubtedly an element of the divine economy. What else is the meaning of the Savior's parable in which he likens the Kingdom of Heaven to a feast?

"A certain man made a great supper, and bade many:

"And! sent his servant at supper-time, to say to them that were bidden, Come, for all things are now ready.

"And they all with one consent began to make excuse. The first said unto him, I have bought a piece of ground, and I must needs go and see it: I pray thee have me excused.

"And another said, I have bought five yoke of oxen, and I go to prove them: I pray thee have me excused.

"And another said. I have married a wife: and therefore I cannot come.

"So that servant came, and showed his lord these things. Then the master of the house, being angry, said to his servant, Go out quickly into the streets and lanes of the city, and bring in hither the poor, and the maimed, and the halt, and the blind.

"And the servant said, Lord, it is done as thou hast commanded, and yet there is room.

"And the lord said unto the servant, Go out into the highways and hedges, and *compel* them to come in, that my house may be filled." [1]

The inference is, that they were "compelled to come in," but not against their own freedom of choice.

Fishers and Hunters.—The God of Israel has set his hand to gather his elect and prepare the world for the sanctifying reign of righteousness. He will accomplish what he has undertaken, using for that purpose every means consistent and available. Christ died to save the souls of men, and save them He will—by mild measures whenever these will avail; but by stern methods, if necessary, after the mild have proved ineffectual. First, the "fishers," with gentle, kind persuasion. Then the "hunters"—war, commotion and destruction. Such is the divine program. [2]

The Day of Wrath—A Refuge From the Storm.—Joseph the Seer prophesied that war would "be poured out upon all nations." Zion, the pure in heart, are to "be the only people that shall not be at war one with another." [3] "And it shall come to pass, among the wicked, that every man that will not take his sword against his neighbor, must needs flee unto Zion for safety." [4] To provide against these and other perils, the Church of Christ was founded—"a standard for the nations," "that the gathering together upon the land of Zion and upon her stakes," might be "for a defense, and for a refuge from the storm, and from wrath when it shall be poured out without mixture upon the whole earth." [5]

Other Judgments.—But war is not the only expression of divine wrath. The strife of nation against nation is but one of many turmoils that the last days are destined to witness. Epidemics of sickness are to play a part in the great retribution. [6] John on Patmos heard a voice from Heaven say: "Come out of her, my people, that ye receive not of her plagues." [7] Through Joseph in America, the same dread oracle proclaimed "a desolating scourge," that "shall go forth among the inhabitants of the earth, and shall continue to be poured out from time to time if they repent not, until the earth is empty and the inhabitants thereof are consumed away and utterly destroyed by the brightness of my coming." [8]

Divine Participation.—And who, after reading what follows, can doubt divine participation in these troubles:

"For I the Almighty have laid my hand upon the nations to scourge them for their wickedness; and plagues shall go forth, and they shall not be taken from the earth until I have completed my work, which shall be cut short in righteousness. Until all shall know me, who remain, even from the least unto the greatest, and shall be filled with the knowledge of the Lord and shall see eye to eye." [9]

After Testimony, Indignation.—The Lord's servants were "to go forth among the Gentiles for the last time," "to bind up the law and seal up the testimony," and "prepare the Saints for the hour of judgment."

"And after your testimony cometh wrath and indignation upon the people.

"For after your testimony cometh the testimony of earthquakes that shall cause groanings in the midst of her, and men shall fall upon the ground and shall not be able to stand.

"And also cometh the testimony of the voice of thunderings and the voice of lightnings, and the voice of tempests, and the voice of the waves of the sea, heaving themselves beyond their bounds.

"And all things shall be in commotion; and surely, men's hearts shall fail them; for fear shall come upon all people." [10]

Again: "The earth shall tremble and reel to and fro as a drunken man; and the sun shall hide his face, and shall refuse to give light, and the moon shall be bathed in blood, and the stars shall become exceeding angry, and shall cast themselves down as a fig that falleth from off a fig tree." [11]

The Question of Cause.—Who will cause these terrible calamities? Not man—that is certain; though his conduct may justify them. Men can stir up strife and precipitate war. They can even bring pestilence and famine. But they cannot stir up tempests and earthquakes, cause whirl winds and tidal-waves, or govern the action of sun, moon and stars. These, with other convulsions of nature, no less than war, famine and pestilence, are among God's judgments upon the workers of iniquity. Satan, "prince of the powers of the air," may be immediately responsible for these fearful disturbances; [12] but he can do only what he is permitted to do by the All-just and All-merciful, who looses him or holds him in check.

The Divine Purpose.—And what is the purpose—the ultimate purpose of it all? Destruction? No, a thousand times no, except in so far as destruction must at times precede reconstruction, and is necessary to preserve what is worth preserving. The world's welfare is the object in view. God's wrath, however fiercely it burns, is not comparable to petty human anger. His work and his glory is "to bring to pass the immortality and eternal life of man," [13] and if, in the process, He uses the powers of destruction, as well as the powers of construction—for "all power" is his, "in heaven and in earth" [14] —it is because such a course has become necessary and is for the best. However severe his chastisements, we can rest assured of this: Hatred of humanity has no place in the heart of Him who "so loved the world" that he "gave his Only Begotten Son" to save it from eternal damnation.

Why Calamities Come.—Calamities do not come up on the world merely to scourge the wicked and avenge the wrongs of the righteous. The primal aim of Divine Punishment is to purify, and if possible save those upon whom the "Great Avenger" lays a chastening hand. The object is to bring sinners to repentance, to throw down the barriers that prevent men from coming to Christ, and turn into the upward path those bent upon pursuing the downward road. The Gospel saves all who are willing to be saved, and who show their willingness by their obedience, their faith by their works. It also aims to save the unwilling and disobedient—here if possible, and if not here, then hereafter. Wars and other woes are sent to put a stop to men's evil practices, lest they add sin to sin and pile up guilt to their greater condemnation. To be swept off the earth and ministered to in the spirit world, is not the worst fate that can befall the wicked. Omnipotence wields the powers of destruction in such a way as to make of them instruments of salvation. It may seem cruel, but in reality it is kind.

Safety With The Priesthood.—The Almighty does not hurl the shafts of affliction against the righteous, especially against helpless innocence; but in pursuance of his benevolent designs, and to effect the greatest good to the greatest number, He permits the destroyer to exercise his agency in a world where good and bad, old and young, all classes and all qualities, dwell. Some of the woes thus launched fall partly upon the choicest of God's children, unless faith be there—as doubtless He intends—faith and the power of the Priesthood, to intervene for their preservation. "The just shall live by faith," it is written, and the Priesthood is a shield to those who bear it and to those who honor its possessors. [15]

The Chastening of the Lord.—"My son," says the ancient Wise Man, "despise not the chastening of the Lord; neither be weary of his correction: For whom the Lord loveth, he correcteth; even as a father the son in whom he delighteth." [16] Bearing in mind this sapient admonition, let us not be doubtful of the Divine Purpose in sending forth the destroyer, whether in the shape of war, pestilence and famine, partly caused by human agency; or in earthquakes, cyclones, and other fierce convulsions, over which man has absolutely no control. They are all phases of "The Battle of the Great God," [17] intent upon clearing the way for the coming of the Perfect One, bringing order out of chaos, overthrowing wrong and establishing right, to the end that the human race may be permanently blest and the righteous possess in peace the heritage prepared for them from the foundation of the world.

Footnotes

1 . Luke 14:16-23.

2 . Jer. 16:16.

3 . D. & C. 87:2.

4 . Ib. 45:68, 69.

5 . Ib. 115:4-6.

6 . Ib. 45:31. "An overflowing scourge—a desolating sickness," to "cover the land."

7 . Rev. 18:4.

8 . D. & C. 5:19.

9 . D. & C. 84:96-98.

10 . Ib. 88:88-91.

11 . Ib. 88:87.

12 . Job 1:19.

13 . Moses 1:39.

14 . Matt. 28:18.

15 . Said President Woodruff, in his address upon the judgments: "Can you tell me where the people are who will be shielded and protected from these great calamities? I'll tell you: The priesthood of God who honor their priesthood, and who are worthy of their blessings. . . . . No other people have a right to be shielded from these judgments. They are at our very doors; not even this people will escape them entirely. They will come down like the judgments of Sodom and Gomorrah, and none but the priesthood will be safe from their fury."

The President meant, no doubt, to include in this reference those who follow the servants of the Lord and are guided by their counsels. He was speaking to a general congregation, and said, in addition to the words just quoted: "If you do your duty, and do my duty, we shall have protection, and shall pass through the afflictions in peace and safety."

16 . Prov. 3:12.

17 . D. & C. 88:114.

ARTICLE TWENTY-SEVEN
THE CONSUMMATION

Time, mighty daughter of Eternity!
Mother of ages and of aeons past!
Assemble now thy children at thy side,
And ere thou diest teach them to be one.
Link to its link rebind the broken chain
Of dispensations, glories, keys and powers,
From Adam's fall unto Messiah's reign—
A thousand years of rest, a day with God,
While Shiloh reigns, and Kolob once revolves. [1]

Gathering the Gatherers.—The Dispensation of the Fulness of Times is distinctively a gathering dispensation. But it stands for more—far more than the assembling of the dispersed House of Israel. It is the spiritual harvest-time of all the ages, the long-heralded Era of Restitution, [2] when the great Garnerer of "all things in Christ" will reveal himself in power and glory, and place the capstone on the temple of heaven-inspired human achievement. The gathering of Israel is only the preface to the book, only the prologue to the play. The gathering of the gatherers—such is the meaning of the preliminary work now in progress, a work in which Gods, angels and men have joined.

The Final Development.—This great era of restoration was made necessary by the departure of the Christian word from the faith delivered to the former-day Saints. But that is not its full significance. In accordance with the foreknowledge of God, and in consonance with his sublime, far-reaching purposes, this vast, all-comprehending period was foreordained from the beginning as the final development of the Divine Plan—"the winding-up scene" of the Creator's work pertaining to this planet. [3]

All in One.—Joseph the Seer, referring to this mighty dispensation, and the object for which it was "ushered in" says:

"It is necessary .... that a whole and complete and perfect union and welding-together of dispensations and keys and powers and glories should take place, and be revealed from the days of Adam even to the present time;

and not only this, but those things which never have been revealed from the foundation of the world, but have been kept hid from the wise and prudent, shall be revealed unto babes and sucklings in this the dispensation of the fulness of times." [4]

Joseph Smith's Work.—These words were uttered by the Prophet less than two years before the tragic termination of his mortal life. He had looked upon the face of God, as did Enoch, Moses, and other seers in times of old. He had communed with Angels, receiving from them the keys of the Priesthood and the principles of the Everlasting Gospel. Thus empowered, he had organized on earth the Church of Christ, the forerunner of the Kingdom that shall stand forever. [5] Wrapt in celestial vision, he had gazed upon the glories of Eternity, portraying in burning eloquence the destiny of the human race, setting forth in vivid plainness the conditions of man's salvation and exaltation in worlds to come. [6] He had preached the Gospel in various parts of his native land, and had caused it to be preached in realms beyond the sea. His glorious career, which was about to end in martyrdom, was signalized by the introduction and practice of sacred principles which he affirmed would bring forth Zion and enable the pure in heart to "see God" and inherit celestial glory—the ultimate aim of all righteous endeavor.

The Divine Presence.—"This," said the Prophet, "is why Adam blessed his posterity; he wanted to bring them into the presence of God." [7] "Moses sought to bring the children of Israel into the presence of God, through the power of the Priesthood, but he could not. In the first ages of the world they tried to establish the same thing, and there were Eliases raised up who tried to restore these very glories, but, did not obtain them. But they prophesied of a day when this glory would be revealed, ... when God would gather together all things in one." [8]

Keys Committed.—The Prophet goes on to say that the Angels who hold the keys of spiritual powers and blessings—"authoritative characters"—men in heaven having children on earth—"will come down and join hand in hand in bringing about this work." [9] At the time of that utterance, this phase of the Latter-day Work had begun, the founder of the Church having received from heavenly messengers the keys of authority and power held by them in past dispensations. The Aaronic Priesthood had been conferred by John the Baptist, [10] and the Melchizedek Priesthood by Peter, James and John. [11] Without this divine authorization the Church could not have been established, the Ensign could not have been raised for the gathering of scattered Israel. Already have I related how the keys of the gathering were committed to Joseph Smith and Oliver Cowdery in the Kirtland Temple.

Elias and Elijah—But more was to follow. In that wonderful record of visions manifested to these Elders, and testified of by them, occurs this solemn affirmation:

"Elias appeared, and committed the dispensation of the Gospel of Abraham, saying that in us and our seed all generations after us should be blessed.

"After this vision had closed, another great and glorious vision burst upon us, for Elijah the Prophet, who was taken to heaven without tasting death, stood before us and said—

"Behold, the time has fully come, which was spoken of by the mouth of Malachi, testifying that he (Elijah) should be sent before the great and dreadful day of the Lord come,

"To turn the hearts of the fathers to the children, and the children to the fathers, lest the whole earth be smitten with a curse.

"Therefore, the keys of this dispensation are committed into your hands, and by this ye may know that the great and dreadful day of the Lord is near, even at the doors." [12]

The Same Yet Not the Same.—"Elias," considered as a name, is the Greek equivalent of the Hebrew "Elijah." Compared references in the New and Old Testaments clearly establish their verbal identity. [13] But Joseph Smith distinguished between "the spirit of Elias" and "the spirit of Elijah," the former a forerunner, the latter holding the sealing powers necessary to complete the work of preparation for Messiah's advent. [14]

Elijah, therefore, is not to be confounded with Elias—that is to say, with the Elias who committed the keys of the Abrahamic dispensation. There are many Eliases, in the sense of the lesser preparing the way before the greater; and by one of them Abraham's keys were restored, in order that the blessings anciently pronounced upon the Father of the Faithful might be extended to his posterity in modern times.

Why Elijah?—"Why send Elijah?" asks the Prophet; and answers his own question thus: "Because he holds the keys of the authority to administer in all the ordinances of the Priesthood; and without the authority is given, the ordinances could not be administered in righteousness." In the same connection he states that "Elijah was the last prophet that held the keys of the Priesthood." [15]

The Restorer's Mission.—Elijah's mission, as made known by modern revelation, represents the establishment of that condition of perfect unity referred to by Joseph the Seer, whose comment thereon is quoted in the third paragraph of this article. "Mormonism," as already explained, does not stand for one Gospel dispensation alone, but for all the Gospel dispensations, extending, like the links of a mighty chain, through the whole course of Time. The Final Dispensation, made effective by the keys of Elijah, will bring together and weld in one the parted links of this universal chain. The restitution of all things—the setting in order of the Lord's House, preparatory to his coming, such is the significance of the mission of Elijah, who turns the hearts of the fathers (in heaven) to the children (on earth), and the hearts of the children to the fathers.

The Welding Link.—But these hearts must not only be turned; they must be bound together, and beat as one. That thought, no less than the other, was in the Prophet's mind when, from his place of retirement during a season of trouble, he wrote repeatedly to the Church regarding an all-important duty devolving upon its members. Said he: "The earth will be smitten with a curse unless there is a welding link of some kind or other, between the fathers and the children." And what is it? "It is the baptism for the dead. For we without them cannot be made perfect, neither can they without us be made perfect." [16]

Without Unity, No Perfection.—Perfection is the great end in view; and without unity there can be no perfection. To bring about this great consummation, the Gospel was instituted, the Savior chosen, Earth created, and the human race placed upon this planet. Nothing imperfect can inherit the Divine Presence—the fulness of God's glory. This important lesson is taught by the principle of marriage—celestial marriage—the sealing of the sexes, not for time only, but for all eternity. "The man is not without the woman, nor the woman without the man, in the Lord." [17] United, they represent completeness, perfection, each being the complement of the other. Husband and wife, parent and child, the living and the dead, must be one, lest it be said of them at the celestial gates, as it was said at the gates of Verdun: "They shall not pass." The Latter-day Saints build temples and officiate therein, the living for the dead, not only to save them, but to bring them into that grand Order of Unity, so necessary to the perfection of God's work.

The Keys of Preparation.—Past and present are related. It is the relationship of parent and child. Neither is complete without the other. What has been and what is must join, before perfection can reign. Without unity and the perfecting power of righteousness, the Saints would be unprepared to receive the King of Kings. Earth, unable to endure the overpowering glory of his presence, would vanish from before his face, like hoar-frost in the rays of the rising sun. [18] That there might be no such calamity, no converting of an intended blessing into a consuming curse, Elijah restored the Keys of Preparation.

The Universal Gathering.—The gathering of the House of Israel is to be supplemented by a greater gathering—the bringing together of all the Gospel dispensations, with all the sacred powers and mighty personages connected therewith. [19] There is to be a general assembly, a universal union, in which sainted souls from all glorified creations will join. [20] All things that are Christs's, both in heaven and on earth, will eventually be brought together, and the divided and discordant parts attuned and blended into one harmonious Whole.

Footnotes

1 . "Elias," Canto 5, p. 37, annotative edition.

2 . Acts 3:21.

3 . D. & C. 77:12.

4 . Ib. 128:18.

5 . Dan. 2:44.

6 . D. & C. 76.

7 . D. & C. 107:56.

8 . Ib. 84:23, 24.

9 . Hist. Ch. Vol. 3, pp. 388, 389.

10 . D. & C. 13.

11 . Ib. 27:12; 128:20.

12 . D. & C. 110:12-16; Hist. Ch. Vol. 3, p. 390.

13 . See Luke 9:54 and 2 Kings 18:38; also James 5:17 and 1 Kings 17:1.

14 . Hist. Ch. Vol. 6, pp. 249, 254.

15 . Hist. Ch. Vol. 4, p. 211.

Elijah the Tishbite, as he is called in Scripture, figured in the history of the Kingdom of Israel about nine centuries before the birth of Jesus of Nazareth. It was a period of idolatry, when the priests of Baal (whom Elijah overthrew) had Ahab the king and his wife, the wicked Jezebel, completely under their sinister influence. Regarding the great Prophet of Restoration, Dr. Geikie, says:

"The immense influence of Elijah during his life is seen in the place he held in the memory of after generations in Israel. He takes rank along with Samuel and Moses; not like the former, as the apostle of a system yet undeveloped; or as the founder of a religion, like the latter; but as the restorer of the old when it was almost driven from the earth. The prophet Malachi portrays him as the announcer of the great and terrible day of Jehovah. His reappearance was constantly expected as the precursor of the Messiah. So continually was he in the thoughts of the people of New Testament times, that both John the Baptist and our Lord were supposed to be no other than he. The son of Sirach (See Apocrypha) calls him a fire, and says that his word burned like a torch, and that it was he who was to gather together again the tribes of Israel from the great dispersion . . . .

"His final coming, it is believed, will be three days before that of the Messiah, and on each of the three he will proclaim peace, happiness and salvation, in a voice that will be heard over all the earth. So firm, indeed, was the conviction of this in the days of the Talmud, that when goods were found which no owner claimed, the common saying was, Put them by till Elijah comes."—"Hours with the Bible," Vol. 4, pp. 65,66.

16 . D. & C. 127, 128.

17 . 1 Cor. 11:11.

18 . Mal. 3:2; 4:1.

19 . D. & C. 27:5-14.

20 . Ib. 76:67; Moses 7:31, 64.

PART SEVEN
POWERS AND PRINCIPLES

ARTICLE TWENTY EIGHT
THE PRIESTHOOD

What "Priesthood" Means.—Divine authority, or the right to rule, inherent in the supreme Source of all power—such is the primal meaning of "Priesthood." It also signifies the men in whom that authority is vested—the servants of the Lord, who officiate for him and administer the laws and ordinances of the Gospel.

Why Necessary.—Divine laws, like human laws, require officers and a government to administer them. God, being in the form of man, cannot be everywhere present in his own person. Immanent by the spirit that proceeds from him, omnipresent by his power, influence and authority, He cannot, as a personage, occupy two places at the same time, any more than he can make something out of nothing or do aught else that is impossible. To say that Deity can do that which cannot be done, is no glorification of Deity. It is sheer nonsense, nothing more.

Since the Supreme Being cannot be everywhere present in person, cannot be in Heaven and on Earth simultaneously, he requires representatives to carry on his work in this as in other parts of the universe. Herein is the prime reason, the fundamental fact, underlying the necessity for a Priesthood and a Church organization.

A Twofold Power.—There are two priesthoods in the Church of Christ, or, more properly, two grand divisions of priesthood, namely, the Melchizedek and the Aaronic, the latter an appendage to the former. [1] This dualism is owing to the fact that Divine Government takes cognizance of and deals with things temporal as well as with things spiritual. Nevertheless, all things are spiritual to Deity. [2] As Eternity includes Time, so the spiritual includes the temporal.

Origin of Names.—The Melchizedek Priesthood was named for Melchizedek, king of Salem. [3] The powers of this priesthood are unlimited. It wields authority over all things. Holding "the keys of the Kingdom of God," it is the divinely ordained "channel through which every important matter is revealed from Heaven." [4] The Aaronic or Lesser Priesthood takes its name from Aaron, the brother of Moses. It operates within a limited sphere, having a special calling to administer in temporal affairs, in material things.

Symbolized by the Soul.—The Government of God, with its two mighty wings of priestly power and authority, corresponds to and is symbolized by the soul. As spirit and body constitute the soul, so the Melchizedek and Aaronic priesthoods constitute the government of the Church of Christ. Through the medium of the body, with its various members and organs, the things of this life are possessed and utilized, while those pertaining to a higher state of existence are apprehended and made use of by means of the spiritual faculties. Even so, by these two priesthoods, differing in powers and prerogatives, yet allied, interwoven and harmonious in their mutual workings, is carried on in all worlds the sublime work of Omnipotence.

Furthermore, to extend the analogy, it is the spirit or higher part of man that controls, directs and supplies the motive power of the body, being the vital mainspring of this wondrous piece of machinery, whose functions are forwarded by the animation resulting from the union of the twain. In like manner, the Melchizedek Priesthood, holding the keys of presidency, controls and directs the entire body of the Church; delegating, however, a portion of its authority to the Lesser Priesthood, that it likewise may wield a legitimate influence and execute the purposes for which it was designed.

"No Man Taketh This Honor."—Men cannot constitute themselves servants of the Lord. They must be called by him—literally called and ordained, or they are not qualified to speak and act in his name and stead. While there is no ban upon doing good, and all are free to promote truth and practice righteousness, and will reap sure reward for so doing, there is no such thing as heavenly sanction upon usurped office and authority. The Scriptures make this fact exceedingly plain. [5] "God will not acknowledge that which he has not called, ordained and chosen." [6]

Christ The Head.—Jesus Christ is the great "Apostle and High Priest," [7] standing at the head of the priestly-kingly Order of Melchizedek. It was originally styled "The Holy Priesthood after the Order of the Son of God;" but this title was changed out of reverence for the Supreme Being, to avoid "the too frequent repetition" of the all-sacred name. Melchizedek's name was substituted, because he "was such a great High Priest." [8] "Apostle means "Messenger," or one who is sent. The use of the term, as one of the titles of the Savior, is warranted by the fact that the Son was sent forth by the Father. [9] He was therefore the Father's messenger. In like manner, those sent forth by the Son are his apostles or messengers, particularly the twelve special witnesses.

Adam Stands Next.—Next to the Savior in divine authority, stands Adam, Ancient of Days, the father of the whole human family. So says Joseph the Prophet, in his great discourse on Priesthood. "The priesthood was first given to Adam; he obtained the First Presidency, and held the keys of it from generation to generation. He obtained it .. before the world was formed. . He had dominion given him over every living creature. He is Michael the Archangel." [10]

Noah's Position.—"Then to Noah, who is Gabriel; he stands next in authority to Adam in the Priesthood. He was called of God to this office, and was the father of all living in his day, and to him was given the dominion. These men held keys first on earth and then in heaven." [11]

These inspired utterances regarding Adam and Noah ought to set at rest the question with which they deal. They are a sufficient answer to the charge, sometimes made, that the Latter-day Saints rank Joseph Smith as next in dignity and power to Jesus Christ. It is fitting that the Prophet himself should supply the refutation.

An Everlasting Principle.—He goes on to say: "The Priesthood is an everlasting principle, and existed with God from eternity, and will to eternity, without beginning of days or end of years. The keys have to be brought from heaven whenever the Gospel is sent. When they are revealed from heaven, it is by Adam's authority." [12]

Succession and Descent.—From Adam, the Priesthood descended through the following line: Abel, Enoch, Noah, Melchizedek, Abraham, Esaias, Gad, Jeremy, Elihu, Caleb, Jethro and Moses. [13] Says the Prophet "The Savior, Moses and Elias gave the keys to Peter, James and John, on the Mount, when they were transfigured before him." He then asks: "How have we come at the Priesthood in the last days?"—and answers thus: "It came down, down, in regular succession. Peter, James and John had it given to them, and they gave it to others." The "others" include Joseph Smith and Oliver Cowdery, the earliest Elders of the Latter-day Church. [14]

Agents of the Almighty.—Inherent in the Priesthood is the principle of representation. So plenary and far-reaching are its powers, that when those holding this authority are in the line of their duty, and possess the spirit of their calling, their official acts and utterances are as valid and as binding as if the Lord himself were present, doing and saying what his servants do and say for him.

This is what it means to bear the Priesthood. It constitutes men agents of the Almighty, transacting sacred business in the interest of the one who sent them. These agents should represent their Principal fairly and faithfully, reflecting, as far as possible, his intelligence and goodness, living so near to him that when their letter of instructions (the written word) falls short, the Spirit that indited it, resting upon them as a continual benediction, can give "line upon line" of revelation, flash upon flash of inspired thought, to illumine and make plain the path they are to tread.

"And whatsoever they shall speak when moved upon by the Holy Ghost shall be scripture, shall be the will of the Lord, shall be the mind of the Lord, shall be the word of the Lord, shall be the voice of the Lord, and the power of God unto salvation." [15]

No Unrighteous Dominion.—A tremendous power for frail mortal man to wield! Yes, and to guard against its abuse, the exercise of this divine prerogative is hedged about with certain conditions and limitations. Thus:

"No power or influence can or ought to be maintained by virtue of the Priesthood, only by persuasion, by long suffering, by gentleness and meekness, and by love unfeigned; by kindness and pure knowledge, which shall greatly enlarge the soul without hypocrisy and without guile, reproving betimes with sharpness, when moved upon by the Holy Ghost, and then showing forth afterwards an increase of love toward him whom thou hast reproved, lest he esteem thee to be his enemy." [16]

Again:

"The rights of the Priesthood are inseparably connected with the powers of heaven, and .. the powers of heaven cannot be controlled or handled only upon the principles of righteousness . . . . When we undertake to cover our sins, or to exercise control or dominion or compulsion upon the souls of the children of men, in any degree of unrighteousness, behold, the heavens withdraw themselves, the Spirit of the Lord is grieved; and when it is withdrawn, Amen to the Priesthood or the authority of that man." [17]

An Echo From the Heights Eternal, where the Gods, in solemn council before the creation of the world, decreed freedom, not tyranny; persuasion, not compulsion; charity, not intolerance, the platform upon which the Lord's servants should stand. There is no room in all the Government of God for the exercise of "unrighteous dominion."

The Other Side.—But there is another side to the question. If the men bearing this sacred authority confine themselves to the lawful use of the powers conferred upon them, doing no other than the things enjoined by divine revelation or inspired by the Holy Spirit—what then? In that event the responsibility shifts to other shoulders; and just how weighty the responsibility is, the Savior himself shows in his parable of the Last Judgment, where is indicated the standard or one of the standards by which He will judge the world. [18]

Before the Bar of God.—When the Son of Man, sitting upon "the throne of his glory," shall require of all nations and of all men a final accounting, and shall put to them the crucial question: "How did you treat my servants whom I sent unto you?" happy the nation or the man who can reply: "Lord, I showed them the respect to which they were entitled—I honored them as I would have honored Thee."

Warning and Exhortation.—Grievous the sin and heavy the penalty incurred by those who mistreat the servants of the Master. But more grievous and more weighty still, the sin and punishment of those who betray them. "See to it," says the Prophet to the Elders of the Church, "that ye do not this thing, lest innocent blood be found upon your skirts, and you go down to hell. All other sins are not to be compared to sinning against the Holy Ghost and proving a traitor to the brethren." [19]

Again that ancient admonition, sounding down the centuries, "Touch not mine anointed, and do my prophets no harm!" blending with the Savior's solemn warning to the world: "Inasmuch as ye have done it unto one of the least of these, my brethren, ye have done it unto Me."

Footnotes

1 . Hist. Ch. Vol. 4, p. 207; D. & C. 107:1-20.

2 . D. & C. 29:34, 35.

3 . Gen. 14:18; Heb. 7:1-21.

4 . Hist. Ch. Vol. 4, p.207.

5 . 1 Sam. 13:9-14; 2 Sam. 6:6, 7; 2 Chron. 26:18-21; Heb. 5:4.

6 . Hist. Ch. Vol. 4. pp. 208, 209.

7 . Heb. 3:1.

8 . D. & C. 107:2-4.

9 . Abr. 3:27; John 14:24.

10 . Ib. p. 386.

11 . Ib.p. 386.

12 . Ib. p. 386.

13 . D. & C. 84:6-17. See also 107:40-52.

14 . D. & C. 13. Ib. 128:20.

15 . Ib. 68:4.

16 . D. & C. 121:41-43.

17 . Ib. vv. 36,37.

18 . Matt. 25:21-46.

19 . Hist. Ch. Vol.3, p. 385.

ARTICLE TWENTY-NINE
CHURCH GOVERNMENT

An Incomparable System.—The Church of Jesus Christ of Latter-day Saints is conceded, even by many outside its pale, to be a most admirable and most thorough system of government. It ought to be; for it is a product of divine wisdom. The Church on Earth is the counterpart, so far as mortal conditions will permit, of the Church in Heaven, as beheld in vision by Joseph the Seer. [1] While the Church founded by him is not yet perfect, it is approximately so, and is destined to attain that condition. It is doubtful that the Church of Christ in any former age had so complete an organization as it possesses at the present time. This wonderful scheme of spiritual-temporal government was revealed from above, and established here below, that the Lord's will might be done on earth even as it is done in heaven.

Earliest Offices.—The earliest offices in the Church were those of Elder, Priest, Teacher and Deacon; all, excepting Elder, callings in the Aaronic Priesthood. [2] Other offices, mostly in the Priesthood of Melchizedek, were evolved as fast as they became necessary. [3] The first Bishops were ordained in 1831, the year after the Church was organized. There was no First Presidency until 1833, and no Stake organization until 1834. The Twelve Apostles and their assistants, the Seventies, were not chosen until 1835. But all these offices and callings were inherent in the two priesthoods conferred upon the founder of the Church before its organization.

First and Second Elders—Other Titles.—Joseph Smith was the first President of the Church. His original title was "First Elder;" Oliver Cowdery being the "Second Elder." The initial use of these titles—an anticipative use—was by John the Baptist, the angel who ordained Joseph and Oliver to the Aaronic Priesthood. He told them of their future ordination to the Melchizedek Priesthood, and of their calling as "Elders" thereunder. [4] As early as the date of the Church's organization, the titles of Seer, Translator, Prophet and Apostle, were conferred upon Joseph, and that of Apostle upon Oliver, by revelation. [5]

Puerile Complaints. In after years President Joseph Smith and his associates were criticised by seceders from the Church, because of additions made to the original list of offices, as the result of growth and development on the part of the infant organization. It was contended that since it came into existence with Elders, Priests, Teachers and Deacons as its governing powers, and this by divine direction, therefore these orders should have been deemed sufficient, to the exclusion of High Priest and other titles claimed to have been added by "ambitious and spiritually blind" leaders. [6] Such objections are manifestly puerile. The faultfinders would have been no more inconsistent, had they contended that a new-born babe should remain a babe, instead of growing up to manhood or womanhood and fulfilling the measure of its creation.

The Correct View.—President George A. Smith, in speaking of the progress of the Church, was fond of using, as a comparison, the growth of a hill of corn—first, a single blade of green shooting up from the soil; then two or three such blades; and afterwards a stalk, with ears of corn and silken tassels pendant. One who made no allowance for the growth of the "hill," might be mystified at beholding it in these various stages of development; but those familiar with the changes incidental to such an evolution would see the matter in a clear light.

Greater Follows Lesser.—What more consistent, more in harmony with correct principle and historical precedent, than for the greater to follow the lesser, as when the Melchizedek Priesthood came to Joseph and Oliver, after their ordination to the Aaronic Priesthood? The lesser prepares the way before the greater. But according to the logic of the Prophet's critics, that first ordination should have been all-sufficient; there should have been no second ordination, and no further development of the Lord's work. It ought to have halted then and there, when the keys of the Lesser Priesthood were given. But the Lord knew best, and his inspired servants knew. There was to be, and there has been, a great and mighty development, as the present status of the Church testifies. It has had a wonderful history and a marvelous growth. Never so strong or so well equipped as now, its future is bright with glorious promise.

Offices in the Aaronic Priesthood.—The offices of the Aaronic Priesthood, graded upward, are Deacon, Teacher and Priest. The presidency of this priesthood is the Bishopric. The Bishop has charge of the Church property. He receives and disburses, under the direction of the higher authorities, the tithes and offerings of the people. A Presiding Bishopric of three have general charge of the funds provided for the support of the poor, for the building of temples, for the creation and maintenance of schools, and for other purposes. The Church's general financial records are also in their keeping. A bishop must be a lineal descendant of Aaron—in which event he can serve without counselors—or else a high priest after the order of Melchizedek, [7] having as his counselors two other high priests of that order. Under the jurisdiction of the Presiding Bishopric, in temporal matters, are the ward bishoprics.

Wards and Stakes.—The Ward is a division of the Stake as the Stake is a division of the Church. A stake, in territorial extent, frequently corresponds to a county, though in populous districts one county may contain several stakes. There are four stakes in Salt Lake City. Each stake has a presidency of three, and a high council of twelve, and these have jurisdiction over all members and organizations in the stake, including the ward bishoprics. Each of the latter constitutes a tribunal for the trial of members who transgress the church laws and regulations. From the decision of the Bishop's Court, either party in a case may appeal to the High Council, and from a decision of this appellate court an appeal may be taken to the First Presidency. They review the evidence, and if any injustice has been done, the case is remanded for a new trial. If a President of the Church were tried, it would be before "The Common Council of the Church," assisted by "twelve counselors of the high priesthood." [8] The extreme penalty imposed by any of the Church tribunals is excommunication.

Administration of Ordinances.—The Aaronic Priesthood administers in outward ordinances, such as baptism, and the sacrament of the Lord's supper. The higher ordinances—confirmations, sealings, adoptions, and other temple ceremonies—must be administered by the Priesthood of Melchizedek.

Offices in the High Priesthood—Quorums and Councils.—The Melchizedek Priesthood comprises, in an ascending scale, the offices of Elder, Seventy and High Priest. The Patriarch, the Apostle, and the President must all be high priests after this order. Each specific body of priesthood is called a quorum, though most of the general priesthood organizations are termed councils.

The General Authorities.—The highest council in the Church is the First Presidency. It is composed of three high priests, one of whom is the President, the others being his First and Second counselors. These three preside over the entire Church. The President is its Prophet, Seer and Revelator, and also its Trustee-in-Trust, holding the legal title to its property.

Next to the First Presidency are the Twelve Apostles. Their special calling is to preach the Gospel or to have it preached, in all nations. The Twelve are equal in authority to the First Presidency, but they exercise the fulness of their powers only in the absence of the higher council. They have the right to regulate and set in order the whole Church, but they act under the direction of the First Presidency. The death of the President dissolves that council, and makes necessary a new organization thereof. The Apostles nominate the President, who then chooses his Counselors, and the three are upheld and sustained by the Church in its public assemblies, called conferences. The duty of the Presiding Patriarch is to bless the Church, give individual blessings to its members, and comfort them with spiritual ministrations. He also assists the Apostles in visiting conferences and missions, and performing other duties as required.

The First Council of the Seventy, seven in number, preside over the entire body of the Seventies. These, however, are divided into quorums of seventy, each quorum having seven presidents of its own. In the absence of the First Presidency and the Twelve, the First Council of the Seventy would preside over the Church, associated with sixty-three others, the senior presidents of the first sixty-three quorums of seventy. The Seventies labor under the direction of the Twelve Apostles. They are independent of the stake presidencies and bishoprics, as quorums, but not as individual members. They are the "minute men" of the Church, subject to sudden calls into the mission field.

The First Presidency, the Twelve Apostles, the Presiding Patriarch, the First Council of the Seventy, and the Presiding Bishopric, constitute the General Authorities of the Church. Their names are submitted to the General Conference, held twice a year, to be voted upon by the members. They are also presented at the stake conferences, held quarterly, to be voted upon, with the stake officers, in like manner.

High Priests, Patriarchs and Elders.—Each Stake has a quorum of high priests, indefinite in number, presided over by three of its members. The High Priesthood holds the inherent right of presidency. All the general authorities, excepting the First Council of the Seventy, must be high priests; and the same is true of stake presidencies and ward bishoprics. In each stake are one or more patriarchs, performing, when active, duties similar to those of the Presiding Patriarch. A Stake has one or more quorums of Elders, each composed of ninety-six members, three of whom preside. Each ward should have one or more quorums of priests (forty-eight), teachers (twenty-four), and deacons (twelve), each with a presidency of three. The ward bishopric presides in a general way over all the quorums of the Aaronic Priesthood in the ward, and over all church members, as individuals, residing therein. The bishop of the ward is ex officio president of the priest's quorum. The Elder's office is the lowest in the Melchizedek Priesthood. The duties of an elder are similar to those of a seventy, though intended to be exercised more at home than abroad.

The Lesser Quorums.—The highest office in the Aaronic Priesthood, except bishop, is that of priest. The bishop, however, is a priest, and officiates as such when sitting as a judge; when presiding over his ward, it is by virtue of the higher priesthood held by him. The priest may preach, baptize and administer the Sacrament, but has not the right to lay on hands and give the Holy Ghost; that being a function of the Melchizedek Priesthood.

The teacher is a peacemaker. He settles difficulties arising between church members in his district; or, if he cannot settle them, he reports them to the bishop. Two or more teachers labor regularly in each of the districts into which a ward is divided. It is incumbent upon them to visit from house to house, to see that no iniquity exists among the members, and that they are attentive to their religious duties. The teachers report monthly, or as often as required, to the ward bishopric. The deacons have charge of the ward property, and they assist the teachers, as the teachers assist the priests.

Auxiliaries—Church Schools. All the organizations named are strictly within the pale of the Priesthood. In addition, there are a number of auxiliary organizations—helps to the Priesthood in the government of the Church—such as relief societies, Sabbath schools, young peoples' mutual improvement associations, primary associations, and religion classes. Church schools, of which the religion classes are an adjunct, exist in many of the stakes. The more notable of the schools are the Brigham Young University at Provo, the Brigham Young College at Logan, and the Latter-day Saints University at Salt Lake City. For the maintenance of its splendid educational system, the Church makes an appropriation of nearly three quarters of a million dollars, annually. All branches of learning find place in the curricula of these institutions, but religion is the principal feature; the object being to develop the spiritual, as well as the mental, physical, and moral faculties of the student—in short, "to make Latter-day Saints." [9]

The Present Status.—At the period of this writing there are eighty-five Stakes of Zion, all located in the region of the Rocky Mountains. The Church's twenty-four outside missions comprise most of the countries of the globe. The Latter-day Saints, in all the world, number about half a million.

Footnotes

1. D. & C. 76:54; 107:93.

2. Ib. 20:38-64.

3. Ib. vv. 65-67. Note.

4. Hist. Ch. Vol. 1, pp. 40, 41, 77, 78.

5. D. & C. 21:1.

6. David Whitmer, one of the Three Witnesses to the Book of Mormon, in a pamphlet published after his excommunication from the Church, put forth such a plea. He also found fault with the Prophet for receiving revelations without the aid of a seer-stone, previously used by him, but laid aside after he had fully mastered his gift, which David seems to have regarded as of less consequence than the stone, which was no longer needed.—"Address to All True Believers in Christ," by David Whitmer, 1881.

7. D. & C. 68:14-21; 107:16, 17, 69-76.

8. Ib. 107:82.

9. For further information on Priesthood and Church Government, the reader is referred to Sections 20, 68, 84, 107, 112 and 114, Doctrine and Covenants; also to Volume 3, p. 385 and Vol. 4, p. 207, History of the Church.

ARTICLE THIRTY
THE LAW OF OBEDIENCE

"There is a law, irrevocably decreed in Heaven before the foundation of this world, upon which all blessings are predicated; and when we obtain any blessing from God, it is by obedience to that law upon which it is predicated."—Joseph Smith. [1]

Pope and His Proverb.—"Order is heaven's first law," said Alexander Pope; [2] and many have accepted the poet's dictum as final. It sounds well, but is it true? President George Q. Cannon denied its truth, affirming order to be an effect rather than a cause, a result flowing from obedience, without which order would be impossible. Obedience, he maintained, is heaven's first law, and the order that reigns there, a condition consequent. Manifestly this is a correct position.

Human and Divine Government.—That obedience is essential to order, must be apparent even to a casual observer of the every-day life of men and nations. All governments demand from their people obedience to the laws enacted for the general welfare. Without it there would be no peace, no protection. Confusion would prevail, and anarchy reign supreme. This is readily conceded by most men as to human governments; but some think it strange that divine government should be administered upon like principles, and for similar though higher ends.

Aliens Must Be Naturalized.—A friend of mine, somewhat of a skeptic, asked me: "Why must I belong to a church, or subscribe to a creed, or undergo any particular ceremony, in order to be saved? I have always done what I thought was right—have been truthful, honest, virtuous and benevolent. Why is that not enough? Why will it not suffice to make my peace with God and pave my way to Heaven?"

I answered: "Suppose you were an alien, born in some country of Europe, or on some island of the sea, and you came to America desiring to become a citizen of the United States. When told that you must declare your intentions, take out naturalization papers, forswear allegiance to any foreign power, and honor and uphold the Constitution and laws of this

Republic, suppose you were to reply: Why, what is the need of all that? I am a good man; I have always acted honorably; am clean, moral and upright in conduct and conversation. Why is that not sufficient to entitle me to vote, to hold office, take up land, and enjoy all the rights and privileges of an American freeman? Do you think such a plea would avail? No, you do not. You see its inconsistency as quickly as the Government would see it and reject your application. You would not expect to become a citizen of the United States on your own terms. Why, then, should you hope for admittance into the Kingdom of Heaven upon any conditions other than those which the King himself has laid down?"

Man's Proper Attitude.—Men must not count upon their personal qualities, when applying for citizenship in the Eternal Commonwealth. The proper attitude is one of humility, not self-righteousness. The Pharisee who prayed, thanking the Lord that he was better than other men, was less justified than the Publican who also prayed, but in a different spirit, meekly murmuring: "God be merciful to me, a sinner." [3] A disposition to laud self, or dictate the terms upon which one is willing to be blest, is anything but modest, anything but reasonable. Truthfulness, honesty, virtue, benevolence—these are precious qualities, treasures enriching the soul under all conditions, inside or outside the Kingdom of Heaven. But they are not valuable enough to purchase a passport into that Kingdom. They go far, but not far enough to secure salvation.

Better Than Sacrifice.—"To obey is better than sacrifice." So said obedient Samuel to disobedient Saul. [4] Abraham's willingness to obey, when the Lord commanded him to offer up Isaac, was accepted in lieu of the offering. A literal sacrifice was not necessary in that case; but the offer to make it was necessary; for thus was symbolized the most important event in all history—the offering by the Eternal Father of his beloved Son for the redemption of the fallen human race. The Patriarch's willingness having been shown, the Lord, who had directed Abraham to offer up his son, sent an angel with the countermanding order: "Lay not thine hand upon the lad." [5] The offering had been accepted, and he who made it was rewarded as abundantly as if the sacrifice had been consummated.

Dead Letter and Living Oracle.—But what if Abraham, when commanded to offer up his son, had refused, citing in support of his position the divine law against homicide, a law dating from the time of Cain and Abel—would that have justified him? No; God's word is his law, and the word last spoken by him must have precedence over any earlier revelation on the same subject. If Abraham, after being forbidden to slay his son, had fanatically persisted in slaying him, he would have been a transgressor, just as much as if he had refused to obey in the first instance. After receiving the second command, he could not consistently plead that he was under obligation to carry out the first. Had he done so, he would have placed himself in a false position, that of honoring the dead letter above the living oracle.

The Will for the Deed.—Let me give this principle another application. A soldier goes forth to fight the battles of his country, goes with a willing heart, offering his life that justice may prevail and freedom endure. Having done his duty, he returns unscathed from the conflict where many went down to death. Is not his offering as acceptable as that of his comrade who makes what is called "the supreme sacrifice?" He certainly offers as much, the only difference being that not as much of his offering is taken.

All honor to those who, during the dreadful war of recent years, perished in the blood-soaked trenches, or fell in the open field with Prussian or Austrian bullets in their breasts! All honor to those who met death by accident or disease, in training camp or at battle-front, on land or on sea, losing their lives while faithfully playing their part in the great world tragedy! Heroes, every one! But the gallant fellows who lived through it all, patiently enduring hardships and privations, dying daily by anticipation, and by willingness to sacrifice all for the common good—be it not forgotten that in spirit they gave as much as any; and the fact that their offering was not taken, does not discount the motive that actuated them, nor diminish the credit due. "As his part is that goeth down to the battle, so shall his part be that tarrieth by the stuff; they shall part alike." [6]

The Just and the Unjust.—All blessings come by obedience. When the Savior said of the Father: "He maketh his sun to rise on the evil and on the good, and sendeth rain on the just and on the unjust." [7] he did not mean that no distinction is made between the two classes. He meant that the Great Judge is just to both—just even to the unjust, sending to them his rain and his sunshine, causing their orchards to bloom and their vineyards to bear equally with those of the righteous, provided similar conditions surround, and both classes are equally obedient to the laws governing the culture of the soil.

They Kept the First Estate.—But rain and sunshine, like all other blessings, are for those who merit them. If the unjust (unjust here) had not "kept their first estate," had not manifested in a previous life some degree of obedience to divine law, they would not have been given a "second estate," would not have been placed where the sunlight and the showers could reach them.

Obedience Must Continue.—In this life, however, further obedience is necessary, in order that greater blessings may come. God's gifts are both spiritual and temporal; but whatever they are, their bestowal is regulated by the great Law of Obedience. A good man may be a poor farmer, and thus fail to raise the full crop that he might have reaped had he been more skillful or more thorough in the practice of his vocation. On the other hand, a bad man may be an expert tiller of the soil, realizing bounteous returns because of his strict observance of the law in that particular department of industry.

Higher Laws and Higher Blessings.—There are greater blessings, however, than those pertaining to the harvest field and the workshop, and they also are to be had only by obedience to the laws governing their bestowal and distribution. One cannot become a member of the Church of Christ by being a successful merchant or stockraiser; and one may hold church membership, yet not be entitled to the privileges of the Temple. It takes more than the skill of a mechanic to get into the Kingdom of Heaven. There is but one way into that kingdom, and he who tries to pick the lock or climb over the wall, will be treated as a trespasser or a robber.

Rod and Rock.—Obedience is the rod of power which smites the rock of divine resource, causing it to flow with the waters of human weal. And the most obedient are the most blest. There are "many mansions" in the great House of God, and the highest are for those who render unto the Master of the House the fulness of their obedience.

Footnotes

1 . D. & C. 130:20,

2 . "Essay on Man," Epis 4, line 49.

3 . Luke 18:10-14.

4 . 1 Sam. 15:22.

5 . Gen. 22:12.

6 . 1 Sam. 30:24.

7 . Matt. 5:45.

ARTICLE THIRTY-ONE
THE DIVINE DOORWAY

The Most Important Personage.—What particular acts of obedience are required from man, in order that the One who redeemed may likewise save and exalt him? What must he do for himself, to the end that he may profit by the great things done in his behalf? In other words, how shall the alien seeking citizenship in the Kingdom of Heaven, obtain it? What are the divine laws of naturalization? The one who can answer such questions, is easily the most important personage of his time. Such a one was Peter, the Galilean fisherman, chief of the twelve special witnesses of the Savior.

The Pentecostal Proclamation.—When Peter, on the Day of Pentecost, preached "Christ and him crucified," and the conscience-stricken multitude, "pricked in their heart," cried out, "men and brethren, what shall we do?" a question was propounded which the most learned philosophers of that age could not answer. Caesar, sitting upon the throne of the world, would have been mystified had the question been put to him—What shall men do to be saved? Not so, the Galilean fisherman. He knew, and he told them straightway:

"Repent, and be baptized, every one of you, in the name of Jesus Christ, for the remission of sins, and ye shall receive the gift of the Holy Ghost." [1]

The Gospel Unchangeable.—These requirements have not changed. They are in force today. They will remain in force so long as the Gospel is preached. The Apostle did not say that these were all the requirements. But he answered the question put to him, and it was the appropriate and sufficient reply for that occasion.

In the Pit.—When Adam and Eve had transgressed the divine command by partaking of the forbidden fruit, it was as if the human race had fallen into a pit, from which they were powerless, by any act of their own, to emerge. They could not climb out, for they knew not how to climb; and even if they had known, there was no means by which to ascend. Human endeavor, unassisted, could accomplish nothing in the way of deliverance. Man in his mortal condition needed revelation, spiritual enlightenment, having forgotten all that he had previously known. He also needed a ladder.

The Gospel of Jesus Christ is the ladder to Freedom and Light. Without it there is no salvation, no exaltation. The Tower of Babel symbolizes the situation. All man's efforts to reach Heaven without divine assistance, must end in confusion and failure.

Self-Help Necessary.—Before there was a Ladder, or while it was not within reach, fallen man could not climb. All his intelligence and skill were unavailing. But the ladder having been let down, if he will use his God-given powers and all the means provided for the purpose, he can mount from Earth to Heaven, round by round. If he refuses to climb, who but himself is to blame for his remaining at the bottom of the pit? The Gospel is not a substitute for self-help. It does not supersede man's efforts in his own behalf. It is the divinely appointed means whereby those efforts are made effectual. It does for man what he cannot do for himself.

Redemption by Grace.—The Gospel of Salvation rests upon the rock of Christ's Atonement—an act of grace, a free gift from God to man, to the wicked as well as to the righteous. All profit by it, for through that atonement, all are brought forth from the grave. This is eminently just. Adam's posterity were consigned to death for no deed of their own doing. It is fitting, therefore, that their redemption should be unconditional.

Salvation by Obedience.—But redemption is not salvation, nor salvation exaltation. Men must "work out" their salvation, [2] and gain exaltation by continuous upward striving. Depending primarily upon the grace of God, salvation and exaltation are likewise the fruits of man's acceptance of the Gospel, and of his steadfast adherence thereto, until it shall have done for him its perfect work.

The First Requirement.—Faith is the first requirement of the Gospel. "He that believeth and is baptized shall be saved." So the Savior declared, when he commissioned his Apostles to "go into all the world and preach the Gospel to every creature." [3] Peter's Pentecostal sermon omitted faith from the list of essentials, doubtless for the reason that those whom the Apostle addressed already had faith, a fact plainly shown by the question put to him. Evidently they believed what he had told them about the crucified Redeemer; else they would not have been "pricked in their heart," and would not have anxiously inquired, "What shall we do?"

In like manner, the Savior, when making his conditional promise of salvation, left out repentance, it being implied, virtually included, in the admonition to believe and be baptized; since baptism is "for the remission of sins"—sins of which man has repented. Faith, not repentance, is the first essential—the initial requirement made of the seeker for salvation.

The Second Step.—The first fruit of faith is repentance. It follows faith as naturally as kindness follows love, as obedience springs from reverence, as a desire to be congenial with, succeeds admiration for, one whose example is deemed worthy of emulation. God commands all men to repent; and a desire to please him and become acceptable in his sight, naturally leads the soul of faith to repentance.

"Sin No More."—Repentance is not that superficial sorrow felt by the wrongdoer when "caught in the act"—a sorrow not for sin, but for sin's detection. Chagrin is not repentance. Mortification and shame alone bring no change of heart toward right feeling and right living. Even remorse is not all there is to repentance. In highest meaning and fullest measure, repentance is equivalent to reformation; the beginning of the reformatory process being a resolve to "sin no more." "By this ye may know that a man repenteth of his sins: Behold he will confess them and forsake them." [4]

What is Sin?—Sin is the transgression of divine law, as made known through the conscience or by revelation. A man sins when he violates his conscience, going contrary to light and knowledge—not the light and knowledge that has come to his neighbor, but that which has come to himself. He sins when he does the opposite of what he knows to be right. Up to that point he only blunders. One may suffer painful consequences for only blundering, but he cannot commit sin unless he knows better than to do the thing in which the sin consists. One must have a conscience before he can violate it. "Where there is no law given, there is no punishment . . . . no condemnation." [5] "He that knoweth not good from; evil is blameless." [6]

Degrees of Damnation.—Souls who know that they have sinned, and who refuse to forsake their sins, will be damned. They damn themselves by that refusal. Damnation is no part of the Gospel. It is simply the sad alternative, the inevitable consequence of rejecting the offer of salvation. Damnation (condemnation) is not necessarily permanent, and it may exist in degrees, the degree being determined by the measure of culpability in the one condemned. Even the damned can be saved if they repent.

The Sin Unpardonable.—It is possible, however, to sin so far and so deeply that repentance is impossible. Shakespeare puts into the mouth of one of his characters—the guilty King Claudius—this speech:

"Try what repentance can: what can it not? Yet what can it when one cannot repent?" [7]

Those who cannot repent are sons of perdition. Their sin is unpardonable, involving utter recreancy to divine light and power previously possessed.

The Washing of Regeneration.—Sin must not only be repented of; it must be blotted out. The soul must be cleansed of it. Baptism is the soul-cleansing process, the divinely instituted means whereby sins are remitted—that is, forgiven and washed away. Immersion in water, symbolizing birth, or burial and resurrection, is the true form of the baptismal ordinance. Baptism is the third principle of the Gospel.

Divine Illumination.—The soul cleansed from sin is in a condition to enjoy the abiding presence of the Holy Spirit, which "dwelleth not in unclean tabernacles." Through this precious gift comes the divine light that "leads into all truth," making manifest the things of God, past, present, and to come. There is a light that illumines, in greater or less degree, every soul that cometh into the world; but the Gift of the Holy Ghost, imparted by the laying on of hands of one divinely authorized to bestow it, is a special endowment, and only those having membership in the Church of Christ can possess it. Each is thus given a direct personal testimony of the Truth, and is founded upon the Rock of Revelation, against which the Gates of Hell cannot prevail.

Gospel Principles Eternal.—The Everlasting Gospel is not an empty phrase. It means just what it says. The principles underlying it are eternal. "Intelligence or the light of truth was not created or made, neither indeed can be." [8] The same is true of faith and repentance. God did not make them. They are self-existent. Such ordinances as baptism by immersion for the remission of sins, and the laying on of hands for the gift (giving) of the Holy Ghost, might indeed be created, and doubtless were; but not the fundamental facts upon which they are based. It did not require a divine edict to make washing (baptism) a prerequisite to cleanliness; nor light (the Holy Spirit) the means of illumination.

A code or system of laws and ordinances can readily be conceived of as a creation. Not so the principles embodied therein. The Gospel, like all other creations, was organized out of materials already in existence— eternal principles adapted to the needs of man and the purposes of Deity. The Supreme Intelligence, recognizing these principles as ennobling and exalting in their tendency, created a plan embodying them as the most effectual means for man's uplift and promotion. That plan, the Gospel of Jesus Christ, is the divinely appointed doorway into the Kingdom of Heaven.

Footnotes

1. Acts 2:38.
2. Phil. 2:12.
3. Mark 16:15, 6.
4. D. & C. 58:43.
5. 2 Nephi 9:25.
6. Alma 29:5.
7. Hamlet, Act. 3, Scene 3.
8. D. & C. 93:29.

ARTICLE THIRTY-TWO
THE SECOND BIRTH

The Edict of the King.—"Except a man be born again, he cannot see the Kingdom of God."

"Except a man be born of water and of the Spirit, he cannot enter into the Kingdom of God." [1]

So said the King of that Kingdom, the only one empowered to prescribe conditions upon which men may become his subjects, or his fellow citizens in the Eternal Commonwealth. Nicodemus, to whom Jesus spoke those words, was a ruler of the Jews, a Pharisee, and, as some suppose, a member of the Sanhedrin, or supreme Jewish council. Favorably inclined toward the unpopular Nazarene, yet too politic to be seen associating with him openly, this man sought him out by night, avowing a belief that he was "a teacher come from God." In response to this confession of faith, Jesus taught Nicodemus the doctrine of baptism.

A Subject of Controversy.—The meaning of the language in which the teaching was conveyed, though perfectly plain to Christians anciently, has been a matter of uncertainty to their successors all down the centuries. From the days of the early Greek fathers of the Christian Church, to the days of St. Augustine, the great theologian of the Western or Roman Catholic division of that Church; from his time to the time of Luther and Calvin, and thence on into the present age, men have disputed over the mystical Second Birth, declared by the World's Redeemer to be the portal of admittance into his Kingdom.

Over the general meaning of the phrase, "Born of Water and of the Spirit," there may have been no serious contention. In all or most of the Christian denominations, it means baptism, the ordinance whereby a person is initiated into the Church. But the meaning of baptism, the significance, form, purpose and effects of the ordinance, and whether or not it is necessary to salvation—these questions have furnished the backbone of the controversy; questions easily answered, problems readily solved, if the Holy Spirit be taken for a guide, and there be no wresting of the scriptures.

The Savior's Example.—The words of Jesus to Nicodemus ought to set at rest the question of necessity. But as a clincher we have the Savior's declaration regarding his own baptism. Jesus came from Galilee to Jordan to be baptized by John. The Baptist, deeming himself unworthy of that high honor, demurred, saying: "I have need to be baptized of thee, and comest thou to me?" Jesus, answering, said: "Suffer it to be so now, for thus it becometh us to fulfill all righteousness. Then he suffered him." [2]

Now, if it was becoming in the Son of God to be baptized, it is becoming in all who follow in his footsteps and hope to be with him hereafter. They must be baptized with the baptism that he was baptized with—the baptism of water and of the Spirit, received by him at the river Jordan nearly two thousand years ago.

King and Subject. There are those who contend that the baptism of Jesus was all-sufficient; that it answered for the whole human race, thereby obviating the necessity of baptism in general. To all such I put this question Can you conceive of a kingdom in which the king is required to obey the laws ordained for its government, while the subjects are not required to obey them? Far more likely, is it not, that the king, rather than the subject, would be exempt from such obedience? But the laws of Christ's Kingdom are just and impartial. They bear with equal pressure upon all. The Son doeth nothing but what he hath seen the Father do, [3] nor does he require from men an obedience that he himself is not willing to render. "Follow Me," is the watchword of his mission.

"To Fulfil All Righteousness."—True, baptism is "for the remission of sins," [4] and in the Savior there was no sin to remit. Why, then, was he baptized? John saw this point, when Jesus presented himself for baptism; and that, no doubt, was one reason why he demurred to the request. We cannot impute sin to the Sinless, but we are in duty bound to accept and obey his instruction. He did not say: Thus it becometh Me to fulfill all righteousness. He put it in the plural, thus giving it general application.

Baptism Not Done Away.—Christ's baptism, whether for original sin—the sin of the world, which he had assumed—or purely as an example, did not do away with baptism, any more than his endurance of the pangs of Adam's race [5] obviated human suffering. Men and women still suffer, notwithstanding that infinite atonement. All must be baptized for the remission of their own sins, notwithstanding the baptism of "the Lamb of God which taketh away the sin of the world." [6]

Exempt From Baptism.—Little children, too young to have sinned, and therefore without need of repentance, are exempt from baptism, and it is a sin to baptize them, involving as it does the vain use of a sacred ordinance.

[7] Redeemed by the blood of Christ from the foundation of the world, their innocence and purity are typical of the saved condition of men and women, who must become like them before entering into the Kingdom of Heaven. As children advance in years, however, they become account-able, and must then yield obedience to the requirements of the Gospel. [8] Eight years is the recognized age of accountability in the Church of Christ. [9]

Redeemed Without Law.—There is another class mentioned in sacred writ, for whom, in the language of the Book of Mormon, "baptism availeth nothing." The "heathen nations," who "died without law," are to be "redeemed without law," and shall "have part in the first resurrection." [10] These, however, are not heirs celestial. Theirs is "the glory of the terrestrial" in the great Kingdom of the Future.

Vicarious Ministrations.—So necessary is baptism, on the part of all capable of intelligent obedience, that the Gospel makes provision for the vicarious baptism of those who pass away without undergoing this ordinance for themselves. Work of this character, when divinely authorized, is acceptable to the Lord; a fact that should occasion little wonder in Christian minds, when it is remembered that the whole fabric of Christianity rests upon the vicarious work wrought by Jesus Christ for the redemption of a world powerless to redeem itself. Men cannot answer by proxy for the deeds done in the body, but there have always been sacred ceremonies that one person might perform for another. Baptism is among them. [11]

For the Remission of Sins.—Baptism is the divinely instituted process whereby sins are remitted. All men have sinned, and in order to bring them back into God's pure presence, where nothing sinful can come, it is necessary that they be first cleansed from sin. Water baptism is the beginning of the cleansing process.

Means and Accessories.—Water, in and of itself, cannot wash away sin; but obedience, typified by the water, can and does, when the ordinance is lawfully and properly administered. [12] The case of Naaman the Syrian, cleansed of leprosy by dipping seven times in the river Jordan, is often cited as an illustration. [13] It was not the water that cured Naaman, but his obedience to the Prophet who had told him to dip seven times in that particular stream. Had he dipped in any other stream, or any other number of times but just seven, his disease would still have clung to him. But he did as he had been directed, and his faith, manifested by his obedience, worked the cure, bringing down the power of God for that purpose. The water was only the medium through which the power operated. Likewise, when Christ anointed the eyes of the blind man with clay, causing him to see, it was faith that wrought the miracle, not the clay, which was only an accessory. It is the same with consecrated oil, as used in the healing ordinance of the Church. [14]

Effect of Baptism.—Baptism cleanses and illumines the soul, and it is by water and by Spirit that the cleansing and illumination come. They are indispensable in the process. The sick can be healed without the use of consecrated oil, or even without the laying on of hands. But no sinner can be baptized—cleansed and illumined—without the water and the Spirit.

Children in Christ.—The effect of baptism is to make men and women childlike—not in ignorance, nor in weakness, but in innocence and humility. "Of such is the Kingdom of Heaven." By baptism, following faith and repentance and administered by divine authority, the soul is "born again," and is typical, in its infant-like purity, of the soul raised to immortality. By baptism we are as effectually freed from sin, as by death, burial and resurrection, the mortal is changed to immortal and ushered into a new existence. Hence, baptism is termed "the washing of regeneration." Regeneration means "new birth."

Early Christian Views.—The earliest Christians did not doubt the necessity of baptism. On the contrary, they strongly insisted upon it, as indispensable to a saved condition. During the Patristic age—that of the post-apostolic Fathers—the conviction that no soul could be saved without baptism was so firm that it led to pedobaptism—the baptism of infants—and to other innovations upon the primitive faith. It was seen that infants could not believe in Christ, nor repent of sins that they had not committed; but it was held that the Church, or those who stood sponsor for the little ones, could believe for them, and they were baptized for original sin, the sin of Adam, which they were supposed to have inherited. Peter's words in promising the Holy Ghost, "For the promise is unto you and to your children." [15] were construed to sustain infant baptism. It was even assumed that the Savior authorized it in saying, "Suffer little children to come unto me."

Pedobaptism.—Holders of such views have never explained why infant baptism did not become prevalent until two or three centuries after Christ; and why such eminent Christians of the fourth century as Gregory of Nazianzum, the son of a bishop; Basil the Great of Cappadocia; Chrysostom of Antioch, and Augustine of Numida—whose mothers were pious Christians—were not baptized until they were over thirty years of age, Paul's affirmation that "children are holy," [16] and the Savior's declaration, "Of such is the kingdom of God," [17] are a sufficient answer to the assumption that children under the age of accountability have need to be baptized. Those who introduced the practice of baptizing infants for original sin, over-looked or were blind to the fact that Christ atoned for original guilt, and that men are accountable for their own sins and not for Adam's transgression.

Other Innovations.—One innovation led to another. Martyrs who had shed their blood in defense of the Church, or for its sake, but had never confessed Christ nor been baptized—what of them? For their benefit another doctrine was introduced. They were held to have been baptized in their own blood. Finally, out of deference to the claims of a far more numerous class—worthy men and women, many of whom had lived and died before the Christian Church was founded, while others, though living contemporaneously with it, were never reached by its missionaries—the idea gradually obtained that baptism was not essential to salvation. All this might have been obviated, and the Church spared much ridicule and skepticism, the result of its rambling inconsistencies, had it kept the key to the situation—Baptism for the Dead.

Gradual Growth of a Heresy.—The idea that baptism is non-essential did not become fixed and popular until many centuries after the Apostles "fell asleep." Saint Augustine, who figured in the latter part of the fourth and in the first half of the fifth century after Christ, and who advanced the notion that water baptism was "the outward sign of an inward grace," held, nevertheless, that no soul could be saved without it—not even infants; though their condemnation, resulting from non-baptism, would be of the mildest character. Augustine's concept of baptism, with some modifications, is the doctrine of the Roman Catholic Church and of the orthodox Protestant churches at the present time. Luther held baptism to be essential to salvation; Calvin and Zwingli did not; and there, in the sixteenth century, it appears, began the schism of opinion concerning it that divides Christendom today.

Footnotes

1 . John 3:3, 5.

2 . Matt. 3:13.

3 . John 5:19.

4 . Mark 1:4; Acts 2:38.

5 . 2 Nephi 9:21, 22.

6 . John 1:29.

7. Moroni 8:8-10, 19, 22.
8. Moses 6:55.
9. D. & C. 68:25-27.
10. Mosiah 3:11; Moroni 8:22; D. & C. 45:54; Ib. 76:72.
11. I Cor. 15:29.
12. Moses 6:60.
13. 2 Kings 5:1-14.
14. James 5:14, 15.
15. Acts 2:29.
16. 1 Cor. 7:14.
17. Mark 10:14; Luke 18:16.

ARTICLE THIRTY-THREE
MEANING AND MODE OF BAPTISM

The Lesser Suggests the Greater.—When Jesus told Nicodemus that man must be born of Water and of the Spirit, he virtually declared the meaning of baptism and prescribed the mode of its administration. It was to prepare the way before a greater principle, that Christ taught and exemplified the principle of baptism. He compared it to birth, the entry into mortal life; and this pointed to resurrection, the entry into immortal glory.

Men's minds, therefore, should be ready to receive something suggestive of birth and resurrection, in the ceremony authorized by the Son of God as the means of admission into his Kingdom. This suggestion is fully realized in the true form of the baptismal ordinance, namely, immersion—going down into the water and coming up out of the water, in the similitude of burial and resurrection, of birth into a higher life.

The Proper Form.—That immersion was the form of the ordinance introduced by John the Baptist, submitted to by the Savior, and perpetuated by his Apostles, is a plain and reasonable inference from the teachings of the New Testament. Jesus, when about to be baptized, must have gone down into the water; for after baptism, he "went up straightway out of the water." [1] When Philip baptized the Eunuch, "they went down both into the water." [2] John baptized "in Aenon, near to Salim, because there was much water there" [3] —another proof presumptive of immersion, the only mode requiring "much water" for its performance.

If this had not been the proper form, Paul would not have compared baptism to burial and resurrection; [4] nor would he have recognized as baptism the passage of the Israelites through the Red Sea. [5] Note also his words to the Corinthians relative to vicarious baptism and in support of resurrection, a doctrine that some of them denied: "Else what shall they do which are baptized for the dead, if the dead rise not at all? Why are they then baptized for the dead?" [6] In other words, why use the symbol of the resurrection, if there be no resurrection—if the symbol does not symbolize?

Additional Evidence.—In addition to what the Bible tells, we have the statements of archaeologists and historians, to the effect that baptism, in the first ages of Christianity, was a dipping or submersion in water. This, in fact, as philologists testify, is the meaning of the Greek word from which the English word "baptism" is derived. Ancient baptisteries and other monumental remains in Asia, Africa and Europe, show that immersion was the act of baptism. The Christian churches of the Orient—Greek, Russian, Armenian, Nestorian, Coptic and others, have always practiced immersion and allow nothing else for baptism. The Western churches preserved this form for thirteen centuries, and then gradually introduced pouring or sprinkling—ceremonies in no way symbolical of birth and resurrection, and therefore not in harmony with the divine purpose for which baptism was instituted.

Clinic Baptism.—Baptisms by pouring or sprinkling were exceptional in the early ages of the Christian Church. They were called clinic baptisms, because administered as a rule to the sick, who could not be taken from their beds to be immersed; but they were rare, and were regarded only as quasi-baptisms. [7]

Immersion Made Optional.—Baptism by immersion was practiced regularly in the Roman Catholic Church until the year 1311, when the Council of Ravenna authorized a change, leaving it optional with the officiating minister to baptize either by immersion or by sprinkling. Even infants were baptized by immersion until about the end of the thirteenth century when sprinkling came into common use.

Luther and Calvin.—Luther favored immersion and sought, against the tendency of the times, to restore it; but Calvin, while admitting that the word "baptism" means immersion, and that this was certainly the practice of the ancient Church, held that the mode was of no consequence. A Greater than Calvin, however, had decreed otherwise, and had set the example that all were to follow.

Modern Methods.—Pouring is the present practice in the Roman Catholic Church; sprinkling in the Church of England and in the Methodist Church. A choice of modes is permitted by the Presbyterians, though sprinkling is the regular form. The Baptists as their name implies, are strong advocates of immersion. The Quakers repudiate baptism altogether.

The Authorized Practice.—The Church of Jesus Christ of Latter-day Saints has but one form of baptism—the one authorized by the Savior and practiced by his Apostles, namely, baptism by immersion for the remission of sins. [8] The Church derives its knowledge of this sacred ordinance, not mainly from the Bible, nor from the Book of Mormon, nor from any other record. It came by direct revelation to Joseph the Seer, restoring that which was lost. Brushing aside the dust and cobwebs of tradition concealing the precious jewel of truth, he brought back the knowledge of the "one Lord, one faith, one baptism" of the ancients. [9]

Baptism and Resurrection.—Baptism was made universal, and became the doorway to the Church of Christ, the Kingdom of God on earth, because it represents resurrection, which is likewise universal and without which no man can enter into the Celestial Kingdom. Christ, the great Exemplar of baptism, was the first to rise from the dead. It was fitting, therefore, that he should undergo the ordinance symbolizing the mighty fact for which he stands—redemption from the grave and eternal life beyond.

Symbolical of the Soul.—Baptism is twofold, corresponding to its subject, the soul, which is both spiritual and temporal. The body is represented by the water; the spirit by the Holy Ghost. Both are essential in the process, since it is not the body alone, nor the spirit alone, that is baptized, but body and spirit in one. Consequently, baptism is administered in a temporal world, where body and spirit can both be present, and where the watery element abounds. A person can believe and repent in the spirit world, but cannot be baptized there. This makes necessary baptism by proxy.

The Blood that Cleanseth.—In reality there are three factors in baptism—the Spirit, the Water and the Blood. Only two of them are used in the ceremony. But without the atoning blood of Christ, there could be no baptism of a saving character. Hence it is written: "The blood of Jesus Christ cleanseth us from all sin." [10]

Three in One.—The Water and the Spirit, representing earth and heaven, are made effectual by the Blood. Man and God are thus reconciled, Christ being the reconciler. There are three that bear record in heaven—the Father, the Son and the Holy Ghost; and there are three that bear witness on earth—the Spirit, the Water and the Blood. Each group corresponds to the other; each three agree in one. Therefore, when a soul is baptized, it must be by Water and by Spirit, made effectual by Blood, and in the name of the Father and of the Son and of the Holy Ghost.

A Divine Exegesis—The Lord explained this principle to Adam thus: "Inasmuch as ye were born into the world by water and blood and the spirit, which I have made, and so became of dust a living soul, even so ye must be born again into the Kingdom of Heaven, of water and of the spirit, and be cleansed by blood, even the blood of mine Only Begotten; that ye might be sanctified from all sin, and enjoy the words of eternal life in this world, and eternal life in the world to come, even immortal glory:

"For by the Water ye keep the commandment; by the Spirit ye are justified, and by the Blood ye are sanctified." [11]

The Mediator.—Spirit, Water and Blood—the three elements of baptism—were combined in the person of Jesus Christ, when baptized by John in the Jordan. Standing upon the river's brink, his sacred from dripping with the waters from which he had just emerged, he was crowned with the Holy Ghost, descending upon him from above. Yet it was necessary that his blood should be shed, in order that the Spirit might come in full force unto his disciples. Not until the Mediator had hung between heaven and earth, were the Apostles endued with power from on High. Then it was that the Spirit of God moved with full effect upon the waters of this world, coming, as in the first instance, that there might be a creation, a new birth, a regeneration for the human race.

Immersion in the Spirit.—So much stress being laid upon immersion, and upon the twofold character of baptism, one may be led to inquire: Why is it not an immersion in the Spirit as well as in the Water? To which I answer: Is it not so? When John the Baptist, proclaiming the Christ, said, "I indeed have baptized you with water, but he shall baptize you with the Holy Ghost," [12] it was baptism in each instance, and baptism signifies immersion. [13]

The Laying on of Hands.—The Holy Ghost is imparted by the laying on of hands. [14] Possibly this ceremony was intended to typify the glorious baptism that Earth will undergo when the Spirit is poured out upon her from on High. The laying on of hands for the giving of the Holy Ghost was an ordinance in the Christian Church for centuries. Cyprian mentions it in the third century; Augustine in the fourth. Gradually, however, it began to be neglected, until finally some of the sects discarded it, while others, retaining the form, "denied the power thereof."

The Fathers Understood.—The Greek fathers of the Church held correct ideas concerning baptism. They termed it "initiation," from its introductory character; "regeneration," from its being regarded as a new birth; "the great circumcision," because it was held to have superseded the circumcision of the Mosaic law; also "illumination" and "the gift of the Lord." [15]

Censured for Truth's Sake.—The Greek Christians of the early centuries, like the Saints of New Testament times, baptized for the remission of sins. They have been censured by modern critics for magnifying the importance of water baptism, and at the same time insisting on the purely ethical or spiritual nature of the rite; for confounding the sign with the thing signified, the action of the water with the action of the Spirit, in the process of regeneration. But they were not any more insistent upon these points than the Apostles themselves.

Augustine's Theory.—St. Augustine is complimented by the same critics for formulating the first strict scientific theory of the nature and effects of baptism. He drew a sharp distinction between "the outward sign"—water baptism—and the inward change of heart resulting from the operation of the Holy Ghost. Yet even he is charged with laying too much stress upon the value of "the outward sign," which he held to be essential to salvation. Protestant theologians have been commended for keeping the "sign" in due subordination to "the thing signified," for justifying themselves by faith, and ignoring to a great extent outward ordinances.

But the Greek Christians, whatever their defects, were nearer right than St. Augustine, and St. Augustine was nearer right than the Protestant theologians who followed him. Baptism, as taught in the New Testament, is not the mere "outward sign of an inward grace." The action of the water and the action of the Spirit are not to be separated in any analysis of the nature and effects of baptism. Both are essential in the soul-cleansing, soul-enlightening process.

A Symbol of Creation.—Every baptism, every resurrection, implies a birth. No seed germinates until it dies, or appears to die, and is buried. The gardener plants that there may be a springing forth of new life from the germ of the old. [16] Coming into this world involves departure out of a previous world, and burial here implies birth hereafter. The sun sets upon the Eastern hemisphere to rise upon the Western, and sets upon the Western to rise upon the Eastern. The setting and rising of the sun; sleep followed by waking; winter with its icy fetters and snowy shroud, succeeded by spring in garments of green, with bright flowers, singing birds and laughing streams; all these suggest baptism, for they symbolize birth, burial and resurrection.

Begotten and Born of God.—We have a Father and a Mother in heaven, in whose image we were created, male and female. We were begotten and born in the spirit before we were begotten and born in the flesh; and we must be begotten and born again, in the similitude of those earlier begettings and births, or we cannot regain the presence of our eternal Father and Mother.

Babes in Christ.—Baptism signifies the creation of souls for the Kingdom of God. The one who baptizes is the spiritual progenitor of the one baptized. This is why the Apostles referred to those who received baptism at their hands as "children of my begetting," "babes in Christ," to be fed "the milk" before "the meat of the word." [17] To baptize is to perform spiritually the functions of fatherhood. Motherhood is symbolized by the baptismal font. Hence, baptism must be by divine authority, must have God's sanction upon it. Heavenly and earthly powers must join, must be wedded for the bringing forth of the redeemed soul; otherwise, the baptism will be unlawful, the birth illegitimate, the act of begetting a sin. Baptisms, like marriages, performed without divine authority, will have no effect "when men are dead."

Suggestive Symbolism.—The significance of baptism and the very form of the ceremony are suggested by the career of that Divine Being whose descent from heaven to earth, and whose ascent from earth to heaven, are the sum and substance of the Gospel Story. Descending below and rising above—such was his experience from the time he left his celestial throne to the time he returned to his glorious exaltation. It is not possible that the sacred ordinance of baptism was intended to symbolize that wonderful event—God's merciful condescension for the sake of fallen man? Was it not instituted in anticipation and as a memorial of that mighty Birth, with its mortal burial and its immortal resurrection?

A Watery World.—Moreover, in the symbolism of the Scriptures, this world is represented by water. [18] "All things are water," said the Greek Thales. At the very dawn of creation, Spirit and Water, the two elements used in baptism, were both present—the one creative, the other createable. [19] "Let the dry land appear!" The very words suggest baptism, birth, creation—the emergence of an infant planet from the womb of the waters. And when the Almighty was about to send the Flood, he said to Noah, concerning the wicked: "Behold, I will destroy them with the earth." [20] Did he mean the watery element which enters so largely into the composition of the earth?

A Double Doorway.—Water represents the temporal part of creation, including the body or mortal part of man. Baptism therefore, in its twofold character, suggests the passing out from this watery world into the spirit world, and thence by resurrection into eternal glory. It is only a suggestion, but it emphasizes for me the reason why the doorway to the Church and Kingdom of God is a double doorway, a dual birth, a baptism of Water and of the Spirit.

Footnotes

1 . Matt. 3:16.

2 . Acts 8:38.

3 . John 3:23.

4 . Rom. 6:3-5; Col. 2:12.

5 . 1 Cor. 10:1, 2.

6 . Ib. 15:29.

7. The first recorded case of clinic baptism is mentioned by Eusebius as having occurred in the third century.

8. 3 Nephi 11:23-29.

9. Eph. 4:5.

10. 1 John 1:7.

11. Moses 6:59, 60.

12. Mark 1:8.

13. President Lorenzo Snow, in describing the effect of the Spirit upon himself, after his baptism in water, says: "It was a complete baptism—a tangible immersion in the heavenly principle or element, the Holy Ghost."—Improvement Era, June, 1919, p. 654.

14. Acts 8:17.

15. Other synonyms were "consecration" and "consummation." Those baptized were understood to have consecrated their lives to God, and to have consummated or completed their preparation for communion with the Church of Christ. Only to such was the sacrament of the Lord's Supper administered.

16. 1 Cor. 15:35-44.

17. 1 Cor. 3:1,2; Heb. 5:13, 14.

18. Dan. 7; Rev. 13, 17.

19. Gen. 1:2.

20. Ib. 6:13.

ARTICLE THIRTY-FOUR
THE GOSPEL'S ACCESSORIES

Many Ways to the Heart.—There is only one way into the Kingdom of Heaven, but there are many ways into the human heart; and the Church of Christ, in its mission of promulgating truth and turning souls to righteousness, has legitimate use for every avenue to that heart. Poetry, music, art in general, as well as science and philosophy—all these can be utilized as auxiliaries in the carrying on of the Lord's manifold work. They may not be essential parts of the divine message, but they prepare the way for its acceptance and are the forerunners of greater things. This, to my thinking, is the main reason why they are in the world. There is something purifying, ennobling, exalting, in all true poetry, true music, real science and genuine philosophy.

The Poet's Mission.—"The poets of the world," says the poetic Dr. Holland, "are the prophets of humanity. They forever reach after and foresee the ultimate good. They are evermore building the paradise that is to be, painting the millennium that is to come, restoring the lost image of God in the human soul. When the world shall reach the poet's ideal, it will arrive at perfection; and much good will it do the world to measure itself by this ideal and struggle to lift the real to its lofty level." [1]

In the light of such a noble utterance, how paltry the ordinary concept of the poet as a mere verse-builder. His true mission is to exalt the ideal, and encourage the listless or struggling real to advance toward it and eventually attain perfection.

Dreamers and Builders.—In this age of money-worship, the poet is often referred to, and at times even ridiculed, as a "dreamer." But the ridicule, when applied to a real poet, a true son or daughter of the Muses, is pointless. The poet *is* a dreamer; but so is the architect and the projector of railroads. All creative minds are dreamful, imaginative, poetic. Were it otherwise, nothing worth while would be created. If there were no dreamers, there would be no builders. Both are necessary to progress. Every art and every science has its share of poetic idealism, of poetic enthusiasm, and must have it, in order to achieve best results.

Well worthy of a place beside Doctor Holland's beautiful thought on poets and their ideals, is the following sentiment on dreamers, from the pen of the popular essayist, James Allen: "As the visible world is sustained by the invisible, so men, through all their trials and sins and sordid vocations, are nourished by the beautiful visions of their solitary dreamers. Humanity cannot forget its dreamers; it cannot let their ideals fade and die; it lives in them; it knows them as the *realities* which it shall one day see and know. Composer, sculptor, painter, poet, prophet, sage, these are the makers of the after-world, the architects of heaven. The world is beautiful because they have lived; without them, laboring humanity would perish." [2]

Poets and Prophets.—Poets are prophets of a lesser degree; and the prophets are the mightiest of the poets. They hold the key to the symbolism of the universe, and they alone are qualified to interpret it.

> Prophets, mightiest of the poets,
> They to whom the Gods tell secrets,
> Doing naught till true revealings
> Have made wise their trusted servants,
> Who in turn make wise the people;
> Bringing past and future present
> For the betterment of all men,
> Earth for every change preparing
> On her pilgrimage to glory. [3]

Rhymes and Rhymesters.—There are rhymesters who are neither poets nor prophets; and there are prophets and poets who never build a verse nor make a rhyme. Rhyme is no essential element of poetry. Versification is an art used by the poet to make his thought more attractive. The rhyme pleases the ear and helps the sentiment to reach the heart—a ticket of admission, as it were. A musical instrument is painted and gilded, not to improve its melodic or harmonic powers, but to make it beautiful to the eye, while its music appeals to the ear and charms the soul. Rhyme sustains about the same relation to poetry, as paint or gold leaf to the piano or organ. Clothing adds nothing to one's stature, to one's mental or moral worth; but it enables one to appear well in society. "The apparel" may "proclaim," but it does not *make* "the man." Neither does rhyme make poetry.

The Essence of Poetry.—The essence of poetry is its idealism, its symbolism. The Creator has built his universe upon symbols, the lesser suggesting and leading up to the greater; and the poetic faculty—possessed in fulness by the prophet—recognizes and interprets them. "All things have their likeness.' [4] All creations testify of their creator. They point to something above and beyond themselves. That is why poetry of the highest order is always prophetic or infinitely suggestive; and that is why the poet is a prophet, and why there is such a thing as poetic prose.

"Consider the lilies of the field, how they grow. They toil not, neither do they spin; and yet I say unto you, that even Solomon, in all his glory was not arrayed like one of these." [5]

That is poetry, real poetry, full of rhythm, yet having no rhyme.

Above and Beyond.—Anything is poetic that suggests something greater than itself. The lilies of the field suggested to the Savior's poetic mind the glory of Solomon. He used them as a means of instilling into the minds of his doubting disciples the great lesson of trust in Providence.

Man, fashioned in the divine image, suggests God, and is therefore "a symbol of God," as Carlyle affirms. [6] But Joseph Smith said it first and more fully. He declared God to be "An Exalted Man." To narrow minds, this is blasphemy. To the broad-minded, it is poetry—poetry of the sublimest type.

Poetic Ordinances.—The bread and water used in the sacrament of the Lord's Supper, represent something greater than those emblems— something above and beyond. The whole sacred ceremony is a poem in word and action.

The same is true of Baptism, which stands for birth, creation, burial and resurrection. Fatherhood and motherhood are both symbolized in the baptismal ordinance, the true form of which is immersion. Any deviation from that mode destroys its poetic suggestiveness, its symbolism.

The Greatest Poet and Prophet.—Jesus Christ, the greatest of all prophets, was likewise the greatest of all poets. He comprehended the universe and its symbolism as no one else ever did or could. He knew it through and through. What wonder? Had he not created it, and was it not made to bear record of him? [7] He taught in poetic parables, taking simple things as types of greater things, and teaching lessons that lead the mind upward towards the ideal, towards perfection. The Gospel of Christ is replete with poetry. It is one vast poem from beginning to end.

What of Philosophy—"Philosophy is the account which the human mind gives to itself of the constitution of the world." So says that great modern philosopher, Ralph Waldo Emerson. [8] In Article Eleven I have pointed out the similarity between Plato's concept of causes that produced the universe, and Joseph Smith's teaching upon the origin and purpose of the great plan of eternal progression. But Joseph did not get his philosophy from Plato. He had it directly from the divine Source of Plato's inspiration. There is no plagiarism in this semi-paralleling of a sublime thought. In like manner Confucius taught, in a negative way, the Golden Rule, afterwards taught affirmatively and more fully by Jesus of Nazareth. Truth, whether uttered by ancient sage or by modern seer, is worthy of all acceptance.

Emerson on "Compensation."—Few things of a philosophic nature appeal to me more strongly than Emerson's great essay on "Compensation." Says that master of thought and expression: "Every excess causes a defect; every defect an excess. Every sweet hath its sour, every evil its good. Every faculty which is a receiver of pleasure, has an equal penalty put on its abuse. It is to answer for its moderation with its life."

"Nature hates monopolies and exceptions. The waves of the sea do not more speedily seek a level from their loftiest tossing, than the varieties of conditions tend to equalize themselves. There is always some leveling circumstance that puts down the overbearing, the strong, the rich, the fortunate, substantially on the same ground with all others."

"The farmer imagines power and place are fine things. But the President has paid dear for his White House."

"The cheat, the defaulter, the gambler, cannot extort the benefit, cannot extort the knowledge of material and moral nature which his honest care and pains yield to the operative. The law of nature is, Do the thing, and you shall have the power; but they why do not the thing have not the power."

"As the royal armies sent against Napoleon, when he approached, cast down their colors and from enemies became friends, so do disasters of all kinds, as sickness, offense, poverty, prove benefactors."

"Our strength grows out of our weakness. Not until we are pricked and stung and sorely shot at, awakens the indignation which arms itself with secret forces. Blame is safter than praise."

"The history of persecution is a history of endeavors to cheat nature, to make water run up hill, to twist a rope of sand. The martyr cannot be dishonored. Every lash inflicted is a tongue of fame; every prison a more illustrious abode; every burned book or house enlightens the world. It is the whipper who is whipped, and the tyrant who is undone."

"The changes which break up at short intervals the prosperity of men, are advertisements of a nature whose law is growth. We cannot part with our friends. We cannot part our friends. We cannot let our angels go. We do not see that they only go out, that archangels may come in."

"The death of a dear friend, wife, brother, lover, which seemed nothing but privation, somewhat later assumes the aspect of a guide or genius; for it commonly operates revolutions in our way of life, terminates an epoch of infancy or of youth which was waiting to be closed, breaks up a wonted occupation, or a household, or style of living, and allows the formation of new ones more friendly to the growth of character." And the man or woman who would have remained a sunny garden flower, with no room for its roots and too much sunshine for its head, by the falling of the walls and the neglect of the gardener, is made the banian of the forest yielding shade and fruit to wide neighborhoods of men." [9]

Divers Teachers.—Philosophy, like poetry, wins its way, where Truth's fulness, preached in power, might offend. The plain blunt message of the prophet who comes proclaiming, "Thus saith the Lord," repels and antagonizes many who will listen to and be impressed by the philosopher, with his cogent reasoning; or charmed by the poet, with his melodious verse and appealing illustrations; or won over by the scientist, with his clear-cut, convincing demonstrations. All kinds of teachers go before the prophet, preparing his way, or follow after him, confirming his testimony. [10]

The Divine Art.—Music softens the heart, thus preparing the way before the Gospel. "The song of the righteous is a prayer unto me," saith the Lord. [11] Nothing brings the good spirit into a meeting more quickly than sweet and soulful singing, especially when choir and congregation join. Tourists come in a constant stream to listen to the organ and the choir in our great Tabernacle. The Gospel is not always preached to them; they do not always desire it. But they are mellowed by the music, and go away with kinder feelings toward, and a better understanding of, the people who build such instruments, organize such choirs, and rear such structures. Their works speak for them. Depraved wretches, such as the majority of Utah's people are falsely represented to be, do not love music, care nothing for poetry and philosophy, do not cultivate the arts and sciences, nor rear tabernacles and temples unto God.

Seeing and Hearing.—In the year 1875 President Ulysses S. Grant came to Utah—the first Executive of the Nation to set foot within the Territory, now a State. It was at a time when, all over this broad land, bitter prejudice against the Latter-day Saints prevailed. It was freely asserted that the man who had finished with the South, would "make short work" of Utah and the "Mormons." Among the places visited by the President and his party during their stay, was the Salt Lake Tabernacle, where he heard the organ played by Joseph J. Daynes. What the President thought of it, I never learned; but Mrs. Grant, her face streaming with tears, turned to Captain Hooper, who had been Utah's delegate in Congress, and said with deep feeling: "I wish I could do something for these good Mormon people." The music had touched her heart, and perhaps the heart of her noble husband; for Grant was noble, though yielding at times to intense prejudice. [12]

No Substitute for the Gospel.—Let it not be supposed, however, that music, poetry, painting, sculpture, science, or any other thing, can take the place of the great uplifting Plan whereby the world, already redeemed, is yet to be glorified. No gift can vie with the Giver, no creature usurp the functions of the Creator. He will use everything true and good and beautiful to melt the hearts of men and prepare them to be saved; but salvation itself comes only by one route—the Gospel of the Lord Jesus Christ.

This is the great Ideal, and it must be honored and maintained as such. In dealing with it, no Procrustean process is permissible. It must not be chopped off because men think it too long, nor stretched out because they deem it too short. It did not come into the world to be mutilated. Revelation cannot bow down to tradition. Truth is the standard—truth as Heaven reveals it—and the opinions and theories of men must give way. The Gospel's accessories are no substitute for the Gospel.

Footnotes

1 . Lessons in Life, by Timothy Titcomb (J. G. Holland)—Lesson 22, "The Poetic Test."

2 . As a Man Thinketh, "Visions and Ideals."

3 . "Love and the Light," p. 68.

4 . Moses 6:63.

5 . Matt. 6:28, 29; Luke 12:27.

6 . Sartor Resartus, 3, "Symbols."

7 . Moses 6:63.

8 . Representative Men, Plato, p. 51.

9 . Emerson's Essays, 3, "Compensation."

10 . A friend of mine, a medical practitioner, was conversing with a learned physician in the great city of London. The subject was the Word of Wisdom (D. & C. 89) wherein the Lord, after deprecating the use of strong drink, tobacco and other things "not good for man," goes on to say that "all wholesome herbs," "every fruit in the season thereof," and all grains are ordained for man's use. "Nevertheless, wheat for man, and corn for the ox, and oats for the horse, and rye for the fowls and for swine and for all beasts of the field and barley for all useful animals, and for mild drinks," etc. The learned man asked: "Where did Joseph Smith get

this information? These teachings are based upon scientific principles, recognized as such by the medical profession; but they are of comparatively recent discovery. They were not known in Joseph Smith's time." My friend, being a Latter-day Saint, did not lose the opportunity thus afforded of bearing testimony to Joseph Smith's mission as a prophet.

11 . D. & C. 25:12.

12 . Before reaching the Tabernacle, President Grant passed up South Temple Street, lined on both sides with sabbath school children, neatly and tastefully attired, waving banners and mottoes of welcome in honor of the nation's chief. Riding in an open carriage, and running the gauntlet of applause and cheers, the honored guest turned to the Governor of Utah, Hon. George W. Emery, who sat beside him, and inquired: "What children are these?" "Mormon children," replied the Governor. "The Silent Man" mused for a moment, and was then heard to murmur, "I have been deceived."

He never was deceived again—in the same way. He could trust his eyes when he looked upon those beautiful children. They were not the product of crime and depravity, not the offspring of savages and criminals. He could trust his ears, too, when he heard that choir and that organ. No one could make him believe, after his visit to the "Mormon City," that its inhabitants were as black as they had been painted.

ARTICLE THIRTY-FIVE
WHAT ARE MIRACLES?

Not Contrary to Law.—Miracles are results flowing from superior means and methods of doing things. They do not happen contrary to law. They are in strict conformity therewith. It could not be otherwise; for the universe, natural and supernatural, is governed by law. But there are greater laws and lesser laws, and the greater have power to suspend the operation of the lesser. When this occurs, people exclaim: "A miracle!" Others say: "It never happened, for it is contrary to law." And indeed it may seem contrary to ordinary law, with the workings of which their everyday experience is familiar. But that does not prove it contrary to some higher law concerning which they may know little or nothing.

Elisha and the Axe.—When the Prophet Elisha relieved the distress of the young man who had lost an axe—a borrowed axe—in the stream on the bank of which he was hewing timber, [1] it may have been supposed, by some skeptical on-looker, that the man of God was working in opposition to law. The account given states that "he cut down a stick" and cast it into the water, and "the iron did swim"—in spite of the fact that it is the nature of iron to sink. The law of gravitation required that the axe remain at the bottom of the stream, unless, by the application of some counter-force, ordinary or otherwise, it could be recovered. The force applied in this case was extraordinary. Elisha invoked a law superior to the law of gravitation, suspending its complete action upon that particular piece of iron. [2]

Scientific Achievements.—Today, iron ships are floating upon every sea. While this is not a miracle such as Elisha wrought, it would have been deemed a miracle in earlier ages of the world, before such wonders became commonplace. The achievements of modern science, compared with past conditions in the same field of thought and action, ought to convince any reasonable mind that the days of miracles are not over.

Light Production.—Men once made light by briskly rubbing together two pieces of wood, until friction generated flame. Gas light or electric light, with the present means of producing them, would have filled the souls of such men with fear and wonder. To them it would have been a miracle.

And yet, to press a button or turn a switch, and thus obtain light, is a very clumsy device—or will be so considered when men learn to make light as God made it on the morning of creation. [3]

"The Earth Moves."—The telegraph, the telephone, the electric car, the automobile, the airship—these and a hundred other marvelous manifestations of scientific power, now quite common, would have been deemed visionary and impossible in former ages. To have avowed even a belief in them would have imperiled one's life or deprived him of his liberty, in the days when Galileo was threatened with torture for declaring that the earth moves, or when women, in later times were hanged or burned as witches for nothing at all. So dangerous is human prejudice, in its fanatical opposition to things new and strange. This, of course, refers only to former ages and to semibenighted peoples. We would not have done as our forefathers did! So each generation thinks. Let us be thankful that the earth "does move," and that the mind of man moves with it, so that perils such as confronted Galileo and others of his class are now less likely to show their ugly features.

The Other Extreme.—But just a word of caution here. We must not rush to the opposite extreme, and become obsessed with that ultra-practical spirit which would make all things commonplace, not only in manifestation, but in origin. Miracles, after all, are facts, not fictions, and some of them have their causes far back of and beyond the known principles of science.

Disbelief in Divine Interposition.—But there is a disposition in these modern days to do away with everything savoring of the supernatural, "Higher Criticism," so-called, seems to regard this as its special mission. Some people, even if they give credence to works of wonder, invariably refer them to ordinary causes—anything rather than acknowledge divine interposition.

Moses and the Red Sea.—For instance, when they read of Moses parting the waters of the Red Sea, they either deny the event in toto, or set Moses and the miracle aside, and substitute some convulsion of nature as the accidental cause of the mighty deliverance, when those waters, after allowing the Israelites to pass through in safety, returned just in time to engulf their pursuing enemies, the Egyptians. [4]

A very convenient earthquake, truly! Nothing could have been more timely! But why could not Divine Power have done it all—done it designedly, in the manner and with the means specified in the sacred narrative? [5] Is God impotent in the presence of Nature—fettered by his own creation?

Alas! these learned theorists believe not in God, and that is why they deny his works and put nature with its blind forces in his stead.

Joshua and the Sun.—They laugh to scorn the idea of Joshua commanding the sun to stand still, deeming it "a sin and a disgrace" that such things should be preached and taught, and denying, of course, that the miracle ever took place. Because, forsooth, the whole solar system would have come crashing down into chaos, had the sun halted for one moment in its decreed course! Yes, that might have happened, such a calamity might have occurred—had there been no God to uphold the solar system and administer the law for its preservation.

"The Lord Fought for Israel."—But there is a God, and he was there as he is everywhere, by his all-protective, all-administrative power—the God to whom Joshua prayed before uttering the sublime command: "Sun, stand thou still upon Gibeon, and thou, Moon, in the valley of Ajalon!" [6] "And the sun stood still, and the moon stayed, until the people had avenged themselves upon their enemies; . . . . for the Lord fought for Israel." [7]

There you have it—it was the Lord's doing. Joshua was merely the instrument, just as Moses had been. But because such things are not happening every day, and because doubt cannot do them, therefore are they impossible to Faith! Such is the logic of those who scoff at the power of Deity and deny even the miracles of the Savior.

Nothing Too Difficult for Omnipotence.—For my part, I see nothing inconsistent in these Bible stories—nothing to justify doubt or denial. A Power that could create the sun and moon and set them whirling in their orbits, could stop them in their decreed course—or stop the earth, so that sun and moon would seem to be stayed—and at the same time uphold the universe, while this part of it remained stationary. Of course, man could not do it; but human power is not the measure of Omnipotence.

What Our Century Needs.—What the Twentieth Century needs, more than anything else, is an honest belief that there is actually a God in heaven, and that his power is superior to man's. The Great Creator has not let out his universe, to be governed by law independently of the Law-giver. The God of Israel is a God who answers prayer, and who works miracles whenever the need arises and conditions warrant—works them according to law. But He administers that law—it does not administer him.

Greater and Lesser Laws.—Some laws are fundamental. The Almighty did not create them; but he controls them and overrules their workings for the welfare of his creatures. According to Joseph Smith, certain laws were "instituted" at the beginning, as a means for human progression. These are eternal principles whereby our great and benevolent Father proposes to save and exalt his children, and give perpetuity to all things necessary for their happiness and glory.

Who, having faith in a Maker of the universe, can question his power to govern that universe, the workmanship of his hands? And if he controls the fundamental laws—those uncreatable, self-existent principles which are as the Constitution of Eternity, surely he can suspend the operation of lesser laws based thereon, setting aside at will his own enactments.

An Illustration.—Suppose a child to be lying at the point of death. The family physician, having done his best and failed, informs the sad-hearted parents that their little one cannot live till morning. Medical science so decrees, in accordance with the law under which the physician has been operating. But, bearing in mind the apostolic injunction, "Is any sick among you? Let him call for the Elders of the Church," [8] the parents send for the Elders. They come and pray over the child, and the prayer of faith "saves the sick," notwithstanding the good doctor's prognostication. A miracle? Yes, if one chooses to call it so. In other words, the suspension of a lesser law by a greater, the former requiring the death of the child, the latter permitting it to live; the lower inoperative in the presence of the higher.

Biggest Things Yet to Be.—Miracles belong to no particular time or place. Whenever and wherever there is sufficient faith and a reasonable demand for its exercise, Divine Power will act, and marvels will result. "There are more things in heaven and earth than are dreamt of" in human "philosophy," and the biggest things are yet to be. God's work is progressive, and the miracles of the future will cause the miracles of the past to pale.

Divine Adaptation.—Progression's highest methods cannot be employed in dealing with undeveloped man. The All-wise adapts himself to the conditions environing those whom he aims to uplift and glorify. "All things are in a scale," rendering necessary a diversity of laws and operations. Even the divine dictum, "Let there be light!" does not represent the last word in light production. God is Light, and has only to appear, and all darkness will flee away. When the sun rises, the moon and stars must "hide their diminished heads." When God dawns upon the world, not even the sun will shine.

Footnotes

1 . 2 Kings 6:1-7.

2 . "What are the Laws of Nature?" asks Carlyle, and continues "To me perhaps the rising of one from the dead were no violation of these laws, but a confirmation, if some far deeper law, now first penetrated into, and by spiritual force, even as the rest have all been, were brought to bear on us with its material force."

"'But is it not the deepest law of Nature that she be constant?' cried an illuminated class: 'Is not the machine of the universe fixt to move by unalterable rules?' Probable enough good friends. . . . . And now of you, too, I make the old inquiry: What those same unalterable rules, forming the complete statute book of Nature, may possibly be?

"'They stand written in our works of science,' say you; 'in the accumulated record of man's experience.' Was man with his experience present at the creation, then, to see how it all went on? Have any deepest scientific individuals yet dived down to the foundations of the universe, and gauged everything there? Did the Maker take them into his counsel, that they read his ground-plan of the incomprehensible All, and can say, This stands marked therein, and no more than this? Alas, not in any wise!" . . . .

"To the minnow, every cranny and pebble and quality and accident, of its little native creek may have become familiar; but does the minnow understand the ocean tides and periodic currents, the trade winds and monsoons and moon's eclipses, by all which the condition of its little creek is regulated, and may, from time to time (unmiraculously enough) be quite upset and reversed? Such a minnow is man; his creek this planet earth; his ocean the immeasurable All; his monsoons and periodic currents the mysterious force of Providence through aeons of aeons."—Sartor Resartus, Natural Supernaturalism, pp. 275-278.

3 . Gen. 1:3.

4 . "Everybody recalls how the Red Sea was rolled aside in order that the Isaraelites under Moses might pass over safely; how the river Jordan, a few later, was driven back, that Joshua and his army might cross; and how Sodom and Gomorrah were overwhelmed with fire and brimstone

for their sins . . . . Geologists are now inclined to believe that the recession of the sea might have been caused by an earthquake pushing up a rock stratum under tremendous pressure. The water would return in some degree upon the subsidence of the stratum. The various miraculous events referred to occurred about the year 1500 B. C., and there is a curious similarity between them. It now appears probable from scientific research that these occurrences were the last of a series of terrific earthquake disturbances that changed the entire surface of the globe." — W. H. Ballou, D. Sc.

5 . Ex. 14:21-31.

6 . Joshua 10:12.

7 . Ib. vv. 13, 14.

8 . James 5:14.

ARTICLE THIRTY-SIX
THE MAINSPRING OF POWER

The Moving Cause.—All power springs from faith. It is "the moving cause of all action" and "the foundation of all righteousness." [1] God did not create the principle of faith, but by means of it he created the worlds, and by means of it he continues to exercise control and dominion over them. It is the faith of Omnipotence that upholds the universe.

A Negative Opinion.—A Christian minister, not of the orthodox school, with whom I was conversing on the subject of faith, tried to convince me that it was anything but an admirable quality. He even called it contemptible, declaring that it consisted of a weak willingness to believe—to believe anything, however improbable or absurd. In short, it was mere credulity, nothing more.

A Spiritual Force.—When I referred to faith as a spiritual force, a principle of power, he said I was attaching to the term a significance that it had never borne, and for which there was no warrant. I then reminded him of the Savior's words: "If ye have faith as a grain of mustard seed, ye shall say unto this mountain, 'Remove hence to yonder place,' and it shall remove, and nothing shall be impossible unto you." [2] Whereupon he flippantly remarked: "Oh, it takes picks and shovels to move mountains."

Picks and Shovels.—And so it does—if one has no better way of moving them. But what about the faith necessary to handle pick and shovel? All energy springs from faith, and whether mountains are moved by man or by his Maker, it is faith that precedes the action and renders it possible. Yet here was a professed minister of Christ, ignoring the teachings of Christ, and denying what all true Christians believe—that the smallest as well as the greatest acts of our lives spring from the exercise of faith.

Misplaced Confidence.—In its incipient stages, faith may at times resemble mere credulity. The untutored savage who was told by one of the early settlers of New England, that if he planted gunpowder it would "grow" gunpowder, believed it, not yet having learned that the white man could lie. He therefore parted with his valuable furs, in exchange for a small quantity of powder, and planted it, showing his confidence in the settler's word. But of course the desired result did not follow; for faith, to be effectual, must be rightly based, must have a reasonable foundation. The Spirit of Truth must inspire it. This was not the case with the poor misguided Indian. He trusted in a falsehood, and was deceived. Still, some good came of it—he ascertained the falsity of the settler's statement. If the planting did not produce powder, it produced a wiser Indian.

Faith's Possibilities.—Had the red man's faith been perfect—an intelligent, rational, heaven-inspired faith—he could have produced gunpowder or any other commodity from the all-containing elements around him. And that, too, without planting a seed or employing any ordinary process of manufacture. The miracles wrought by the Savior—his turning of water into wine, his miraculous feeding of the multitude, his walking on the waves, healing of the sick, raising of the dead, and other wonderful works—what were they but manifestations of an all-powerful faith, to possess which is to have the power to move mountains, without picks and shovels, my skeptical friend to the contrary notwithstanding? Faith is not to confounded with blind ignorant credulity. It is a divine energy, operating upon natural principles and by natural processes—natural, though unknown to "the natural man," and termed by him "supernatural."

"As a Grain of Mustard Seed."—When the Savior spoke of the faith that moves mountains, he was not measuring the quantity of the faith by the size of the mustard seed. Neither was it an Oriental hyperbole. Jesus was speaking literally. Mountains had been moved before by the power of faith; [3] then why not now? [4]

An Impelling Force.—Faith is the beating heart of the universe. Without it nothing was ever accomplished, small or great, commonplace or miraculous. No work ever succeeded that was not backed by confidence in some power, human or superhuman, that impelled and pushed forward the enterprise.

Those Who Believe.—It was not doubt that drove Columbus across the sea; it was faith—the impelling force of the Spirit of the Lord. [5] It was not doubt that inspired Jefferson, Franklin, and the other patriot fathers to lay broad and deep the foundations of this mighty republic, as a hope and a refuge for oppressed humanity. It is not doubt that causes nations to rise and flourish, that induces great and good men in all ages and in all climes to teach and toil and sacrifice for the benefit of their fellows. It is faith that does such things. Doubt only hinders what faith would achieve. The men and women who move the world are the men and women who believe.

Mahomet and Islam.—Carlyle, in splendid phrasing, depicts the wonderful change that came over the Arabian people when they abandoned idolatry, the insincere worship of "sticks and stones," and became a believing nation. "It was as a birth from darkness into light; Arabia first became alive by means of it. A poor shepherd people roaming unnoticed in its deserts since the creation of the world; a hero-prophet was sent down to them with a word they could believe; see, the unnoticed becomes world-notable, the small has become world-great; within one century afterward Arabia is at Granada on this hand, at Delhi on that—glancing in valor and splendor and the light of genius, Arabia shines through long ages over a great section of the world. Belief is great, life-giving. The history of a nation becomes fruitful, soul-elevating, great, so soon as it believes." [6]

Achievements of Christendom.—The same philosophy, with far greater emphasis, applies to Christendom and its glorious achievements all down the centuries. What has caused Christian nations to flourish so mightily? What has enabled Christianity, in spite of its errors, to survive the wreck of empires and to weather the storms of time? Faith in the Christ, imperfect though that faith has been. The faith of any people—its trust in and reliance upon some power deemed by it divine—constitutes its main source of strength.

Faith Must Be Genuine.—But faith must be genuine. Pretense and formalism will not avail. Hypocrisy is the worst form of unbelief. Honest idolatry is infinitely preferable to dishonest worship. Better burn incense to Diana, believing it to be right, than bow down to Christ in hollow-hearted insincerity. Mighty Rome did not fall until she had ceased to worship sincerely the gods enshrined within her Pantheon. Glorious Greece did not succumb until her believers had become doubters, until skeptical philosophy had supplanted religious enthusiasm, and the worship of freedom, grace and beauty had degenerated into unbridled license and groveling sensuality. No nation ever crumbled to ruin until false to itself, false to the true principles of success, the basic one of which is *To Believe*.

Germany's Mistake.—The world in recent years has witnessed the sad spectacle of a great nation, or the ruling powers of that nation, turning from Christ and substituting for Christian faith a godless pagan philosophy. Discarding the just and merciful principles of the Gospel, and adopting the false notion that might makes right, the fallen Teutonic empire has shown, by the revolting cruelties practiced in pursuance of that doctrine, what science (kultur) is capable of, when it parts company with God and morality. The land of Goethe and Wagner, and alas! the land also of the Hohenzollern and the Hindenburg, far from winning the "place in the sun" that she so coveted, has lost the proud place already held by her when the mad ambition of her military chiefs plunged her into ruin. The one thing that can now redeem her and lift her up out of the pit into which she has fallen, is faith in the true God, and the works by which that faith is made manifest.

According to Their Faith.—God deals with men ac-according to their faith. The Savior wrought mighty miracles, by his own faith, but most of them were faith abounded in the hearts of the people. In other places he did not do many mighty works, "because of their unbelief." Faith is a gift from God, and they who serve him best have most of it. Faith is the soil that brings forth miracles. "All things are possible to them that believe."

Footnotes

1 . D. & C. Lectures on Faith, Lec. 1, pp. 1, 2; See also Heb. 11.

2 . Matt. 17:20.

3 . Ether 12:30.

4 . It is my belief that the Savior, in his reference to the mustard seed, meant that if man would obey the divine law given for his government as faithfully as that tiny germ obeys the law given for its government, he could wield infinitely more power than he now possesses. Solid stone pavements are upheaved and cracked asunder by the gradual growth or expansion of a seed or root buried underneath. Such things indicate a hidden force even in the lowliest creations. It is written that the earth "filleth the measure of its creation, and transgresseth not the law." (D. & C. 88:25). If man were that obedient, he would have the power to "move mountains."

5 . 1 Nephi 13:12.

6 . "Heroes and Hero Worship," Lec. 2.

PART EIGHTH
BEYOND THE HORIZON

ARTICLE THIRTY-SEVEN
THE SPIRIT WORLD

Not Heaven.—That there is a Spirit World, and that it is closely connected with the material world—the one we now inhabit—has been a tenet in the religious philosophy of wise and good men all down the ages. In the minds of many people, the Spirit World and Heaven are synonymous terms, indicating one and the same place. But in reality there is a wide difference between them. A State of rest, such as the spirit life is understood to be for the righteous—though "rest" should not be interpreted as idleness or want of occupation—might easily pass for heaven, when contrasted with this life of pain, sorrow and trouble. But that is only relative. It is not saying too much—indeed it may be saying too little—to affirm that there is just as much difference between the spirit world and heaven, as between the mortal and the spiritual phases of man's existence.

Here on Earth.—According to Parley P. Pratt, the Spirit World is the spiritual part of this planet—or, to use his exact language: "The earth and other planets of a like order have their inward or spiritual spheres, as well as their outward or temporal. The one is peopled by temporal tabernacles, and the other by spirits." "As to its location," he says, "it is here on the very planet where we were born." [1]

All Things Before Created.—The proposition that Earth has a spiritual as well as a temporal sphere is a reassertion of the doctrine of duality, embodied in ancient and modern revelation, and particularly emphasized by Joseph the Seer. A careful reading of the Book of Genesis (the King James version) discloses, though somewhat vaguely, the fact of this duality, as applied to the works of creation. Thus, after giving an account of the earth and of all things connected therewith, the sacred writer says:

"These are the generations of the heavens and of the earth when they were created, in the day that the Lord God made the earth and the heavens, and every plant of the field before it was in the earth, and every herb of the field before it grew: for the Lord God had not caused it to rain upon the earth, and there was not a man to till the ground." [2]

"Not a man to till the ground"—and yet man had been created, as well as the plants and herbs that existed "before they grew." The apparent contradiction—apparent though not real—was explained by the Prophet when, by the Spirit of Revelation, he revised the Scriptures, giving a more ample account of the creation than the ordinary Bible contains. From that account the following sentences are taken:

"For I the Lord God created all things of which I have spoken, spiritually, before they were naturally upon the face of the earth. . . . . And I the Lord had created all the children of men; and not yet a man to till the ground. For in heaven created I them; and there was not yet flesh upon the earth, neither in the water, neither in the air . . . . Nevertheless, all things were before created." [3]

First Spiritual, Then Temporal.—In other words, there were two creations—or rather, the creation had two phases, the first spiritual, the second temporal. When the Creator made man and beast and fish and fowl, he made them twice—first in the spirit, then in the body; and the same is true of the trees, the shrubs, the flowers, and all other created things. They were made spiritually and temporally, the spirit and the body constituting the soul. [4]

Not Far Away.—The Spirit World is not a thing afar off. Our thoughts need not sail away millions of miles into space to find it. According to the best evidence we possess, it is near to us—right around us. We have but to emerge from the body, and we are in the spirit world. Out of it we came, and unto it we shall return. "The spirits of the just," says the Prophet Joseph, "are not far from us;" they "know and understand our thoughts, feelings and motions, and are often pained therewith." [5]

Just and Unjust.—The spirits of the unjust likewise inhabit the spirit world, though they are separated from the righteous, and are not in a state of rest. Light and darkness divide that realm, each domain having its appropriate population. So far from being Heaven, part of the spirit world is Hades or Hell. Referring to the class who people that part, the Prophet says: "The great misery of departed spirits ... is to know that they come short of the glory that others enjoy and that they might have enjoyed themselves; and they are their own accusers." [6]

Jesus and the Penitent Thief.—"In the spirit world," says Parley P. Pratt, "are all the varieties and grades of intellectual beings which exist in the present world. For instance, Jesus Christ and the thief on the cross both went to the same place." That is to say, they both went to the spirit world.

Jesus, it will be borne in mind, had been crucified between two thieves, one of whom derided him, insulting his dying agonies. The other, being penitent, prayed: "Lord, remember me when thou comest into thy kingdom." To him the Savior said: "Today shalt thou be with me in paradise." [7] Because of this utterance—which Joseph Smith declared to be a mistranslation, maintaining that "paradise" should read "world of spirits" [8]—uninspired minds have drawn the conclusion that the penitent thief was promised immediate heavenly exaltation, for repenting at the last moment and professing faith in the Redeemer. This notion is still entertained. The criminal who has forfeited his life and is under sentence of death, because unfit to dwell among his fallen fellow creatures, is made to believe that by confessing Christ, even on the scaffold, he is fitted at once for the society of Gods and angels, and will be wafted to never-ending bliss.

A False Doctrine.—Jesus never taught such a doctrine, nor did any authorized servant of the Lord. It is a man-made theory, based upon faulty inference and misinterpretation. The Scriptures plainly teach that men will be judged according to their works, [9] and receive rewards as varied as their deeds. [10] It was best for the thief, of course, to repent even at the eleventh hour; but he could not be exalted until prepared for it, if it took a thousand years. When Christ said: "I go to prepare a place for you, that where I am there ye may be also," [11] he was not speaking to murderers and malefactors, but to his pure-minded, right-living disciples, those only to whom such a promise could consistently be given.

What Goes on There.—Jesus Christ and the thief both went to the world of spirits, a place of rest for the righteous, a place of correction for the wicked. "But," as the Apostle Parley goes on to say, "the one was there in all the intelligence, happiness, benevolence and charity which characterize a teacher, a messenger anointed to preach glad tidings to the meek, to bind up the broken-hearted, to comfort those who mourned, to preach deliverance to the captive, and open the prison to those who were bound; or, in other words, to preach the Gospel to the spirits in prison, that they might be judged according to men in the flesh; while the other was there as a thief, who had expired on the cross for crime, and who was guilty, ignorant, uncultivated, and unprepared for resurrection, having need of remission of sins and to be instructed in the science of salvation."

Thus is told in part what goes on in the spirit world. "It is a place," continues our Apostle, "where the Gospel is preached, where faith, repentance and charity may be exercised, a place of waiting for the resurrection or redemption of the body; while to those who deserve it, it is a place of punishment, a purgatory or hell, where spirits are buffeted until the day of redemption."

Alma's Teaching.—To the foregoing should be added the testimony of Alma the Nephite, upon the same subject:

"Now concerning the state of the soul between death and the resurrection—Behold, it has been made known unto me by an angel, that the spirits of all men, as soon as they are departed from this mortal body, yea, the spirits of all men, whether they be good or evil, are taken home to that God who gave them life.

"And then shall it come to pass that the spirits of those who are righteous, are received into a state of happiness, which is called paradise; a state of rest; a state of peace, where they shall rest from all their troubles and from all care, and sorrow.

"And then shall it come to pass, that the spirits of the wicked, yea, who are evil—for behold, they have no part nor portion of the Spirit of the Lord; for behold, they chose evil works rather than good; therefore the spirit of the devil did enter into them, and take possession of their house—and these shall be cast out into outer darkness; there shall be weeping, and wailing, and gnashing of teeth; and this because of their own iniquity; being led captive by the will of the devil.

"Now this is the state of the souls of the wicked, yea, in darkness, and a state of awful, fearful, looking for the fiery indignation of the wrath of God upon them; thus they remain in this state, as well as the righteous in paradise, until the time of their resurrection." [12]

A Vision of Redemption.—President Joseph F. Smith, only a short while before his death, saw in a "vision of the redemption of the dead," the Savior's visit to the world of spirits, as recorded in the first epistle of Peter. [13] The President's account of what he beheld follows:

"I saw the hosts of the dead, both small and great, and there were gathered together in one place an innumerable company of the spirits of the just ... They were filled with joy and gladness, and were rejoicing together because the day of their deliverance was at hand... The Son of God appeared, and preached to them the everlasting gospel.

"I perceived that the Lord went not in person among the wicked and disobedient who had rejected the truth, to teach them; but behold from among the righteous he organized his forces and appointed messengers, clothed with power and authority, and commissioned them to go forth and carry the light of the gospel to them that were in darkness, even to all the spirits of men.

"I beheld that the faithful Elders of this dispensation, when they depart from mortal life, continue their labors in the preaching of the gospel....

among those who are in darkness and under bondage of sin in the great world of the spirits of the dead." [14]

Personal and Proxy Ministrations.—The new light here thrown upon the subject proceeds from the declaration that when the Savior visited the inhabitants of the spirit world, it was by proxy, and not in person, so far as the wicked were concerned. He ministered to the righteous directly, and to the unrighteous indirectly, sending to the latter his servants, bearing the authority of the Priesthood, and duly commissioned to speak and act for him. President Smith's pronouncement modifies the view commonly taken, that the Savior's personal ministry was to both classes of spirits. [15]

A Temporary Abode.—Thus we see that the Spirit World is not Heaven, except in a relative sense, and then only in part. It is a temporary abode for God's children, while undergoing processes of purification and development, as a preparation for better things beyond. Heaven, on the other hand—heaven in the highest degree—is the permanent home of the perfected and glorified.

Footnotes

1 . Key to Theology. Chapt. 14.

2 . Gen. 2:4, 5.

3 . Moses 3:5, 7.

4 . D. & C. 88:15; Moses 3:9.

5 . Hist. Ch. Vol. 6, p. 52.

6 . Ib. Vol. 5, p. 425.

7 . Luke 23:43.

8 . Hist. Ch. Vol. 5, pp. 424, 425.

9 . Rev. 20:12, 13.

10 . D. & C. 76.

11 . John 14:2, 3.

12 . Alma 40:11-14.

13 . 1 Peter 3:18-20.

14 . Gospel Doctrine, pp. 596-601.

15 . Compare 3 Nephi 15:21-24; D. & C. 76:112.

ARTICLE THIRTY-EIGHT
SPIRIT PROMPTINGS

Spirit Memories.—Writing one day upon the subject of spirit memories, and the influence exerted upon the affairs of this life by the awakened recollections of a former experience, I found myself indulging in the following reflections:

Why are we drawn toward certain persons, and they toward us, independently of any known previous acquaintance? Is it a fact, or only a fancy, that we and they were mutually acquainted and mutually attracted in some earlier period of our eternal existence? Is there something, after all, in that much abused term "affinity," and is this the basis of its claim? More than once, after meeting someone whom I had never met before on earth, I have wondered why his or her face seemed so familiar. Many times, upon hearing a noble sentiment expressed, though unable to recall having heard it until then, I have been thrilled by it, and felt as if I had always known it. The same is true of music, some strains of which are like echoes from afar, sounds falling from celestial heights, notes struck from the vibrant harps of eternity. I do not assert pre-acquaintance in all such cases, but as one thought suggests another, these queries arise in the mind.

The Shepherd's Voice.—When it comes to the Gospel, I feel more positive. Why did the Savior say: "My sheep know my voice?" Can a sheep know the voice of its shepherd, if it has never heard that voice before? They who love Truth, and to whom it appeals most powerfully, were they not its best friends in a previous state of existence? I think so. I believe that we knew the Gospel before we came here, and it is this knowledge, this acquaintance, that gives to it a familiar sound.

Very much in the same vein, I once wrote to President Joseph F. Smith—he at the time in Utah, and I on a mission in Europe. Here is his reply:

President Smith's View.—"I heartily endorse your sentiments respecting congeniality of spirits. Our knowledge of persons and things before we came here, combined with the divinity awakened within our souls through obedience to the gospel, powerfully affects, in my opinion, all our likes and dislikes, and guides our preferences in the course of this life, provided we give careful heed to the admonitions of the Spirit.

"All those salient truths which come so forcibly to the head and heart seem but the awakening of the memories of the spirit. Can we know anything here that we did not know before we came? Are not the means of knowledge in the first estate equal those of this? I think that the spirit, before and after this probation, possesses greater facilities, aye, manifold greater, for the acquisition of knowledge, than while manacled and shut up in the prison-house of mortality. I believe that our Savior possessed a foreknowledge of all the vicissitudes through which he would have to pass in the mortal tabernacle.

"If Christ knew beforehand, so did we. But in coming here, we forgot all, that our agency might be free indeed, to choose good or evil, that we might merit the reward of our own choice and conduct. But by the power of the Spirit, in the redemption of Christ, through obedience, we often catch a spark from the awakened memories of the immortal soul, which lights up our whole being as with the glory of our former home." [1]

"A Glance Behind the Curtain."—Closely akin to these reflections, are some pointed and telling lines in which the poet Lowell expresses his conviction regarding the influence of the unseen world upon the world visible. The action of the poem from which the lines are taken deals with Oliver Cromwell and John Hampden, English patriots, who are represented as about to flee from the tyranny of King Charles the First, and seek a new home overseas, joining the little band of Puritans who have already found a haven on western Atlantic shores. Hampden urges flight, but Cromwell hesitates. Something within tells him not to go—tells him that Freedom has a work for him to go—tells him that Freedom has a work for him to do, not in America, but in his own land, where he afterwards overthrew the royal tyrant, became Lord Protector of the Commonwealth, and broadened and deepened the foundations of English liberty. The opening verses of the poem contain the crux of the whole matter under discussion:

> We see but half the causes of our deeds,
> Seeking them wholly in the outer life,
> And heedless of the encircling spirit world,
> Which, though unseen, is felt, and sows in us
> All germs of pure and world-wide purposes.
>
> The fate of England and of freedom once
> Seemed wavering in the heart of one plain man.
> One step of his, and the great dial-hand
> That marks the destined progress of the world

In the eternal round from wisdom on
To higher wisdom, had been made to pause
A hundred years.

That step he did not take—
He knew not why, nor we, but only God,
And lived to make his simple oaken chair
More terrible and grandly beautiful,
More full of majesty than any throne,
Before or after, of a British king. [2]

A Well Warranted Conviction.—How much of fact and how much of fiction, are here interwoven, matters not for the purpose of this argument. It was the poet's belief that such things could be, a belief shared by myriads of Christian men and women, and confirmed by a multiplicity of experiences.

Columbus and "The Voice."--In another poem--"Columbus"--Lowell sets forth the same idea, that of whisperings or suggestions from beyond the "veil" hiding the spirit world from this world of flesh and blood. The great mariner is supposed to be standing on the deck of his ocean-tossed vessel, soliloquizing over the situation surrounding him: A yet undiscovered country ahead, a mutinous and grumbling crew behind, threatening to put him in irons and turn the ship's prow toward Spain, if sight of the promised shore of India--for which Columus set sail--came not with the break of dawn. A world of care weighs him down, a sense of solitude and utter loneliness, but his soul hears "the voice that errs not," and is patient and trustful to the hour of complete triumph. [3]

Nephi and the Spirit.—That it was indeed "the voice that errs not" which inspired Columbus, upholding and urging him on to the consummation of the great enterprise he had undertaken, we have sacred and indisputable evidence. Long before Columbus crossed the ocean, an American prophet and seer, Nephi by name, looking down the vista of twenty centuries, forecast the career of that man of destiny, telling how "the Spirit of God" would impel him to cross "the many waters" to this "promised land;" and how the same Spirit, moving upon others, would induce them to follow in the wake of the mighty explorer. That prophet beheld in vision the war for American Independence, the successful struggle of the oppressed colonies against the mother country, and the founding here of a free government, a heaven-favored nation, destined to foster and give protection to the growing work of God in after days. And this revealing Spirit—so Nephi affirms—was more than an inward monitor: "I spake unto him as a man speaketh, for I beheld that he was in the form of man; yet, nevertheless, I knew that it was the Spirit of the Lord! and he spake unto me as a man speaketh with another." [4]

The Holy Ghost.—Evidently it was the Holy Ghost who communed with Nephi, though he is here spoken of as "the Spirit of God, and 'the Spirit of the Lord." "The Holy Ghost is a personage of spirit," [5] and though not in a tabernacle like the Father or the Son, he is nevertheless in human form, and Nephi beheld him and conversed with him.

The Unerring Guide.—The experience of Columbus differed from that of Nephi, notably in this particular: Nephi "beheld," while Columbus was moved upon—yet it was the same Spirit in each instance. It was of the Holy Ghost that the Savior was speaking, when he said to his disciples: "He will guide you into all truth." [6] The mission of the Holy Ghost is to make manifest the things of God, past, present and future, explaining the purpose of this mortal life, revealing to man his eternal origin and destiny, and answering the otherwise unanswerable questions—whence? whither? and why?

Wordsworth's "Intimation."—It was this Spirit that inspired the poet Wordsworth, bringing the forgotten past to his remembrance, and prompting the utterance of the noble thoughts embodied in these lofty lines:

> Our birth is but a sleep and a forgetting;
> The soul that rises with us, our life's star,
> Hath had elsewhere its setting,
> And cometh from afar;
> Not in entire forgetfulness,
> And not in utter nakedness,
> But trailing clouds of glory do we come
> From God who is our home. [7]

Truth and Bigotry.—The big thought was too broad for the narrow, rigid orthodoxy of Wordsworth's time, which could allow for the pre-existence of the Son of God, but not for that of the race in general. "And now, O Father, glorify thou me with thine own self, with the glory which I had with thee before the world was." [8] This wonderful prayer from the lips of the Savior was too plain to be misunderstood. It was clear that Jesus Christ, "the Word" that was "in the beginning with God," and "was God," before he "was made flesh," [9] had lived before this life. But man, "mere man," was an earth-worm, made out of nothing, and consequently had no pre-existence. So Christian orthodoxy maintained; and Wordsworth had to recant or half-way deny that his heaven-inspired "intimation" meant as much as his bigoted censors seemed to fear. Nevertheless,

> "Got but the truth once uttered, and 'tis like
> A star new-born, that drops into its place,
> And which, once circling in its placid round,
> Not all the tumult of the earth can shake."

The truth uttered by the great "poet of nature" touching the previous life, was probably accepted by thousands of advanced thinkers; and their acceptance helped to prepare the way for a more positive and more complete presentation of the great doctrine of man's pre-existence. In this connection the subjoined verses from the pen of a "Mormon" poet, tell their own eloquent story:

> O my Father, thou that dwellest
> In the high and glorious place!
> When shall I regain thy presence,
> And again behold thy face?
> In thy holy habitation
> Did my spirit once reside;
> In my first primeval childhood
> Was I nurtured near thy side.
>
> For a wise and glorious purpose
> Thou hast placed me here on earth,
> And withheld the recollection
> Of my former friends and birth.
> Yet, ofttimes a secret something
> Whispered, "You're a stranger here,"
> And I felt that I had wandered
> From a more exalted sphere.
>
> I had learned to call thee Father,
> Through thy Spirit from on high;
> But until the Key of Knowledge
> Was restored, I knew not why.
> In the heavens are parents single?
> No, the thought makes reason stare!
> Truth is reason-truth eternal
> Tells me I've a Mother there.
>
> When I leave this frail existence,
> When I lay this mortal by,
> Father, Mother, may I meet you

In your royal courts on high?
Then, at length, when I've completed
All you sent me forth to do,
With your mutual approbation
Let me come and dwell with you. [10]

How wonderfully clear and comprehensive!—past, present and future circumscribed in brief compass, the mystery of the former life unfolded, the meaning of all existence made plain.

Maeterlinck and "The Bluebird."—Maeterlinck, the Belgian poet, author of "The Bluebird," in that section of his dramatic masterpiece entitled "The Kingdom of the Future," deals with the pre-mortal life, and with the spirits of little children waiting to be brought down to earth to be born here. Old Father Time is there with his barge, gathering in the tiny passengers, holding back some whose turn is not yet, and permitting others whose birth-hour is about to strike. The barge being filled, he sails away, and mingling with the sweet strains of children's voices, hailing the distant planet that is to be their new abode, rises from below the song of the mothers coming out to meet them. When the poet's inspired mind conceived this beautiful creation, had he heard of Eliza R. Snow and her invocation to the Eternal Father and Mother?

The Same Note.—I do not impute plagiarism in such cases. There is no monopoly of Truth. It reveals itself to whomsoever it will, and sometimes it tells to several persons, at different times and places, the same thing. Suffice it, that Eliza R. Snow, when she sang of the "first primeval childhood," sounded the identical note subsequently struck by Maurice Maeterlinck, when portraying so tenderly and so tellingly the heavenly origin and earthly advent of the spirits that tabernacle in mortality.

Fame's Partiality.—Inspiration was kind to both poets, but fame has been somewhat partial. Some day, when bigotry is dead and prejudice no longer has power to blind men's eyes to the truth and pervert their judgment, the just claims of all inspired teachers will be recognized, if not recompensed. Meanwhile the world will go on glorifying one and crying down another, as it always has done. It will continue "tossing high its ready cap" in honor of Maeterlinck, the Belgian poet, for the beautiful truths set forth in his sublime symbolic drama; little realizing that the American prophet, Joseph Smith, and some who sat at his feet learning wisdom from his lips, taught the same and greater truths long before Maeterlinck was born.

Communications from the Departed.—Many instances might be given of the action and influence of "the other world" upon this world

The experiences of the Latter-day Saints alone would fill volumes. I refer particularly to those connected with the gathering up of genealogies for use in temple work, and the work itself done vicariously for the benefit of the departed. By dreams and visions, by voices and other manifestations, spirits "behind the veil" have made known their wishes to surviving relatives in the flesh, so that their left-over tasks might be done for them, the records of their ancestors secured, and they in like manner redeemed through sacred ordinances performed in their behalf and necessary to their progress and happiness in spheres beyond.

Footnotes

1 . Gospel Doctrine, pp. 15, 16. "Columbus."

2 . J. R. Lowell's Poems, "A Glance Behind the Curtain."

3 . Ib. "Columbus."

4 . 1 Nephi 11:11; 13:10:19.

5 . D. & C. 130:22.

6 . John 16:13.

7 . Wordsworth's Poems, "Intimations of Immortality," first published in 1807.

8 . John 17:5.

9 . Ib. 1:1-14.

10 . Eliza R. Snow's "Invocation," L. D. S. Hymn Book.

ARTICLE THIRTY-NINE
DO THE DEAD RETURN?

Hamlet and the Ghost.—I had always thought it strange that a great Christian poet like Shakespeare, after portraying, as he does in "Hamlet," an interview between the Prince of Denmark and his father's ghost, should refer to the spirit world as "that undiscovered country from whose bourne no traveler returns." Had not the ghost returned from that very "country," for the special purpose of this interview?

While deeming it contradictory, my admiration and reverence for the immortal bard induced me to minimize and even excuse the apparent inconsistency. In his behalf I argued that it was Hamlet, not Shakespeare, who interviewed the Ghost at Castle Elsinore; that it was the prince and not the poet who soliloquized relative to the non-returning "traveler." I took the ground that Shakespeare, in writing the play of "Hamlet," was not presenting the author's autobiography, and should not, therefore, be held responsible for the idiosyncrasies of "the melancholy Dane;" he being mad, and mad people having the right to say what they please, no matter how much they contradict themselves or speak and act inconsistently.

A Better Defense.—But all the while there was a better defense for both Shakespeare and Hamlet—it a certain hypothesis be well founded, the supporters of which would have us believe that the famed soliloquy, "To be or not be," wherein the allusion to the spirit "traveler" occurs, originally had place nearer the beginning of the play and before Hamlet had seen the Ghost. Not Shakespeare, therefore, nor Hamlet, but some one who tampered with the poet's masterpiece after his death—"a custom more honored in the breach than the observance"—is to be held responsible for the incongruity. Such is the suggestion put forth by one or more literary savants. Allowing it to be true, Shakespeare and the Bible are thus reconciled, and Hamlet is no longer in the attitude of disputing the sacred account of the risen Savior's personal appearing to his disciples, after his return from the spirit world. [1]

Belasco and "Peter Grimm."—That the creator of Hamlet and Macbeth believed in spirits, and made plentiful use of them as part of his "celestial machinery," is evident from the works of the master dramatist; and that his talented disciple, David Belasco, likewise favors such usage, is plainly shown in that intensely interesting book and play, "The Return of Peter Grimm." Let me briefly review the story.

Peter Grimm, an honest, elderly Dutch-American, carrying on the business of florist at Grimm Manor, a suburb of New York City, has a friend and family physician in Alexander McPherson, who, I need not say, is a Scotchman. He is also a spiritualist, deeply interested in the laws of psychic phenomena, and exceedingly tenacious of his occult views.

Grim is bluntly skeptical upon the subject, and he and his Scotch friend have many a warm debate thereon. Finally McPherson proposes a compact to this effect: Whichever one of the twain shall pass away first, his spirit will return, if possible, and communicate with the other, making known the secrets of the after life. Grimm laughs at the idea, even ridicules it, but at last consents, and with a flash of humor suggestive of his name, says: "If I find I am wrong, when I come back I will apologize."

A little later the florist dies suddenly of heart failure. He passes into the spirit world, and there obtains leave to "revisit the glimpses of the moon," as Hamlet puts it; in other words, to return to Grimm Manor and rectify a mistake made by him while in the flesh—a mistake affecting the happiness of his adopted daughter Kathrien, who, yielding to his insistence, has given up the man she loved, and has agreed to marry Grimm's nephew, Frederic. This young man is a villain, whose unworthiness his uncle discovers after his arrival in "the undiscovered country," from which he now proposes to "return" and prevent the marriage previously planned.

The wrong is to be righted by the delivery of a message. But how "get the message across?" That is the problem of the play. "Not every one can receive a communication from the spirit world." So McPherson has said in one of his conversations with Grimm, adding that "the receiver must be a sensitive, a medium."

Strange to say, the old Scotch physician is of no help whatever in the predicament now facing his departed friend. He knows all about spirits—is saturated with the lore of the subject; but he is not a "sensitive," and cannot therefore "receive."

The spirit of Grimm, re-entering his old home, makes persistent efforts to be seen or heard by some member of the household; but all in vain. None of his family, none of his friends, can behold him or hear his pathetic pleadings. Yes—there is one who can; a little invalid boy, Frederick's illegitimate child, who is wasting away with a fever. The veil is thin between him and the spirit land, to which he will accompany Peter Grimm, after the latter's earthly errand is accomplished. This little lad is a "sensitive."

He sees the spirit, receives the message, and the threatened misalliance is averted, Kathrien and her worthy lover being happily reunited.

Fiction and Fact.—Such is the story of Peter Grimm and his return from the world of spirits. It is pure fiction, of course; but fiction often supports fact, and is even less strange, as a well-worn proverb affirms. Nevertheless, it will be seen from what follows that I am not in absolute harmony with Belasco's ingenious presentation of the spiritualistic theme. My views upon the subject are not based upon the theories of men; they are founded upon the revelations of God.

Spirits in Prison.—That the inhabitants of the spirit world, or some of them, return at times and communicate with mortals, I am perfectly well assured. But I am not convinced that any and every spirit is at liberty to return, whatever the "compacts" that may have been entered into beforehand. Some spirits are "in prison." [2] Of what avail would a compact be in their case, unless their jailor or some higher power were a party to it? Evidently the spirits that communicate with mortals are not of that class, unless it be in exceptional cases, where leave of absence has been granted for some special reason.

A House of Order.—God's house is a house of order, and the spirit world is a room in that house. This being the case, it is only reasonable to conclude that before anything important or unusual can take place there, the Master of the Mansion must first give consent. Otherwise confusion would prevail, and the divine purpose for which the veil was dropped between the two worlds might be thwarted.

Unembodied and Disembodied Spirits.—Spirits are of two kinds—the unembodied and the disembodied; that is to say, those who have not tabernacled in the flesh, and those who after taking bodies on earth, have passed out of them. It matters not which class is considered; in any case, permission from the Great Father would have to be obtained before one of his children, either an unembodied or a disembodied spirit, could make itself manifest to mortals.

The Question of Receptivity.—Moreover, as Belasco, through Dr. McPherson, aims to show, not every mortal is qualified to receive a message from "the other side." One must be fittingly endowed, must have the proper gift, in order to get a communication of that kind. [3] Earthly ties would not necessarily govern. Other and higher relationships are involved. There must be capacity as well as a desire to receive. Because men like Moses and Joseph Smith saw God, is no sign that any man can see him. "Choice seers" were they, very different from ordinary men. All human beings can obtain blessings from heaven, but not always in the same way. There are diversities of gifts and varying degrees of receptivity. Wireless telegraphy furnishes a hint in this connection. Unless there be a receiving station with an apparatus properly attuned, a message launched upon the ether would find, like Noah's dove, "no rest for the sole of her foot." [4]

Future Occupations.—In one of the supposed conversations between Peter Grimm and Doctor McPherson, the subject of future occupations is discussed. The "compact" having been entered into, the Doctor says: "I would like you to find out, if you can, what we do in the other world. I would like to know if I have got to go on being a bone-setter throughout all eternity." Grimm's reply is characteristic: "Well, you would stand a better chance for success, having practiced it all your life here, than a novice who simply took it up there, wouldn't you?"

The florist's argument is logical, but like the question that called it forth, somewhat misapplied. "A spirit hath not flesh and bones." [5] Bone-setting, therefore, does not belong to the spirit world. Nevertheless, there must be occupations in the future life, of which those in the present life may be regarded as typical, or in the nature of a preparation, leading up to loftier employments. If a follower of Joseph Smith were asked: "How do you expect to spend eternity?" he would not agree with that clergyman who said, in answer to the same question: "I expect to spend the first million years gazing upon the face of the Savior." The Latter-day Saint would be very apt to reply: "I expect to do hereafter what I have learned to do here, but with more perfect means and in higher and better ways."

"And every power find sweet employ In that eternal world of joy."

Evil Spirits at Large.—A very important question now arises: How may good or bad spirits be known? For every spirit is not good, nor is every spiritual manifestation genuine. There are frauds and counterfeits innumerable. Even if real spirits and actual manifestations are alone considered, we must still be on our guard against deception. There are many evil spirits in this world—spirits that have never had bodies. They are here by permission or toleration of the Most High, against whom they rebelled when the Savior was chosen. Satan and his legions, those cast out of heaven, are all wicked spirits, and they wander up and down the world, endeavoring to lead mortals astray. Wherever possible, they take possession of the bodies of men and even of the lower animals. [6] Therefore is power given to the Priesthood to "cast out devils." [7] Against these fallen spirits, mortals must be ever on the defensive, lest their souls be ensnared. Temptation, however, is an important factor in man's probation; for by resisting it, the soul is developed and made stronger. This is probably one reason why the pernicious activity of such spirits is tolerated. Punished in part by being denied bodies, the full penalty for their misdeeds—the second death—is yet to be visited upon them.

Spiritualism a Reality.—Spiritualism is not altogether what some people imagine. Despite the frauds connected with it, it is a reality, and was recognized as such long before Sir Oliver Lodge and Sir A. Conan Doyle proclaimed their conversion thereto, thus lending to it the prestige of their illustrious names. But all realities are not righteous. Because there is a devil—an actual demon and his dupes, is no reason why we should associate with them, confide in them, or accept their evil communications.

How can We Know?—There are bad spirits as well as good, and the vital question is: How can we know the difference between them? Let us at this stage consult an expert—for there are such—one who came in contact with spiritual forces to a marvelous extent, not only receiving messages from other worlds, but also interviewing the messengers. Joseph Smith knew the difference between good and evil communicants, and here is his testimony concerning them:

Expert Testimony.—"When a messenger comes, saying he has a message from God, offer him your hand, and request him to shake hands with you.

"If he be an angel, he will do so, and you will feel his hand." [An angel is a resurrected being, with a body as tangible as man's.]

"If he be the spirit of a just man made perfect, he will come in his glory; for that is the only way he can appear.

"Ask him to shake hands with you, but he will not move, because it is contrary to the order of heaven for a just man to deceive; but he will still deliver his message.

"If it be the Devil as an angel of light, when you ask him to shake hands, he will offer you his hand, and you will not feel anything [he also being without a body]. You may therefore detect him." [8]

In another place, the Prophet says: "Wicked spirits have their bounds, limits and laws, by which they are governed; and it is very evident that they possess a power that none but those who have the Priesthood can control." [9] To his declaration that "a man is saved no faster than he gets knowledge," he adds that if men do not get knowledge, including the knowledge of how to control evil spirits, the latter will have more power than the former, and thus be able to dominate them. This is precisely the condition of "the spirits in prison." They are dominated by a power which they cannot control. They are in Hell, and Satan sways the scepter over his own dominion.

Seek Knowledge Aright.—To those in quest of spiritual light, this word of counsel: Seek it only in the Lord's appointed way. Follow the advice of the Apostle James and the example of Joseph the Prophet. [10] Never go upon the Devil's ground. Keep away from all deceptive influence. One may believe in hypnotism, without being a hypnotist, without surrendering one's will to the will of the person exercising that power—a very dangerous power when wielded by an unprincipled possessor. In like manner, one may believe spiritualism real, without becoming a spiritualist, without attending "seances," without consulting "mediums," without putting trust in planchettes, ouija boards, automatic pencils, false impersonations, or in any way encouraging the advances of designing spirits, who thus gain an ascendancy over their victims, leading them into mazes of delusion, and often into depths of despair. Go not after them; and if they come to you, put them to the test. "Try the spirits." [11] If they speak not according to revealed truth, if they conform not to divine standards, "it is because there is no light in them." [12]

The Great Return.—Yes, the dead, or the departed, do return. They are no more dead than we are. Nay, not so much. The Savior's reappearance after death to his amazed and incredulous disciples—what was that but a return, a real return, from the realm of the departed, where in the interim between his crucifixion and resurrection, he "preached to the spirits in prison?" Moreover, the ascended Lord promised another return, or his angel promised it for him, when the "men of Galilee" stood "gazing up into heaven," after "a cloud" had "received him out of their sight." [13] That glorious return is nigh. All the signs so indicate. May the kingly Traveler from heaven to earth meet a royal welcome when he appears!

Footnotes

1 . Luke 24:36-39.

2 . 1 Peter 3:18-20.

3 . 1 Cor. 12:4-11.

4 . Gen. 8:9.

5. Luke 24:39.

6. Acts 19:13-16; Mark 5:12, 3.

7. Ib. 16:17; Hist. Ch. Vol. 5, p. 403.

8. D. & C. 129:4-8.

9. Hist. Ch. Vol. 4, p. 576.

10. James 1:5; Hist. Ch. Vol. 1, pp. 4, 5.

11. 1 John 4:1.

12. Isa. 8:20.

13. Acts 1:9-11.

ARTICLE FORTY
THE GOAL ETERNAL

Dante and the Divine Comedy.—In the thirteenth century a great Italian poet, the immortal Dante, produced a wonderful work, "La Divina Comedia"—in English, "The Divine Comedy." In one part of the poem the author represents himself as passing through Hades. In the first circle of the infernal depths, a region called "Limbo"—described by a footnote in my copy of the work as a place "containing the souls of unbaptized children and of those virtuous men and women who lived before the birth of our Savior"—he comes upon such characters as Homer, Virgil, Plato and others of their class, and the spirit guide who is conducting him through "the realms of shade," says:

> —Inquirest thou not what spirits
> Are these, which thou beholdest? Ere thou pass
> Farther, I would thou know, that these of sin
> Were blameless; and if aught they merited
> It profits not, since baptism was not theirs,
> The portal to thy faith. If they before
> The Gospel lived, they served not God aright;
> And among such am I.
> For these defects
> And for no other evil, we are lost;
> Only so far afflicted, that we live
> Desiring without hope. [1]

And this was all that thirteenth century theology could say for worthies of that stamp—the best and brightest spirits of their times. Blameless, and yet in hell, "desiring without hope," simply because they had lived on earth when the Gospel was not on earth, and had not been baptized! Whether or not, as some think, it was the intent of the poet to covertly satirize such teachings, is immaterial at the present time. It is sufficient that he had such teachings to satirize.

Truth's Restoration Imperative.—If any reader of mine wishes to know why Joseph Smith and "Mormonism" came into the world, he need look no further to find one of the cardinal reasons. It is furnished in those lines from Dante's masterpiece, setting forth the orthodox tenet and teaching of the Christian Church regarding the spirits of the good who depart this life without undergoing the baptismal ordinance. This, and that other man-made doctrine, that half to be damned, regardless of any good or evil done by them—little children being included in both classes—were widely preached in Christendom at the time of the advent of "Mormonism." It was imperative that a prophet should arise, that the pure primitive faith should be restored, and God's word go forth once more on its mission of justice and mercy.

"According to Their Works."—Whatever Christian theology may have taught, or whatever it may teach, in support of such doctrines, the fact remains that the Gospel of Christ does not, and never did dispose of men's precious souls in that unrighteous, unreasonable, unscriptural manner. It does not prejudge, nor save nor damn, regardless of men's deserts. Rewarding all according to their works, [2] it gives to every creature, living or dead, the opportunity to accept or reject it before final judgment. [3] God is not trying to damn the world; he is trying to save it—but not independently of the principles of truth and righteousness.

A Nautical Illustration.—I was crossing the Atlantic on an ocean-liner, and had been fortunate enough to secure a first-cabin berth, the only one remaining unsold when I made my purchase. There were upwards of a hundred passengers in that part of the vessel. The second-cabin compartment contained perhaps twice as many; and in the steerage were several hundred more.

The first-cabin berths were the best furnished and the most favorably situated for comfort, convenience and safety. The passengers were shown every courtesy; their food was of the choicest; the captain and other officers were their associates, and they enjoyed the full freedom of the ship. They might go down onto the second-cabin deck, or lower down, into the steerage, and return without hindrance or question. They had paid for these privileges, and were therefore entitled to them.

But it was different in the lower compartment. There the food was not so good, the berths were less comfortable, and the privileges fewer. The second-class passengers could descend into the steerage, but were not permitted upon the first-cabin deck.

Conditions in the steerage were even less favorable. The food was still poorer, and the restrictions were yet more rigid. The occupants of that section were not allowed even second-class privileges. They had to remain right where they were. Having paid only for steerage accommodations, these were all that they could consistently claim.

A Likeness of Human Destiny.—I was struck with the analogy existing between the things that I beheld and the higher things which they seemed to symbolize. I saw another illustration of the proverb, "The earthly typifies the heavenly," and received fresh confirmation of the poetic truth: "All things have their likeness." That ocean-going steamer was a likeness of human destiny, projecting the eternal future of Adam's race, as made known by divine revelation. All souls rewarded according to their works—their varied works—and saved and glorified in the "many mansions" of the Father. [4]

Celestial Glory—The Church of the First Born.—"And this is the testimony of the gospel of Christ concerning those who come forth in the resurrection of the just:

"They are they who received the testimony of Jesus, and believed on his name, and were baptized after the manner of his burial; . . . .

"That by keeping the commandments they might be washed and cleansed from all their sins, and receive the Holy Spirit by the laying on the hands of him who is ordained and sealed unto this power;

"And who overcome by faith, and are sealed by the Holy Spirit of Promise, which the Father sheds forth upon all those who are just and true . . . .

"They are they who are the Church of the First-born.

"They are they into whose hands the Father has given all things—

"They are they who are priests and kings, who have received of his fulness and of his glory . . . .

"Wherefore, as it is written, they are Gods, even the sons of God—

"Wherefore, all things are theirs, whether life or death, or things present or things to come, all are theirs and they are Christ's and Christ is God's . . . .

"These shall dwell in the presence of God and his Christ forever and ever . . . .

"These are they whom he shall bring with him, when he shall come in the clouds of heaven, to reign on the earth over his people.

"These are they who shall have part in the first resurrection.

"These are they who shall come forth in the resurrection of the just.

"These are they who are come unto Mount Zion, and unto the city of the living God, the heavenly place, the holiest of all.

"These are they who have come to an innumerable company of angels, to the general assembly and church of Enoch, and of the first-born.

"These are they whose names are written in heaven, where God and Christ are the judge of all.

"These are they who are just men made perfect through Jesus the mediator of the new covenant, who wrought out this perfect atonement through the shedding of his own blood.

"These are they whose bodies are celestial, whose glory is that of the sun, even the glory of God, the highest of all, whose glory the sun of the firmament is written of as being typical." [5]

In other words—if the maritime metaphor be allowed—they were first-cabin passengers over the sea of mortal life. They gave to the great Captain the fulness of their obedience, and received from him the fulness of recognition and reward. All privileges, all possessions, are theirs. They associate with divine beings, and are themselves divine.

Terrestrial Glory.—Concerning those who attain to a terrestrial sphere, "whose glory differs from that of the Church of the First-Born, as the moon differs from the sun," the Vision goes on to say:

"Behold, these are they who died without law.

"And also they who are the spirits of men kept in prison, whom the Son visited and preached the gospel unto them, that they might be judged according to men in the flesh.

"Who received not the testimony of Jesus in the flesh, but afterwards received it.

"These are they who are honorable men of the earth who were blinded by the craftiness of men.

"These are they who receive of his glory, but not of his fulness.

"These are they who receive of the presence of the Son, but not of the fulness of the Father;

"Wherefore they are bodies terrestrial, and not bodies celestial, and differ in glory as the moon differs from the sun.

"These are they who are not valiant in the testimony of Jesus; wherefore they obtain not the crown over the kingdom of our God." [6]

Continuing the comparison: These voyagers paid only for second-rate privileges. They "drew the line," giving a part but not all of their allegiance to Him who hath said: "Thou shalt have no other gods before me." The things of this world were more precious in their eyes than the riches that perish not and that thieves cannot steal. They loved Truth, but not wholeheartedly. They loved money and pleasure more, and strove for fame and the applause of this world, rather than for the approval of heaven. Though clean of conduct and honorable in deal, they were not zealous for Christ, and knew not the meaning of self-sacrifice. These are worthy of the Kingdom, but not of the Crown; and they shine, not like the golden sun, but like the silvery moon, with a diminished or secondary radiance, with reflected rather than with original light.

Telestial Glory—Servants of the Most High.—As for those who inherit telestial conditions, differing from the terrestrial as the stars differ from the moon—were they not symbolized by the steerage and its occupants?

"These are they who are thrust down to hell. These are they who shall not be redeemed from the Devil, until the last resurrection," at the close of the Millennial reign. Criminals of every type and grade, they "suffer the wrath of God until the fulness of times, until Christ shall have subdued all enemies under his feet and shall have perfected his work." They receive not of "his fulness in the eternal world, but of the Holy Spirit through the ministration of the terrestrial; and the terrestrial through the ministration of the celestial. And also the telestial receive it of the administering of angels who are appointed to minister for them, or who are appointed to be ministering spirits for them, for they shall be heirs of salvation." [7]

The heirs telestial are those who "receive not the Gospel, neither the testimony of Jesus, neither the prophets, neither the everlasting covenant." According to the Vision, they "were as innumerable as the stars in the firmament of heaven, or as the sands upon the seashore." Concerning this vast multitude, the voice of the Lord was heard, saying:

"These all shall bow the knee, and every tongue shall confess to Him who sits upon the throne forever and ever.

"For they shall be judged according to their works, and every man shall receive according to his own works his own dominion in the mansions which are prepared.

"And they shall be servants of the Most High, but where God and Christ dwell they cannot come, worlds without end." [8]

The Damned Can Be Saved.—Yes, such is "Mormonism's" astounding declaration—and not only saved, but glorified, if they will repent. The glorified planets are God's kingdoms, and "all kingdoms have a law given"—celestial, terrestrial or telestial. Whosoever inherits any of these kingdoms, must abide the law pertaining to that kingdom. If he cannot abide "the Law of Christ," he must inherit a glory other than the celestial—even a terrestrial or a telestial glory. If he cannot abide a telestial law, he is "not meet for a kingdom of glory;" and if he willeth to abide in sin, and altogether abideth in sin, then must he "remain filthy still." [9]

Sons of Perdition.—One class alone remains outside salvation's pale, permanently condemned—they who commit the unpardonable sin, the sin against the Holy Ghost. For them there is no forgiveness. But one must receive the Holy Ghost before he can sin against it, must have knowledge and power sufficient to entitle him to celestial exaltation; and then prove utterly recreant to the great light that has come to him. Such a sin can be committed only by men equipped with every qualification for the highest degree of eternal glory. It is an offense so heinous that the sinner cannot repent. This is what makes his case hopeless; salvation being predicated upon repentance. If he could repent, he could be forgiven; but being unable to repent, incapable of reformation, he cannot be reached by the pardoning power.

They who commit the sin unpardonable are as first-cabin passengers who, in the full enjoyment of every privilege and advantage pertaining to that highly favored condition, wilfully throw all away, and recklessly fling themselves overboard, to go down in unfathomable depths. Sons of Perdition, these—"the only ones on whom the second death shall have any power"—"the only ones who shall not be redeemed in the due time of the Lord." They "deny the Son, after the Father has revealed him. Wherefore, he saves all except them." [10]

Desires As Well as Deeds a Basis of Judgment.—But the final word was not yet spoken. At a date subsequent to that upon which Joseph and Sidney received this wonderful manifestation, the heavens were again opened to the Prophet, and he beheld the glory—the transcendent glory of the Celestial Kingdom, [11] He saw that little children, those "who die before they arrive at the years of accountability," are saved in that kingdom. He also saw his brother Alvin—a good and worthy man, but one who had not been baptized, he having died before the Gospel came—saw him in celestial glory! Joseph marveled at the sight, wondering how Alvin could have risen to so exalted a plane. Then came the voice of the Lord to him, saying: "All who have died without a knowledge of this gospel, who would have received it if they had been permitted to tarry, shall be heirs of the celestial kingdom of God; also all that shall die henceforth without a knowledge of it, who would have received it with all their hearts, shall be heirs of that kingdom; for I, the Lord, will judge all men according to their works, according to the desire of their hearts." [12]

Mormonism's Magnanimity.—And yet "Mormonism" is said to be narrow, small and illiberal. Narrow, forsooth! Then where will you find breadth? Where find justice, mercy, magnanimity, if not in a religion that saves the living, redeems the dead, rescues the damned, and glorifies all who repent? "Mormonism" a small thing? It's the biggest thing in the universe! It is the Everlasting Gospel, the mighty soul-ship of the dispensations, launched in the days of Adam upon the heaving ocean of the ages, and now on its last voyage over the stormy billows of Time to the beaconing coast of Eternity.

Footnotes

1 . Hades or Hell, Canto 4, lines 29-39.

2 . Rev. 20:12.

3 . I Peter 4:6.

4 . John 14:2.

5 . Vision of Joseph Smith and Sidney Rigdon, D. & C. 76:50-70. See also 131:1. Compare 1 Cor. 15:40-42.

6 . D. & C. 76:72-79.

7 . D. & C. 76:84-88.

8 . D. & C. 76:110-112.

9 . Ib. 88:21-40.

10 . D. & C. 76:31-44.

11 . February 16th, 1832, was the date of Joseph and Sidney's vision; January 21st, 1836 the date of the other manifestation.

12 . Hist. Ch. Vol. 2, p. 380. Compare Alma 29:4,5.

We are not to infer that Alvin Smith or anyone else could inherit celestial glory, without receiving the fulness of the

Gospel. It was a prophetic vision, showing what would be when Alvin had done his part, and the part that he could not do had been done for him. The same vision showed the parents of the Prophet—Joseph and Lucy Smith—in celestial glory; and yet at that time they were still alive on earth. We are not to infer that Alvin Smith or anyone else could inherit celestial glory, without receiving the fulness of the Gospel. It was a prophetic vision, showing what would be when Alvin had done his part, and the part that he could not do had been done for him. The same vision showed the parents of the Prophet—Joseph and Lucy Smith—in celestial glory; and yet at that time they were still alive on earth.